CREATIV
UNIVERSI

Reimagining Education for Global Challenges and Alternative Futures

Anke Schwittay

BRISTOL
UNIVERSITY
PRESS

First published in Great Britain in 2021 by

Bristol University Press
University of Bristol
1–9 Old Park Hill
Bristol
BS2 8BB
UK
t: +44 (0)117 954 5940
e: bup-info@bristol.ac.uk

Details of international sales and distribution partners are available at
bristoluniversitypress.co.uk

© Bristol University Press 2021

British Library Cataloguing in Publication Data
A catalogue record for this book is available from the British Library

ISBN 978-1-5292-1364-5 hardcover
ISBN 978-1-5292-1365-2 paperback
ISBN 978-1-5292-1366-9 ePub
ISBN 978-1-5292-1367-6 ePdf

Cover design: Nicky Boroweic
Front cover image: Shutterstock_238305940
Bristol University Press uses environmentally responsible print partners.
Printed in Poole, UK by CMP

Contents

List of Figures, Tables and Images

Figures

Tables

Images

List of Abbreviations

ESD	Education for Sustainable Development
HE	Higher Education
NGO	non-governmental organization
SDGs	Sustainable Development Goals
SSE	Social and Solidarity Economies
STEM	science, technology, engineering and mathematics
UN	United Nations

Acknowledgements

This book would not exist without the many inspiring colleagues and students at the School of Global Studies at the University of Sussex who nurtured my first inkling that writing a book about teaching would be a worthwhile, if daunting, endeavour. I especially thank Beth Mills and Demet Dinler for your belief in this project from the beginning, for your constant and enthusiastic support, for sharing ideas about and experiences from your own teaching and for being a careful sounding board at all stages of this writing journey. Thank you for seeing the importance of this work as much as I do. Meike Fechter and Alice Wilson joined me in a COVID-book-writing group that sustained us through the long and lonely months of 2020: thank you for reading, commenting, encouraging as well as sharing with me your own thoughts about teaching. I would also like to thank Gurminder Bhambra, Andrea Cornwall, Fae Dussart, Paul Gilbert, Farai Jena, Anna Laing, Alan Lester and Lyndsay Mclean for discussing your modules with me. Even though COVID prevented me from visiting most of your classes, learning about your teaching has played a crucial part in formulating the ideas of this book. I did get to observe the serious games workshops taught by Dominic Kniveton; thank you Dom for inviting me into your classroom. Conversations with Evan Killick, Melissa Lazenby, Mario Novelli and Linda Waldman were also helpful in developing my ideas. And thank you Buzz and Andrea for trusting me with the head of department role so early on; even though it might seem strange that such an admin-intensive role should allow time for conducting research and planning a book, being head of department gave me the space, opportunity and courage to converse, think and write about teaching in more serious ways. A post-head of department sabbatical gave me the time to put my ideas onto paper.

Just as important as fellow educators have been the students who participated in the interviews for this book; thank you Alice, Charlotte, Evie, Harry, Hein, Holly, Jamie, Joanna, Juliette, Kotryna, Lette, Liam, Lola, Mary-Jane, Nalishua, Roseanne and Yuvinka for your time. Without your perspectives this would be a very incomplete and one-sided account. I especially thank Cristina Palacio Cano, Diana Garduño Jiménez, Kendra

Quinn, Lydia Bennett-Li and Ruthie Walters for engaging in longer exchanges and for sharing some of your thoughts on my blog. They were some of the most popular posts! To all the students on my Activism for Social Change and Development and Urban Futures modules over the years, thank you for your positive presence in our classes, whether in person or virtual, and for being open to trying out new activities even though they might have seemed a bit daunting or dubious at first. It takes courage not only to teach but also to learn in new ways. I especially thank the autumn 2019 cohort of the Urban Futures module for participating in my research by responding to the weekly questionnaires and allowing me to use your creations and reflections in my book. As you can see, co-learning with you really shaped the activities in many chapters of this book, making it more concrete and relevant. Thank you also to the autumn 2017 cohort of Disasters, Environment and Development for allowing me to observe your serious games; they were truly eye-opening as to the potential of creativity for a different kind of learning.

In La Paz, my research would not have gotten off the ground without the early and ongoing support from Juana Roca. Thank you for helping me to establish contacts with so many academics, for being my guide through La Paz, Bolivian politics, decolonization and Buen Vivir, and for many insightful and provocative conversations. I also thank Alfredo Seoane, Elizabeth Jiménez and all CIDES colleagues for the warm reception and probing discussions at your institution. Interviews with Oscar Bazoberry, Ivonne Farah, Olga Jarra, Jose Nuñez del Prado, Pablo Regalsky and Fernanda Wanderley helped me to understand the joys and challenges of teaching Bolivian students. Talking to Marilia, Stefanie and Abraham added very important student perspectives. Thank you all for taking the time to talk to me. I hope that this book continues our *hablamos entre equals* and that we will be able to resume this in person in the future. I also thank Anders Burman, Hanne Halland, Anna Laing, Mieke Lopes Cardozo and Nancy Postero for general conversations about Bolivia and Belén Luna Sanz for introducing me to *torta de leche* and the many neighbourhoods of La Paz. My research in Bolivia was supported by a Faculty Opportunity Fund from the University of Sussex.

Conversations with academics and educators beyond Sussex have been numerous over the years. Particularly inspiring were meetings at the University of Edinburgh's Design for Change MA; thank you Arno Verhoeven, Rachel Harkness and Martin Craig. Thank you also to Jamie Cross, Alice Street and Julie Huang for making my stay in Edinburgh enjoyable and thought provoking. At the Stanford school Leticia Britos Cavagnaro and Ulrich Weinberg at the Potsdam d.school were helpful interlocutors, even though I never made it to Potsdam because of COVID. I would also like to thank Paul Braund, Ruth Barcan, Arturo Escobar, Keri Facer and Craig Hammond for your encouraging comments at various stages of this project. Able research assistance for various chapters was provided by Finley Braund, Hongling Pang and Caixuan (Susan) Ji, the latter two supported by the University of Sussex International Junior Research Associate Fellowship.

The book's companion website, www.creativeuniversities.com, was designed with funding from the Impact Acceleration Account (IAA) and the Higher Education Innovation Fund (HEIF) from the University of Sussex and I would like to thank Mike Collyer and Lorna Hards for their help in securing these grants. Clementine Thompson's research for the website and Genna Print's webdesign were instrumental in making the site beautiful and useful.

I thank Paul for introducing me to design thinking and doing and developing my understanding its ways through our many many conversations and projects together. Thank you also for always being there throughout this writing journey. My book would be much less beautiful and searching without your keen eye, creative interventions and persistent insistence to ask more questions, keep an open mind and push further. Your drawing of the critical-creative pedagogy guiding star is a wonderful summation of the main ideas of my book and your cover designs brought the long search for the perfect cover to a fitting creative solution. Helga and Gerold, thank you for always believing in me and for accompanying me through the various Bauhaus museums, just before lockdown put an end to all travel. And to Finley and Rory, thank you for being my teachers on this journey of life, I hope that when you go to uni some of your teachers will inspire you as much as you have me to use your talents and energy for creating the right kinds of alternative futures.

1

Invitation

In 2010, as a faculty member at the Centre for Development Studies at the University of Auckland, I was teaching a course on microfinance to a group of postgraduate students from New Zealand and the Asia-Pacific. One afternoon, one of the most engaged students in the class came to my office hours and asked me, in a tone somewhere between anger and resignation, whether there was any hope left for development. Was microfinance, a popular and widely celebrated development intervention that she had until now regarded very positively,[1] really just another in a long line of programmes that was not working? And, if so, was there anything that was actually helping marginalized people? And what did these doubts mean for her own plans to work in development upon graduation? The student was right. Based on my own research into microfinance I was highly critical of the practice and conveyed that to my students, obviously to great effect. The student's questions did not bring me satisfaction or pride in my successful teaching but, rather, a sense of discomfort and unease. Especially because this was not the first time that I had heard such comments. Like many of the University of Sussex students whom I interviewed for this book eight years later, this particular student had "hit the wall"[2] and was feeling "defeated" by what she was learning. She felt "heart-broken to learn about difficult issues and see that there is no direct answer or solution". And she was questioning her career path and identity as somebody who wanted to help make a difference in the world.

To be clear, students, who sometimes come to their studies with a self-admitted idealistic plan of "working for the United Nations (UN) and saving the world", mostly appreciate critical teaching. They understand why it is necessary to learn that development is much more complex and complicated than they had initially assumed, that it is rooted in historical colonial injustices that give rise to persistent inequalities, structured by a global system of power where Northern institutions dictate the fate of millions of marginalized people. Students recognize the need to interrogate their own positionalities and privileges and to query their everyday and historical

1

complicities. Comments such as "people need to have their idealistic ideas challenged because otherwise they would reproduce harmful stereotypes and practices", and "if we don't study that development projects can have bad outcomes because well-meaning and naïve people lead international development we can become those", show that students take these necessary critical perspectives on board.

And yet, over time I started feeling that I was also letting my students down, especially those who come to university after living, travelling or volunteering abroad, where they have encountered situations of poverty, marginalization and injustice that they feel need to be changed. As the generation that has consistently been told that they can make poverty history, they want to do something about it. They arrive at university eager to learn more about how to participate in these changes in the right ways, sometimes fuelled by misgivings after their own volunteering experiences that show them that things are not as fun, easy and simple as presented in the promotional literature. These students have been taking my courses with great interest, but often leave them disillusioned and demoralized because nothing seems to work. Every possible action, including popular interventions such as participatory development and microfinance, leads to unintended and often negative consequences. As one student said "you wish there was a bit more hope, you could think of creative solutions but in the end I had to find them for myself". This got me thinking – what if I could help students find creative ways, through my teaching, to move beyond the seeming impasse produced by relentless critique?

Already in 1927, Alfred Whitehead argued that

> A university is imaginative or it is nothing – at least nothing useful ... A university which fails [to impart information imaginatively] has no reason for existence. This atmosphere of excitement, arising from imaginative consideration, transforms knowledge. A fact is no longer a bare fact: it is invested with all its possibilities. It is no longer a burden on the memory: it is energising as the poet of our dreams, and as the architect of our purposes. (Whitehead, 1929, p 17)

What if *my* teaching could offer students openings where they could see only closure? What if I could design teaching activities that engaged students' creativity to help them imagine different responses than the ones they understood were not working?

Outline of a critical-creative pedagogy

In trying to find answers to these questions, I began to develop what I call a 'critical-creative pedagogy' that does not abandon critique but complements it with creativity. Rather than just teach students to deconstruct, this pedagogy can also inspire them to rebuild. Rather than just teach students to take apart, it can also foster their capacities to put together again, in radically new ways. Rather than just teach students to understand the legacies of the past and the failings of the present, it can also encourage them to imagine possible alternative futures. *Creative Universities* is the result of my educational journey towards realizing this pedagogy, whose contours I briefly sketch here and will fill with detail throughout the chapters of the book. Critical-creative pedagogy consists of four strands that interweave and support each other, forming an expandable sphere that can be as small or all encompassing as one wants it to be (Image 1.1).

The *first* strand is 'whole-person learning' (James and Brookfield, 2014, p 228), which has experiential, embodied and emotive elements that invite students to bring not only their intellects but also their bodies, feelings and senses into the classroom. In addition, students' past and present experiences in class, on campus and outside university are important sources of knowledge that can inform their own and their peers' learning. A *second*

Image 1.1: Critical–creative pedagogy 'guiding star'

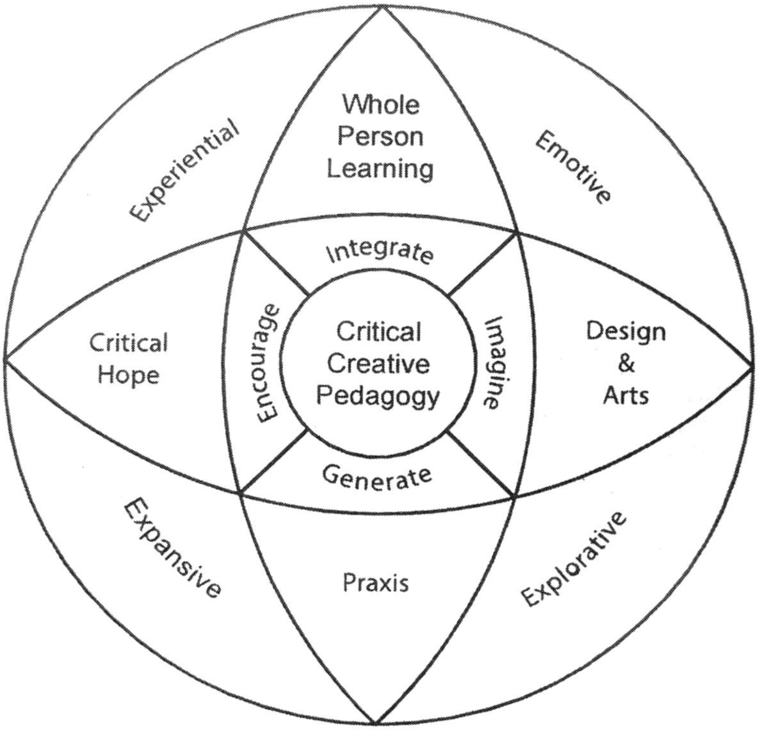

strand is the incorporation of creative methods from design and the arts, which are particularly apt to engage students' imagination. Especially, design thinking and practices can develop their abilities for open-ended inquiry and iterative experimentation, help them to learn in the absence of (easy) solutions and draw attention to the materiality of this learning. The *third* strand is found in praxis, understood as action informed by theory. This means that a critical-creative pedagogy engages with global challenges not in a contemplative mode but in a forward-looking one that considers possible responses, especially heterodox ones, and how students could work towards creating these individually and collectively. Praxis therefore incorporates elements of problem-based, practical and applied learning. This connects closely to the *fourth* strand, which is critical hope. A critical-creative pedagogy assumes a hopeful stance, in an informed way where hope is aware of its own conditions of possibility. Critical hope does not lead to unrealistic optimism or naive solutionism but is reparative in addressing past injustices and destruction and active in engaging with contemporary challenges.

Together, whole-person learning, creative methods, praxis and critical hope provide a pedagogical approach that can help students to better understand global challenges and imagine alternative responses to them. According to Sarah Amsler,

> knowing that there are alternatives 'out there' and in principle is not enough to make concrete and critical hope in social change possible ... The construction of paths and bridges, of spaces and infrastructures for learning, of signposts for way-making, and of way-stations to nourish us on the journey, is essential work. (2015, p 17)

It is this work that a critical-creative pedagogy undertakes, and as I bring it to life throughout my book I hope to inspire readers to consider how its contents might unfold in their own pedagogical practice.

While *Creative Universities* is grounded in my own teaching in the fields of global development and anthropology, its arguments are also relevant for other social science disciplines that study current global social, economic and ecological challenges.[3] This broader relevance comes from both of my home disciplines being capacious: interested in holistic understanding of contemporary worlds, their historical roots and, to some extent, future trajectories. This is especially the case for global development, where teaching focuses on issues affecting marginalized people and what is being and can be done to address them.[4] In other words, I wrote this book with a large audience in mind, hoping that it will speak to all educators who want to help students better understand global challenges and also enable them to imagine responses to these challenges.

There is one caveat, however: I do not have an educational scholarship background and therefore do not engage with the rich pedagogical scholarship literature. In its absence, the diverse fields I do draw on – design, solidarity economies, transition studies and complex systems thinking, among others – provide lateral and cross-fertilizing perspectives that can enrich teaching in novel ways. This, then, is a partial account that aims for breadth rather than depth in tackling diverse challenges and casts a wide net in its search for alternative responses to them. As a result, extensive debates will be summarized and nuanced positions simplified, a risk I am willing to take in order to provide accessible entry points for educators and students interested in creatively reimagining teaching and learning.

Writing with courage

Publishing a book about teaching as an anthropologist rather than a pedagogical scholar has taken courage. Because social scientists do not usually research or write about their own teaching, it is not a common or high-profile topic, 'perhaps reflecting a broader failure in the academy to subject our teaching to serious critical reflection and to consider it worthy of serious writing and publication' (Cameron et al, 2013, p 349). But most social scientists do teach, spending many hours crafting syllabi, reading lists, virtual learning sites, lectures and seminars and then delivering them to students. This demanding pedagogical work often leaves little time or space for reflections or conversations. This is partly systemic, when teaching loads are increasing, when core modules with mandatory content need to be taught, when fixed learning outcomes ask for conformity and when conventional modes of assessment are the norm. Academics come more alive when they can develop specialist modules based on their own research interests, and many still have relative freedom to design and deliver such modules as long as they incorporate basic requirements. But precisely because we all teach, writing about teaching hits close to home, touches daily activities of which we are protective, through which we might partly define ourselves. Being told that our teaching is not creative enough might be the last thing we want to hear. It is also not the message of this book.

Creative Universities aims to be a starting point for discussions about teaching and an invitation to explore some of the book's ideas in practice. It wants to prompt rather than prescribe, be experimental rather than exhaustive. I share my own insights and activities, as well as the work of my colleagues at the University of Sussex and students' reactions to our teaching, to encourage readers to imagine possible applications and adaptations in their own classrooms. I also recognize that everybody's situation and context is different and, in this sense, my book is an example of an 'anti-methods pedagogy' that does not offer standardized methodological recipes or ready-made pedagogical solutions (Macedo, 1997, p 1).

Instead, it provides a map to enable readers to retrace my journey and in the process forge their own paths. I invite fellow educators to be courageous and experimental themselves; as Paolo Freire wrote in his *Letter to Those who Dare to Teach*: 'it is impossible to teach without the courage to try a thousand times before giving up' (cited in Darder, 2009, p 575). To facilitate such experimentation, my ideas and suggestions do not require a wholesale overhaul of modules or courses and can be adapted for individual seminars or workshops.[5] After all, 'it is legitimate to dream in steps rather than leaps', and small steps are what this book offers (Amsler, 2014, p 288). That the great majority of its teaching activities have been taken from existing practice shows their feasibility, offering what one reviewer described as 'pragmatic optimism'.

Writing a book about teaching in the middle of a global health pandemic proved particularly challenging. Even though I was on leave to write this book throughout 2020 and therefore only watched the sudden move to remote and then blended teaching from afar, the COVID-19 pandemic cast a deep shadow over my writing. In the depths of lockdown in March and April, when I was just getting into the flow of things, I also began to question my entire project. After all, the subtitle of my book is 'reimagining teaching for global challenges and alternative futures', and we were facing the biggest challenge of the century. Observing and living the fumbling early responses of the UK government to the pandemic showed the difficult trade-offs that have to be made in response to complex challenges, but because this pandemic was outside of my expertise I was not able to address it in a substantial manner.

In addition, my pedagogy is built around face-to-face teaching and now it seemed that such teaching, which remains my preferred way of interacting with students, was disappearing overnight. In the course of a few weeks, the role of digital technologies in all — including higher education — classrooms changed necessarily and radically, overcoming many individual and institutional resistances to online teaching in the process. This shift strengthened the agendas of technology evangelists who have been expounding the benefits and potentials of digital technologies for years, and there are undoubtedly many: online courses that provide access to education to those students who would otherwise be excluded because of financial, time or visa constraints, immersive technologies that enrich teaching, platforms that connect students for collaborative cross-border learning are just a few examples. As the pandemic has lingered, digital technologies have also continued to enable staff and students who cannot return to classrooms for health and other reasons to teach and learn.

And yet, I believe that there is a continued central place for face-to-face teaching, that direct rather than digitally mediated pedagogical interactions provide unique and valuable modes of learning and that physical engagement with others and the wider world are important ways of learning. In addition, the COVID-induced necessities have not overcome the limitations of digital educational technologies.[6] The introduction of such technologies has too often resulted in 'digital accounting systems that have come to both responsibilise and punish learners, enabling surveillance and an ever more narrow definition of education as techno-cratic preparation for employment' (Facer, 2018b, p 200). Educational technologies are embedded in social, political and economic contexts, and if these are 'competitive, individualised, exploitative – the technologies will be harnessed to those agendas. In and of themselves technologies will neither liberate nor transform education' (p 201).

Technologies can exacerbate existing inequalities or introduce new ones, when richer universities are able to use the latest and most innovative teaching tools – immersive virtual environments, augmented reality, artificial intelligence – while under-resourced universities and their students are left further behind. They can reinforce individualizing tendencies when students learn by themselves in their homes or dormitories, and stand in the way of social interactions and collaborations. Technologies raise different questions of inclusiveness and accessibility and need to cater as much to content delivery as to relationship building. They can expand their surveillance affordances from students to faculty, whose teaching can now be recorded, monitored and used in new ways that could curtail the freedom that is left in course design and threaten jobs in the long run. Against this backdrop, I will reflect on the role that digital technologies can play in critical-creative teaching in the upcoming chapters, albeit briefly.

Finally, I need to acknowledge the limits that come from writing, and working, within the belly of the beast that are universities operating in the neoliberal higher education (HE) regime. There have been many calls for the wholesale rejection or radical overhaul of universities, alongside arguments that as long as students are paying exorbitant tuition fees, no meaningful changes are possible. Critics observe that working within the system not only helps to sustain it but also compromises the radical potentialities of more emancipatory educational models (Bessant et al, 2015). I understand these critiques, and yet, I agree with bell hooks who writes that 'the classroom remains the most radical space of possibility in the academy' (hooks, 1994) and with Boaventura de Sousa Santos on the importance of teaching revolutionary ideas in reactionary institutions (cited in Harcourt, 2017). In doing so, I try to walk my own talk. As I aim to teach critical hope, I remain hopeful myself that there is value in working in the cracks in the system and that individual transformative practices in the classroom, when connected with others, can multiply, amplify and affect larger changes. Adhering to a personal prefigurative politics, I aim to enact in my own teaching the possibilities

I want students to imagine and create. Following J.K. Gibson-Graham (2008), I believe in the performative nature of academic work, in its potential to open up spaces for a pedagogical politics of possibilities where alternatives can germinate and be nurtured rather than analysed out of existence.

Of course I recognize that co-optation is an ever-present danger, but I do not see it as a necessary condition of working within universities. Granted, proposing to be more creative in our teaching, and for students to be more creative in their learning, could easily become part of the market-driven HE regime. It could be drafted into employability efforts for a future workforce ready to compete in the knowledge economy and creative industries. It could also become an additional requirement for already stretched faculty and overwhelmed students. I am acutely mindful of these possibilities and address them in the first part of each chapter, where I decentre mainstream educational practices. Teaching is a deeply moral, ethical and political endeavour and

> we must take responsibility for the specific normative values and objectives of all our projects; remain vigilant about how power works through ostensibly liberatory practices such as dialogue, witnessing and cooperation; and be critically aware of the possibility that such practices can easily be deployed for conservative and repressive ends. (Amsler, 2014, p 281)

However, rather than call for resignation and refusal, these dangers demand 'vigilant exercises of self-scrutiny and self-cultivation' (Gibson-Graham, 2006, p xxvi). This is best done from a position of generative theorizing.

Generative theory

In this book, I propose the use of what I call 'generative theory' – a theory that is able to generate possibilities – to inform critical-creative teaching. This theory is grounded in the writings of J.K. Gibson-Graham on academic practices as performative projects that create alternatives, and on academic subjects as 'world-makers' who have 'a constitutive role in the worlds that exist, and ... power to bring new worlds into being' (2008, p 614). These subjectivities encompass committed educators, involved researchers and scholar-activists.[7] Becoming such academic subjects is not easy because

> we are trained to be discerning, detached and critical so that we can penetrate the veil of common understanding and explore the root causes and bottom lines that govern the phenomenal world. This academic stance means that most theorizing is tinged with scepticism and negativity, not a particularly nurturing environment for hopeful, inchoate experiments. (p 618)

Gibson-Graham (2006) find the sources of such negative or, in their words, 'strong' theorizing in certain (leftist) practices, as articulated by Eve Sedgewick's analysis of paranoia that is all-knowing to protect itself against surprises, Walter Benjamin's writings about melancholia that looks back towards certainties and Saul Newman's arguments about moralism that aims for the purity of powerlessness. Taken together, paranoia, melancholia and moralism result in strong theory that dismisses experimental practices as always already co-opted, tainted or inadequate. This in turn reinforces dominant political-economic structures rather than questioning them and 'render[s] the world effectively incontestable' (Gibson-Graham, 2006, p 6). Instead of subscribing to strong theory's scepticism and suspicion, Gibson-Graham use Sedgewick's 'weak' theory to practise openness towards the new. Weak theory cultivates a beginner's mindset that refuses to know too much and supports rather than discredits the emergence of alternatives. It entails reduced reach, localized purview and attenuated explanations, in order to hold open spaces in which possibilities can grow, rather than foreclose them from the outset with overwhelming or destructive critique.

To escape the negative connotations of 'weak', I propose the term 'generative theory', which also highlights its ability to actively create possibilities. In the context of global challenges, generative theorizing engages in identifying their root causes, manifestations and impacts and then takes a partial, cautious and nurturing approach to addressing these. It does not aim for absolute diagnosis and grand solutionism but for finding work-arounds, accommodations and fixes while recognizing their incompleteness, impurities and imperfections. Generative theory has an experimental and open stance towards responses to global challenges, an attention to multiplicities and ambiguities. It seeks connections and collaborations and is willing to consider rather than judge. It embraces the unexpected, celebrates surprises and is interested in building up rather than tearing down. Generative theory enables a critical-creative pedagogy by ensuring that its critical component does not overwhelm its creative sibling, putting both on an equal footing where they can nurture each other. My own generative theorizing throughout this book shows its potential for reimagining education.

Whether to practise negative or generative theory is not only a pedagogical decision but also a political and ethical one, shaped by a commitment to become a condition of possibility rather than impossibility. It does not deny or ignore the existence of oppressive and exploitative structures that work against the realization of possibilities, but 'encourages us to deny these forces as fundamental, structural, or universal reality and to instead identify them as contingent outcomes of ethical decisions, political projects, and sedimented localized practices' (Gibson-Graham, 2006, p xxxi). It also does not mean suspending critique, but places it alongside generativity and care. Gibson-Graham's writings are replete with references to surprise, invention and playfulness. These resonances with creativity are not coincidental, as for Gibson-Graham practising creativity is a technique that enables academics to become new ethical subjects of possibility. This entails bringing things from different domains together to generate something new and then transferring this to areas where it can be useful. This is in line with much general thinking on creativity.

The radically creative university

Creativity is a complex, contested and context-specific phenomenon with intellectual, emotional, practical and ethical dimensions. In spite of this multidimensionality, there are characteristics of creativity that resonate across the vast scholarly and popular literature on the topic; these include originality, curiosity, playfulness, divergent thinking, risk taking, openness to new experiences and an ability to tolerate ambiguity and accept uncertainty. With a systematic review of this literature being beyond the scope of this chapter, I will briefly survey some of the recent research on creativity in education.[8] There is general agreement that teaching and learning are inherently creative processes, even though they might not always be recognized as such. In the literature, creativity is often connected to pioneers in alternative and child-centred education such as John Dewey, Rudolf Steiner and Maria Montessori, who argued that education should draw out the inborn abilities of each child. In the context of adult education, Paolo Freire showed the importance of education engaging people's natural artistic and creative expressions and harnessing these for personal and social change. For him, learning was about 'being in the world through creative practice' (quoted in Pope, 2005, p 53).

For HE in particular, scholars have identified being imaginative, original, exploratory, analytical and communicative as key aspects of pedagogical creativity (Jackson and Shaw, 2006; Figure 1.1). Such creativity entails looking at things from different and multiple perspectives and includes 'domain bridging', which is the mash-up of disparate ideas, from making unusual and surprising connections across different areas or from putting unrelated things together (Staley, 2019). In other words, pedagogical creativity entails the 'ability to leap out of familiar habits into new idea spaces' (Robinson, 2001, p 185). Similarly, pedagogical imagination means being able to 'move away from the well-trodden, to sniff out the subtle indicators of possibility, and to move sideways and beyond into seeing many different aspects of a situation or individual and their potential' (James and Brookfield, 2014, p 60). This does not preclude critique, because creativity must be grounded in critique in order to work with an informed understanding of the contexts and conditions of particular situations. Each creative action has an element of critique, as new ideas need to be critically evaluated in order to become

Figure 1.1: Five elements of pedagogical creativity

⇒ Imagination – move beyond the obvious

⇒ Originality – add to what already exists

⇒ Exploration – be open to the emergent

⇒ Analysis – think critically about new ideas

⇒ Communication – explore different modes

Source: Author, adapted from Jackson and Shaw, 2006, p 90.

meaningful, while critical thinking itself is a creative process. Therefore, instead of operating as a binary, critique and creativity are interlinked and best seen as a continuum.

Creative capacities are latent in all individuals. As everyday creativity, human originality is found across diverse activities of everyday lives in individuals constantly adapting, innovating, being flexible and trying out new ideas (Richards, 2007). Both the process of being creative and the creative outcomes to which it gives rise are important. Creativity can operate on several levels, from individual creativity found in practices that are new for a particular person, to social creativity that creates novelty for a group, to historical creativity that takes humankind and history as its points of reference (Robinson, 2001). This last version most closely corresponds to elite conceptions of creativity and is often found in artistic or scientific breakthroughs. Alongside these, everyday creativity celebrates the creative achievements of individuals in the context of their own lives, while also being meaningful to others. Ken Robinson therefore defines creativity as 'imaginative processes with outcomes that are original and of value' (p 118). Everyday creativity means that every educator and student has creative capabilities that can be developed and nurtured through pedagogical practices. These must be inclusive and accessible to different learners.

This was brought home to me during a university-wide teaching event at Sussex, when I suggested that we need more creativity, imagination and hopefulness in our teaching and was told by another participant that this could be off-putting to some students, or indeed staff. To address such concerns, broad and flexible ideas and practices of creativity are needed within which all students can find possibilities for learning. This works best when teachers model creativity in their own classroom practices and are honest with students about feeling pushed out of their comfort zones, which can be a scary prospect. That creative teaching might not fit all students or educators is often acknowledged by scholars in this area, such as Alison James and Stephen Brookfield, for whom it depends on personal preferences, teaching styles and curriculum requirements. Such teaching will therefore be received with 'complex and contradictory' responses from both colleagues and students, ranging from enthusiastic embrace, to ambivalent attempts, to cynical questioning or outright refusal (2014, p 228).

Importantly, James and Brookfield also warn that if students feel that they are not creative or transformational enough, creative teaching can become a form of control or disciplinary power. In light of this, making explicit the normative values of our pedagogical projects and being aware of their implications and consequences is crucial. But the authors also argue that 'students remember imaginative classroom moments as some of the most powerful events in their learning trajectories' (p xiv). This happens when students are given opportunities to explore a multiplicity of creative possibilities through finding the medium or form of expression that works best for them, obtaining the skills to work within the medium and having the freedom to experiment (Robinson, 2001). Such open-ended practice entails attention to process over product, valuing students' creative explorations of and engagement with challenges as important in and of themselves, rather than looking only at the final outcomes of these engagements.[9]

While creative capacities are latent in all learners, childhood creativity is often lost when students move through the mainstream education system (Robinson, 2001). This is due to the system's emphasis on academicism, encompassing logico-deductive reasoning, linear moves from causes to effects and propositional knowledge supported by evidence of observation. The focus of academic education is on knowledge assimilation and critical analysis, to be tested through the achievement of learning objectives and outcomes-based assessments that leave little room for the unexpected that is an integral part of creative teaching. There are also particular challenges in the context of HE, where calls for more creativity are usually linked to the importance of education for developing students' personal potentials as fully as possible, including preparing them for rapidly changing workplaces. Such a linkage to economic imperatives parallels arguments by policy makers and university senior managers for more of a particular kind of creativity.

This is the corporate-managerialist creativity that emerged during the mid-20th century as a Euro-American response to problems associated with rapid social and technological changes and aimed to bring about scientific discoveries, technological inventions, commercial competition and military superiority (Pope, 2005). Building on these foundations, the rise of the knowledge economy at the end of the 20th century led to a focus on creativity as a tool for corporate growth and national economic competitiveness, leading Pope to call this corporatist creativity 'one of the most prized commodities of capitalism' (p 23). It has renewed itself with the emergence of the creative industries as a key economic sector. As I show in Chapter 6, in HE such instrumentalist creativity has resulted in a human resources-driven and employment-oriented version of creative education that is focusing on competencies and skills for student employability above all else. By contrast, I follow Sarah Amsler (2014) in arguing for radical creativity that moves outside of mainstream capitalist growth agendas and instead searches for alternative futures.

Imagining alternative futures

A critical-creative education informed by radical creativity can better enable students to understand and address global challenges through imagining and working towards alternative futures. My language is deliberate – I am not proposing to solve current problems (although they undoubtedly need to be solved), because solutionism is too often associated with technological fixes, economic growth and scientific advances that need to be questioned rather than celebrated. Practices of working towards are gradual, modest and meandering and therefore lend themselves to creative approaches. They also need to engage students' imagination, because 'we cannot build a future we cannot imagine' (Elgin, 1991, p 5). Our imagination allows us to consider not just what is, but what can be, as it can broaden the scope of what is perceived as possible. However, there is always more than one possible future, and whose version of the future counts involves considerations of power and politics. A clearer understanding of the relationship between education and futuring can unpack universities' roles in shaping diverse futures. Keri Facer shows that 'futurity is embedded at the heart of the educational process' and has given rise to three main future orientations in education (2018b, p 202).

First is 'the future as a landscape for rational choice making', where education contributes to rendering its contours knowable, identifying preferable actions and assessing the impact of decisions (p 203). If COVID-19 has taught us anything, it is the fallacy of such instrumentalist assumptions. Second is a colonial orientation that aims to persuade students of particular visions of the future, be they progressive or conservative, and to shape their attitudes and behaviours towards these. While this is an enticing proposition, especially for critical educators, it needs to acknowledge its own ethical agendas, potential conflicts of interest and possible temptation for adults to abdicate their responsibilities towards present challenges. This relates to the third orientation, where education serves as a bulwark against an unknown and potentially dystopian future, becoming the silver bullet that will solve all problems. These orientations not only overestimate the power of education and neglect the importance of other factors, but also see educational success as the sole means of achieving personal and social goods. Too often, these future visions are dominated by prescriptive economic mandates and technological visions. By contrast, when futures are seen as sites of possibilities that students can explore, rather than being predetermined by teachers and other adults, educational spaces can become places of experimentation with potential alternative futures.

This raises the question of alternatives to what? Rather than simply meaning different or unusual, in this book I propose radical alternatives to conventional, orthodox, hegemonic interventions. Each chapter begins with a decentring of mainstream perspectives and practices, to show that the alternatives I subsequently present are dissident, heterodox, unruly. At times I use these qualifiers, but even when I do not, the language of alternatives refers to multiple, diverse and plural responses to contemporary challenges that differ from and often work against mainstream interventions. In conceptualizing these alternatives, I draw especially on the work of Arturo Escobar, an anthropologist of (post)development who has turned his thinking towards pluriversal alternatives that are grounded in social movements in his native Columbia and other indigenous cosmovisions and that incorporate ideas of design, political ecology, feminist economics and political ontology, among others (Escobar, 2017, 2020). Many of these alternatives feed into the emerging field of transition studies, which bring together pure, applied and engaged research on transformational actions by drawing on diverse academic disciplines as well as social movements, activist networks and radical civil society organizations (Escobar, 2015).

What unite these various fields are transition discourses that call for heterodox transformations, because contemporary crises cannot be solved from within the current epistemological, economic and political paradigms that have been instrumental in creating these crises. According to de Sousa Santos 'we have modern problems for which there are no modern solutions', or, as Colombian activists put it, 'we cannot construct our world with more of the same ... What's possible has already been done; now let's go for the impossible' (cited in Escobar, 2020, pp 6, 45). This leads Escobar and others to argue that we 'need to step outside of existing institutional and epistemic boundaries if we truly want to envision the worlds and practices capable of bringing about the significant transformations seen as needed' (p 13). It also implies moving away from a worldview dominated by Euro-American history and thought that presents itself as universal, and moving towards a pluriverse constituted by a multiplicity of distinct but mutually entangled and partially connected worlds that co-constitute each other. Undertaking this shift requires deep transformations in ways of being, knowing and making in the world, including the relocalization of economic activities and the reconstitution of the communal to embrace non-human beings. In each chapter I consider some of the knowledges, orientations and politics that can help students to imagine such alternative visions and link these to particular transition examples, such as transition design in Chapter 3, solidarity and community economies in Chapter 4 and Buen Vivir in Chapter 5.

Like Escobar, I look especially to Latin America for the emergence of alternatives. The region has a long history of alternative thought, including dependency theory, liberation philosophy and theology, hybridity and participatory action research. More recently, the modernity/coloniality research programme is shaping decolonial thinking in many universities through non-Eurocentric epistemologies. Similarly, a long history of social movements, from the Zapatistas and many other indigenous movements to the Landless Workers Movement and the World Social Forum, has inspired activists around the world, often linked up through transnational networks. Correspondingly, Latin American scholars and activists 'have pushed ahead much further and with wider public appeal in their efforts to develop deeper concepts of alternatives than their counterparts in Europe' (North and Cato, 2017, p 295). This has given rise to 'hope movements [as] the collective action directed to anticipate, imperfectly, alternative realities to arise from the openness of the present one' (Dinerstein and Deneulin, 2012, p 585). Hope therefore plays an important role in imagining heterodox alternatives. Like creativity, it is a wide-ranging concept that has been explored from many different disciplinary angles (for a good summary see Webb, 2007). Hope is both personal and social, has to be actively cultivated and is often seen as 'a precondition for any form of action, and indeed, as generative of action' (White, 1996, p 9).

In education, Freire advanced a notion of radical hope as 'the active refiguring of epistemological, ontological and axiological conditions necessary for renewing society and alleviating human suffering' (Lake and Kress, 2017, p 69). Besides being a central part of Critical Pedagogy, hope has also been connected to a pedagogy of possibility (Barcan, 2016) and incorporated into proposals for a utopian pedagogy (Hammond, 2017). In all cases, 'in order to pursue pedagogy as a mechanism for transformation, liberation and social justice, it is essential that active, militant and constructive hope be one of its key foundations' (p 107). Often, creativity is seen to play an important role in cultivating such hope. However, like creativity, hope can be and has been commodified, emblazoned on T-shirts and sloganized beyond any meaningful content (Lake and Kress, 2017). More insidious perhaps are accusations of hope as naive, trivial and childish, made by those for whom 'hopelessness is what the contemporary ethos demands as we attend to the serious business of trying to adapt to circumstances that are increasingly alienating and oppressive' (p 72). As a result, hope as a form of resistance is neutralized rather than harnessed for transformative action. To recuperate this potential, critical hope has been one of the animating sentiments of my project.

Researching teaching

Creative Universities is my own 'performative ontological project' of making hope and possibility more present, credible and viable in HE classrooms

(Gibson-Graham, 2008, p 626). The book has emerged from my teaching journey, which began as a teaching assistant at the University of California, Berkeley. Upon finishing my PhD in Anthropology there, I co-founded the RiOS Institute, a research group bringing design and anthropology approaches to Silicon Valley organizations using technology for development. In this context I delivered interactive workshops to diverse groups that included technology company chief executive officers, social entrepreneurs and World Bank officials, which have informed my ideas for active teaching. I also undertook contract teaching at Berkeley, including designing a course on social entrepreneurship, technology and development for students at the School of Information. As part of the course, students were placed with local organizations, which introduced me to some of the challenges of work experiences described in Chapter 6, and also to transdisciplinary teaching. During a summer working at a semi-rural community college I taught the fundamentals of anthropological theory to students who were often the first in their families to go to college and challenged me to find accessible and creative ways of conveying complex concepts. Last but not least, a term teaching at a sustainability-focused business school introduced me to project-based teaching. It was designing learning experiences for such diverse audiences that sowed the seeds of critical-creative pedagogy.

In 2009 I took up a position at the Centre for Development Studies at the University of Auckland in New Zealand, a small postgraduate programme that allowed me to continue experimenting with practice-focused teaching, while also exposing me for the first time to decolonial practices through Mātauranga Māori and Pacific philosophies as a distinct way of knowing and being in the world.[10] In 2014 I joined the University of Sussex's School of Global Studies, becoming head of the Department of International Development two years later. This meant that, in addition to my own teaching, I was now thinking about teaching more than ever and was having more and more conversations with colleagues and students. A year later, I began focused research for this book.

This research has consisted of 'journey interviews' with 30 undergraduate students who had just finished their degree course, usually in international development and often combined with anthropology, geography, international relations, economics, sociology or a language. In these interviews I asked students about their experiences of studying at Sussex, about their modules and how they were taught, their views on development and social change and their own roles within both. I interviewed several of my colleagues about their teaching, in addition to the many informal conversations I had at Sussex and other universities. I also observed some of my colleagues' classes, which I selected because of their teaching content and format and because they were consistently mentioned by students as having been transformative and impactful.

Last but not least, I drew on my own teaching practice, particularly a postgraduate module on Activism for Social Change and Development and a third-year undergraduate module on Urban Futures, both of which incorporate some of the teaching activities I describe in the following chapters. Besides formal module evaluations, I gathered student feedback on a voluntary basis through weekly anonymous surveys, follow-up interviews with interested students and written reflective accounts. Following Sussex University ethics protocol, I obtained informed consent from all students and conducted all interviews with them once marks had been finalized. Having conducted all of my empirical research at my current home university has provided advantages of deep contextual knowledge, personal situatedness and long-term sustained engagement. But there are also limitations resulting from this unique setting and small sample, and I therefore need to acknowledge the particular context of the University of Sussex.

Sussex was established in 1961 as a public university just outside Brighton in the south-east of the UK, being the first of the new or 'plate glass' universities set up by the UK government after the Second World War. The term was coined by Michael Beloff (1970) in reference to the architectural style of these universities, which used steel and glass rather than red brick and traditional Oxbridge forms. In the case of Sussex, architect Basil Spence's 'modernist architecture with brutalist flourishes' was inspired by the beauty of the South Downs in which the university is located (Ijeh, 2015). It combined the old and the new, mixing concrete and red brick, which is now mainly greyed by age and pollution, and organizing the first buildings around a central quadrangle with modernist arches. What was novel about Sussex was its break with academic traditions through progressive teaching in multidisciplinary schools that brought together social and natural sciences, for example.

Early on, the university developed a reputation for radical student activism that manifested in support for anti-apartheid and anti-Vietnam war struggles, including a group of students preventing then government advisor Samuel Huntington from speaking on campus and throwing red paint over a visiting US diplomat. Student protests also encompassed (rent) strikes, assessment boycotts and the periodic occupations of administrative buildings; they continue in various forms, as I show in Chapter 6. The forerunner to the School of Global Studies where I teach was the School of African and Asian Studies (AFRAS), which challenged existing ideas around colonialism, race and gender and hosted scholars and activists from the global South. In the late 1960s, the UN asked Sussex researchers for science policy recommendations; the ensuing report became known as the Sussex Manifesto, and, while initially deemed as too radical to be included in official UN reports, it did influence UN thinking around the role of science and technology in development. Forty years later, a new Manifesto was written by academics in the Science, Technology and Policy Research Unit (SPRU), Global Studies and the Institute of Development Studies, which is co-located on campus. This critical mass of people working in challenge-related areas has contributed to Sussex being repeatedly ranked first in the world for development studies.

However, Sussex is no educational utopia. Adam Tickell, Sussex's vice-chancellor at the time of writing, became known as the 'neoliberal beast' during the first wave of staff pension strikes in 2018. Sussex became a hotspot of protests during that and more recent strikes. During this time, the university has also been receiving research funding from questionable philanthropic sources.[11] A 2016 report, commissioned by senior management after a domestic violence case involving a student and her doctoral supervisor was initially handled in grossly inadequate ways, speaks of 'the performance of activism' and shows the persistence of structural inequalities around race, gender and sexuality, institutional privilege and deep divisions between staff and senior management.[12] In 2019 the university's pro-vice-chancellor for Education and Students launched a top-down Pedagogic Revolution that, amid COVID, refocused on 'the digital pivot'. But Sussex is also home to the faculty-initiated Active Learning Network[13] and a great number of inspiring, passionate and committed educators. While I have learned much from working with them, I also wanted to expand my perspective beyond HE institutions in the Global North, which led to a period of research in Bolivia.

In 2019 I conducted a series of interviews with academics and students at various universities in La Paz to obtain a Global South perspective on social science teaching. Having been trained as a Latin Americanist and conducted ethnographic research with traditional healers and indigenous peoples in north-western Argentina (Schwittay, 2003), I have closely followed developments in the region over the years. Tapping into this regional and linguistic knowledge, when I was thinking about a second research site Bolivia came to mind for a number of reasons: it has been a long-standing experimental location for mainstream development interventions, including economic shock therapy and International Monetary Fund-mandated structural adjustment in the 1980s,[14] and more recently having strong social, popular and indigenous movements that have given rise to a number of economic, ecological and epistemological alternatives (Gudynas, 2011). This has included the pioneering work of the Taller de Historia Oral Andina,[15] which has contributed to creating an indigenous counterpublic sphere and alternative history forged by indigenous intellectuals (Rivera Cusicanqui, 1986). '

It also led to the election of Evo Morales as the country's first indigenous president in 2006, following many years of indigenous and working-class insurrection. Some scholars have interpreted Morales' ascent as an example of a 'world reversal' or civilizational change, in spite of his failure to move outside the established capitalist order after his election (Escobar, 2020, p xxxvi). His broken promises eventually led to him being forced from office in 2019, although his MAS party won subsequent elections in 2020. Following Morales' election, decolonization became part of Bolivia's official government agenda, with education playing a key role. This included decolonizing the national education system itself, with the aim of

> putting an end to ethnic borders that influence opportunities in the area of education, work, politics and economic security, where no one is privileged on the basis of race, ethnicity or language. It also signifies to avoid favouring conceptualisations of the Western world as if they are universal, yet valuing the knowledge, skills and technologies of the indigenous civilisations. (Congreso Nacional de Educacion, cited in Lopes Cardozo, 2012, p 24)

HE in particular was identified as central to not only implementing but also generating decolonizing politics, with resulting dissonances between state-mandated educational reforms, including indigenous universities, and activist counter-institutions that drew on indigenous cosmologies and ontologies in more substantial ways (Burman, 2012).

Consequently, many of my conversations with educators at public, private and indigenous universities centred on the complicated relationship of Bolivian academics to this official agenda, but also on larger questions of decoloniality, knowledge traditions and the role of university education for different student groups. These conversations made me aware of the importance of national educational contexts, the contested nature of alternative visions and their embeddedness in local politics. Throughout this research, I grappled with 'the ethical implications of the Global North looking to [educational] people and communities whom they have historically exploited and colonized as resources for their own salvation today' (Amsler and Facer, 2017, p 13). Within this context, how could I build research relations that were 'not parasitic but collegial' (p 13)? Sharing my own knowledge and opening myself up to interrogation and critique, being respectful of academics' intellectual choices and articulating epistemologies from the Global South with Northern ones were some of my strategies. These were guided by a spirit of *hablamos entre equales*, a phrase my interlocutors and I coined to characterize our dialogues among equals.

The journey ahead: knowing what, being how, doing for

Each of the following chapters addresses a particular challenge, showing how the strands of critical-creative pedagogy manifest in teaching students new knowledge related to the challenge, cultivating orientations that help students activate that knowledge and informing a politics through which students can use their learning to imagine and work towards alternatives (Table 1.1).

Here is a brief overview of what's to come. In Chapter 2 I elaborate the critical side of critical-creative pedagogy by drawing selectively on the cannon of Critical Pedagogy, in a broad arch that spans from John Dewey to Paolo Freire to Maxine Greene and Sarah Amsler, as a critique of the current neoliberalized university. In parallel, I incorporate calls for the decolonization of the westernized university, which will be explored through the writings of Oliveira Andreotti, Boaventura de Souza Santos and Ramon Grosfoguel. I then explore the emergence of academic identities in relation to generative theory and to teaching that counters students' saviourism. The chapter concludes with two teaching activities, body mapping and writing an urban manifesto, that constitute students as embodied and situated learners.

Chapter 3 introduces design, to consider how classrooms can be expanded in future-oriented ways. Concepts such as design thinking and wicked problems introduce students to open-ended and iterative modes of inquiry appropriate for understanding complex challenges, while orientations of becoming comfortable with ambiguity and acting with humility help them to imagine responses to them. Design also brings into focus the materiality of teaching, through emphasizing the importance of spaces and materials, while drawing attention to the resource politics in which these are embedded. Two teaching activities show the value of scenario building for helping students envision alternative futures. Chapter 4 argues for the need to reclaim economies by firstly opening up orthodox economics through pluralist and heterodox teaching. I draw on various examples of relocalizing economic activities, such as pluralist and solidarity economies in Bolivia and diverse community economies, to explore alternative practices that move away from mainstream capitalist logics. Closely related to this are the two teaching activities presented in this chapter, which include students creating personal diverse economy portfolios and designing plans for a cooperative as an alternative economic space.

A focus on repairing ecologies takes centre stage in Chapter 5, where I question mainstream green growth and sustainable development agendas by showing the potential of deep ecology and sustain-ability[16] as disruptive alternatives. Concrete examples, such as Buen Vivir in Bolivia and complex systems thinking, highlight the fundamental interrelations and interdependencies among all living beings. The chapter's teaching activities focus on creative ways of engaging students with sustain-ability issues, such as designing and playing serious games to understand the effects of climate change and mapping campus ecosystems as a basis for enacting change. This

Table 1.1: Key chapter insights

	2 Academic identities	3 Designing futures	4 Reclaiming economies	5 Repairing ecologies	6 Prefiguring alternatives
Knowledge learning about	*neoliberal HE decolonial	*wicked problems *design thinking	*diverse economies *social embeddedness	*Buen Vivir *complex system thinking	*prefiguration *activism
Orientations being (open to)	*unlearning *decolonizing	*ambiguity *humility *empathy	*heterodox *alternative economic subjects	*trans-disciplinary *uncertainty	*hopeful *transgressive
Politics practising	*anti-saviourism	*resource equalities	*applied knowledge	*eco-centrism	*possibilities

Source: Author.

leads directly into Chapter 6 in which I consider praxis as a central element of teaching. Against mainstream employability agendas, I use pedagogical examples focusing on decolonial movements and activism to ask how teaching changes students and students, in turn, change teaching. I look at the activism campaigns that were created by students in my own activism module, as well as at climate change activism among Sussex students, as concrete instances of students using their learning to imagine alternatives and beginning to enact them in powerful and inspiring ways.

The book concludes with a proposal for several speculative capstone projects that show the potential of a critical-creative pedagogy informed by the knowledges, orientations and politics from all chapters writ large across universities and what it would take to realize this potential. The questions in Figure 1.2 can be used as a guide for readers to make this book their own: imagine how it can be useful in your area of teaching and feel free to add to this list! Finally, you can find resources for some of the teaching activities on the book's companion website, www.creativeuniversities.com

Figure 1.2: Reading questions

⇒ What are the most urgent challenges in my field of teaching?

⇒ Which key concepts do I want my students to learn about in critical-creative ways?

⇒ How would the values and orientations presented in this book be relevant in my classes?

⇒ What are heterodox alternatives in my discipline?

⇒ How would I translate the activities into my own classroom?

⇒ What other possibilities do exist?

Source: Author.

2

Remaking Academic Identities

It's day two of the Decolonial Pedagogies conference at Sussex, and 15 people sit on the floor of a large, light-filled room, waiting for the start of a body-mapping workshop. The conference handbook describes body mapping as 'a flexible and creative tool to explore our inner worlds [that] can be used as a visual dialogue with ourselves to unpack facets of our experiences and as a way to communicate these to others'. The workshop facilitator begins by briefly tracing the origins of body mapping in social activism and shows some of the powerful body maps that have been created by artist-activists in a variety of contexts. Explaining that today's session will focus on participants' relationships with power, she asks them to reflect on questions such as: Who has power over us? What do we have power for? Who do we have power with? Rather than discussing these different dimensions on a theoretical level, participants explore how they connect with different parts of their bodies. They begin by tracing the outlines of their bodies on large sheets of paper and then set about filling these with colours, patterns, slogans and images. Their creative practice is guided by the facilitator's prompts: How are your feet grounding and situating you? What and who do you hold dear and treasure close to your hearts? With whom do your fingers connect you for support? The smell of paint, glue and other crafty materials suffuses the room, against a backdrop of music and the hum of low conversations as the facilitator moves around to talk to each participant. An atmosphere of concentrated yet animated making soon takes over as everybody works on creating their unique body maps.

Body mapping is a good example of critical-creative pedagogy that engages whole-person learning, incorporates artistic practices and often fosters critical hope in participants. Body mapping can therefore be used in university classrooms for students to explore their own positions vis-à-vis social change projects. This personal dimension of teaching and learning is at the heart of this chapter, which focuses on the unmaking and remaking of educator and student subjectivities. To begin a book on critical-creative pedagogies with the personal lays important groundwork for later chapters that focus more explicitly on global economic, ecological and social challenges, because any participation in projects to address these challenges starts from one's own location. Therefore, building students' understanding of their own positionalities and privileges through critical analysis and creative experimentation is a first step towards imagining and creating personal and collective change in university classrooms. This work generates new knowledges about decolonization for students, together with orientations of unlearning and letting go of personal certainties and ambitions. Both can result in a politics of anti-saviourism that questions uncritical aspirations to help and save.

Educators engaged in this pedagogical project operate within particular environments, and I begin the chapter by analysing the neoliberalization of contemporary universities and how critical pedagogy has emerged in resistance to it. Alongside, movements to decolonize the westernized university have begun to counter the theoretical and pedagogical dominance of Eurocentric knowledge through the introduction of epistemic diversity. These larger contexts present both challenges and opportunities for critical-creative educators committed to the necessary personal–professional transformations. In the second half of the chapter I describe two teaching activities: the first one shows how body mapping can be used in university classrooms to support alternative narratives of students' selves and their relations to others, and the second locates students as situated learners in their day-to-day surroundings.

Resisting the neoliberalized university

Neoliberalism is an attack on all public institutions, including universities. Fuelled by decades of 'economistic, utilitarian and technocratic discourses about schooling and higher education, combined with the gradual institutionalization of managerialism and marketization', universities in the UK and other countries have become commodified, privatized and corporatized (Amsler, 2014, p 275). These processes have been critiqued in great detail by especially Critical Pedagogy scholars, and my brief summary will draw especially on the work of Henri Giroux (2014), Sarah Amsler (2011) and Stephen Cowden and Gurnam Singh (2013). Beginning this chapter with HE's current neoliberal context also highlights the constraints it creates for any change project within universities: constraints that are real but not insurmountable.

In the UK, the privatization of universities has been driven by public funding cuts and the introduction of university fees, which means that universities need to attract ever-increasing numbers of students, to commercialize research and to create links with businesses. Besides instituting market-driven operational logics, these changes have affected the governance of universities. These are now run by executive officer -like vice-chancellors and their senior managers, who are replacing collective forms of governance with top-down decision making. Forms of audit, surveillance and professionalization have introduced bureaucratic norms and market values of efficiency and returns on investment. If there is participation by academics it is often tokenistic, as democratic institutions are undermined, intellectual autonomy is eroded and dissent is suppressed. Amsler shows how, as early as the mid-1980s, academics in the UK were seen by vice-chancellors as obstacles in this managerial project, needing to be re-educated to embrace the ongoing changes with more enthusiasm.

For many new academics, such forms of control are compounded by conditions of precarity, as they are increasingly hired on short-term and part-time contracts. The resulting casualization of academic labour leads to overwork, stress and demoralization and is sometimes combined with self-disciplining and self-censorship. The COVID-19 pandemic has exacerbated these exhausting working conditions, as shifting to online and blended teaching was time consuming and often meant learning new skills, students' pastoral needs increased and many academics have been facing uncertain futures. Throughout this, the need for academics to be both service providers to student consumers and entrepreneurial subjects generating income for their universities has not changed. Individuals respond to these conditions in different ways, ranging from cynicism, accommodation and retreat to defiance, protest and a search for transformations.

When university education becomes a financial transaction where students and their families pay upwards of £9,000 a year to study, they are encouraged to see themselves as customers entitled to demand value for their money. This becomes especially visible during times of module evaluations, surveys like the National Student Survey and faculty strike action. Education, until the COVID pandemic increasingly taking place in over-crowded classrooms or during evening hours to accommodate the rising numbers of students, centres on employability prospects, workplace-related skills and labour market demands. In the process, knowledge is commodified and pedagogy is instrumentalized in the form of prescriptive, outcomes-driven learning and competency-based curricula. In this focus on 'technically competent dissemination of information' (Cowden and Singh, 2013, p 30), intellectual knowledge becomes regarded as too difficult or irrelevant. This has particular implications for the arts, humanities and social sciences, which are often sidelined in a focus on STEM (science, technology, engineering and mathematics) subjects.[1] And even in the critical social disciplines, educators can find it increasingly difficult to get students to query the dominant values of consumption and competition that they encounter in their everyday lives on and off campus. As discourses of public values, social responsibility and civic education become dismantled in public spheres, education for democracy, equality and justice seems ever more remote.

Especially relevant for a critical-creative pedagogy is the foreclosure of possibilities for alternative pedagogical actions that accompanies the neoliberalization of education. Sarah Amsler and Keri Facer show the disciplining effects of an 'anticipatory regime' in UK education policy, for example through the use of digital data to statistically calculate and predict outcomes or through testing to identify latent risks, with the aim to minimize future ones. This regime aims to control educational outcomes and reinforces managerial and bureaucratic power. It also 'systematically diminishes opportunities for creative emergence and spaces of political possibilities in order to reproduce itself', by marginalizing and censuring academics who work against it (2017, p 9).

Amsler and Facer have situated these processes within a wider political construction of hopelessness, where spaces of possibility are contracted or foreclosed altogether, through discourses of inevitability, the dismantling of democratic structures and the diminishing of political agency. This has important implications for the abilities of students to imagine alternatives: 'adequate responses to ecological, economic and political crises require radical modes of thinking and acting which people formed and socialized through formal education in the Global North – despite being able to identify the problem – are ill-prepared to imagine or engage in' (p 7). Many of the writings diagnosing the current HE condition make for truly depressing reading, painting a dystopian picture for its future. They are based on strong theory subscribing to the 'narrative of neoliberalism as global capitalism's consolidating regulative regime' and therefore seem to leave little room for changes (Gibson-Graham, 2006, p 4).

But the authors of these accounts also acknowledge that universities remain important places to contribute to imagining alternatives. They show that the neoliberalization of HE has been met with ongoing resistance, including student and faculty protests, strikes and occupations. The 2010 UK student protests against university funding cuts and tuition fee rises, for example, have been identified as a 'politics of possibility' (Amsler, 2011, p 79). Rather than lamenting the death of (public) education, student protestors celebrated the birth of a movement and the corresponding opening up of possibilities through creative resignification of spaces of action. Henri Giroux argues that such resistance

demands a politics and pedagogy that refuses to separate individual problems from public issues and social considerations ... [It] displaces cynicism with hope, challenging the neoliberal notion that there are no alternatives with visions of a better society, and develops a pedagogy of commitment that puts into place modes of critical literacy in which competency and interpretation provide the bases of actually intervening in the world. [It] invokes the demand to make the pedagogical more political by linking critical thought to collective action, human agency to social responsibility, and knowledge and power to a profound impatience with a status quo founded upon deep inequalities and injustices. (2014, pp 46–7)

Showing students the interconnectedness of personal and collective practices and politics is an important element of critical-creative teaching. It is also at the heart of Critical Pedagogy, with its aim of 'self-other-world transformation' (Lake and Kress, 2017, p 69). As I have shown, Critical Pedagogy's proponents such as Henri Giroux, Peter McLaren and Michael Apple have been at the forefront of critiques against the neoliberal university.

The term Critical Pedagogy emerged in the 1980s 'from a long historical legacy of radical social thought and progressive educational movements, which aspired to link practices of schooling to democratic principles of society and transformative social action in the interest of oppressed communities' (Darder et al, 2009, p 3).[2] The intellectual tradition of the Frankfurt School, with its critique of rising authoritarianism and the increasing bureaucratization of everyday life, as well as the work of Antonio Gramsci and Michel Foucault, was foundational. Equally central has been the Marxist notion of human beings co-constructing knowledge from their material experiences in and of the world. Critical Pedagogy educators also draw on the ideas of John Dewey, a founding figure of the progressive educational movement in the US, who advocated for public education in the services of democracy and freedom.

Particularly important for a critical-creative pedagogy are Dewey's ideas around experiential learning, which he aimed to realize with varying success at his own experimental school in Chicago. In *Education and Experience*, Dewey, writing in 1938, argued that education must engage students' experiences, including through interacting with their environments. Experiential education subscribes to an active, contextual and relational concept of learning that establishes a temporal connection between the past and the present to shape the future. This is linked to a sense of possibility, based on Dewey's realization that imagining future worlds is also important for better understanding the present one: 'it is by a sense of possibilities opening before us that we become aware of constrictions that hem us in and of burdens that oppress' (2005, p 360). For Dewey, learning has a moral dimension that involves personal reflection and social interaction and can result in action (Roberts, 2008). The relationship between reflection and action is also central to the work of another foundational critical educator.

Paolo Freire introduced a Global South perspective to Critical Pedagogy.[3] His ideas started to become known in the Global North when, forced into political exile from his native Brazil, he became a visiting professor at Harvard University in the early 1970s, at the same time as *Pedagogy of the Oppressed* was translated into English. For Freire, critical education is 'the practice of freedom, the means by which men and women deal critically and creatively with reality and discover how to participate in the transformation of their world' (2000, p 34). Such education focuses on developing radical knowledge that departs from lived experiences of oppression and marginalization to create opportunities for personal and social transformations. This necessitates the development of a critical consciousness that recognizes, for example, 'hunger as more than just not eating, as the manifestation of a political, economic and social reality of deep injustice' (Freire, cited in Lake and Kress, 2017, p 65).[4] Such a reframing of personal deprivation as social and political problems takes place through praxis, which is the cycle of reflection, dialogue and action grounded in the exploration of learners' own knowledge and dialogical interaction with teachers.[5]

Freire was highly critical of what he called banking education, where teachers deposit information into passive students who memorize and regurgitate it. He saw this not only as objectifying and alienating but also as taking away students' creative power. More generally, he argued that those in power are opposed to any educational experiments that could stimulate students' critical–creative faculties, while his own humanistic education placed a profound trust in these capacities. Freire also subscribed to a concept of radical hope grounded in a refusal to accept the world as it is and in a recognition of human and social incompleteness, which makes change possibly. Radical hope is a moral and political act of daring to envision alternative futures because 'to build a better tomorrow needs to happen through transforming today. Different tomorrows are possible [and] necessary to reinvent the future. Education is indispensable for this reinvention' (Freire, cited in Hammond, 2017, p 107).

The creative dimension of critical–creative pedagogy draws on two Critical Pedagogy scholars in particular. Fellow Brazilian Augusto Boal and his experimental theatre for the oppressed complements some of the overtly theoretical and text-based ideas of Critical Pedagogy with more practical and affective ways of teaching. In a similar vein, Maxine Greene was a staunch advocate of the integration of the arts into education as sources of personal reflection and inspiration. According to Greene, the arts and literature open up spaces of possibility by 'giving play to our imagination, enlarg[ing] the scope of lived experience and reach[ing] beyond from our own grounds' (2009, p 84). Fiction, when allowed to be studied as an art form with all its mysteries and aesthetic pleasures, can nurture individual desires, hopes and expectations. Poetry is often non–linear and filled with imagery and unusual connections that can further inspire students' imaginations. Both 'alter the vision of the way things are; it opens spaces in experience where projects can be devised, the kinds of projects that maybe bring things closer to what ought to be' (1997, p 17). Such personal reflections connect to pluralistic actions towards community and public change through the work of social imagination, which is 'the capacity to invent visions of what should be and what might be in our deficient society' (1995, p 5). Similarly to Dewey, Greene also showed that it is through imagining a better future that individuals find the present wanting and in need of change.

More recently, Sarah Amsler's work on pedagogies of possibility and becoming has important implications for a critical-creative pedagogy. Based on her research with popular educators, social movements and cultural activists in the UK, Amsler (2015) identifies non-formal educational practices that recognize cognitive, affective and material processes of learning. These practices have creative, aesthetic and relational learning at their centre; they are open ended, slow and not easily controlled or bureaucratized. She argues that 'to educate the imagination, we can explore … not only the cognitive dimension of learning but also the epistemological, affective and material conditions of learning how to think, feel, do and be in liberating ways' (2014, p 281). Together with Keri Facer, Amsler (2017) has studied radical and utopian experiments with autonomous, often anti-colonial and indigenous education in the Global South, which incorporate socially and ecologically relational and holistic modes of learning. These experiments shift the focus from neoliberal to (de)colonizing universities.

Decolonizing the westernized university

Decolonization has been defined as

> an umbrella term for diverse efforts to resist the distinct but intertwined processes of colonization and racialization, to enact transformations and redress in reference to the historical and ongoing effects of these processes, and to create and keep alive modes of knowing, being, and relating that these processes seek to eradicate. (Stein and Andreotti, 2016, p 978)

There is a voluminous literature on the discourses, practices and politics of decolonization, especially in the HE context. Here 'de-colonization has multiple meanings, and the desires and investments that animate it are diverse, contested and sometimes at odds with each other' (Andreotti et al, 2015, p 22). Nevertheless, common themes focus on epistemological hegemony and diversity, the continued predominance of a westernized university model and multiple responses to it, and an emphasis on praxis over theory.

Modern universities have profited from colonization in multiple ways, ranging from the expropriation of indigenous lands to the use of slave labour and funding through wealth extracted from colonial enterprises (Stein and Andreotti, 2016). Universities in turn participated in these enterprises through the production of knowledge in disciplines such as anthropology, geography and, later, development studies, which enabled and legitimized colonial exploitation and administration. Colonial knowledge practices continue when universities reproduce epistemic hierarchies, with Western knowledge positioned as universal and superior and alternative knowledge being commodified, neglected or taught as folkloric and local varieties. De Sousa Santos has called this 'epistemicide', which 'was not just essential for the European colonial project, but remains central to the current system of Eurocentric knowledge production' (Laing, 2020, p 5).

In many academic disciplines, the canon is populated by mainly Western, male thought. Dominant social theory, for example, has been produced by male thinkers from Italy, France, Germany, the UK and US; these countries make up 12% of the world population, which belies any claims to the universality of the knowledge produced for human experience (de Sousa Santos, 2017). Another dimension of universities' coloniality is that 'we find the same structures of knowledge in Westernized universities everywhere in the world ... Be they in Dakar, Buenos Aires, New Delhi, Manila, New York, Paris or Cairo, they have fundamentally the same disciplinary divisions and racist/sexist canon of thought' (Grosfoguel, 2012, p 83). What Grosfoguel calls the 'monocultural, monoepistemic and monocosmological' Eurocentric knowledge framework is used to educate national elites and can result in their rejection of local knowledge systems as inferior. This in turn contributes to the perpetuation of current political and economic systems and the suppression of alternatives. It also means that the authors of marginalized knowledges are regarded as objects of study only, rather than as knowledge-producing subjects, while their knowledge is appropriated by the westernized academy (Tuhiwai-Smith, 2013).

This system is being challenged on multiple fronts, which have taken specific forms in different localities, from the Rhodes Must Fall movement in South Africa, the Universidad de la Tierra in Mexico, Mātauranga Māori in New Zealand and Why Is My Curriculum White? in the UK. Stein and Andreotti (2016) have mapped different decolonizing responses in US and UK universities. On one end are weak responses that advocate for increased diversity through the inclusion of marginalized staff, students and perspectives into persisting institutional structures of knowledge and power hierarchies. A stronger response departs from a critique of these structures, showing their ongoing reproduction of racial and economic exclusions and their exploitative effects on marginalized groups. Here, actions include calls for empowerment, redress and the redistribution of resources. Stronger responses have resulted in important institutional transformations such as desegregation, the establishment of ethnic and women's studies departments or even government-sponsored indigenous universities, which can be transformational but also undermined by tokenism and co-optation.

The third set of responses is therefore more radical and considers the limits of a university system that is funded and managed by capitalist markets and neoliberal governments. Radical campaigners argue that 'reform is not possible and what is needed is to imagine and create radically different, unknown futures for higher education and beyond' (Stein and Andreotti, 2016, p 980). Their practices include appropriating university resources for more heterodox projects and experimenting with autonomous alternatives. Importantly, Stein and Andreotti argue that 'people tend to strategically and incoherently make use of different approaches, often at the same time' (p 980). This speaks to the ambiguous, open-ended and sometimes contradictory character of decolonizing efforts in HE.

Decolonization entails the transition from a uni-versity dominated by Eurocentric knowledge to pluri-versities characterized by 'epistemic diversity', which challenge this dominance (de Sousa Santos, 2016, p 18). Such diversity includes delegitimized 'epistemologies of the south' that are still too frequently absent from university curricula. To redress this exclusion, de Sousa Santos proposes a 'sociology of emergences' that amplifies alternatives born from non-Eurocentric understandings of the world and how to transform it. These alternatives are growing in 'committed, polyphonic pluriversities' that engage in struggles for social, economic and ecological justice through pluralistic pedagogies that encompass unconventional ways of learning (2017, p 377). They foster individual and institutional creativity and experimentation to subvert the dominance of market-value disciplines that further neoliberal university agendas. By contrast, non-market-value disciplines like the humanities and critical social sciences have the potential to become sites of resistance, especially when they build alliances with social movements and popular education institutions outside the university system. In *Decolonizing the University*, de Sousa Santos describes several examples of such 'sub-versities' in Latin America, where they have emerged from Freire's and others' path-breaking work. Latin America is therefore an important site of educational alternatives, which have emerged from struggles against colonialism and coloniality.

Eurocentric dominance in Latin America began with the 15th-century conquest that set individualized European knowledge expressed through written language against 'collectively constructed oral narratives and pictoideographic representational systems of the Amerindians', with the latter regarded by colonial powers as irrational and idolatrous (Mansell, 2013, p 20). This co-constitution of superior and inferior knowledges located the latter in a position of exteriority to European thought, including its critical schools. From this position Latin American scholars, such as those belonging to the Modernity–Coloniality–Decoloniality school, have created a radically alternative knowledge system that is grounded in experiences of conquest and domination as well as subsequent decolonial struggles for autonomy and freedom (Walsh, 2007). As the Bolivian Quechua-Aymara intellectual Fausto Reinaga wrote: 'our struggle comes from afar, from the same instance that the Spanish hordes invaded the Confederation of Amer-Indian people ... and is against all European vestiges ..., all that maintains us in dependence, in mental colonialism, in blindness without finding the light' (1970, p 15).

There are important connections to Freirean pedagogy, with its rejection of monological approaches to literacy and learning. Students' passive reception of knowledge through banking education establishes power relations that recall the colonial processes of denying and annihilating other knowledges (Mansell, 2013). Freire sees an alternative in dialogical education that also begins with what is exterior and marginalized, in his case the knowledge of the oppressed individuals he was teaching. Dialogue is equally central to decolonization, where 'concepts need to be conceived as invitations to dialogue and not as impositions. They are expressions of the availability of the subject to engage in dialogue and the desire for exchange' (Maldonado-Torres, 2007, p 256). Both Critical Pedagogy and decolonizing university programmes provide an important context for critical-creative pedagogy, informing especially its critical elements. In the next part of the chapter I show how critique can be complemented with creativity, beginning with educators' own experiences.

Cultivating critical-creative educators

The practice of critical-creative teaching makes particular demands on educators who will need courage to cede control in the classroom, commitment to step out of their comfort zones, confidence to make room for the unexpected and energy to persevere. Once again, Freire provides guidance. Reflecting on his own experiences, he emphasized the importance of teachers' humility grounded in courage, self-confidence and respect for self and others. He exerted teachers to denounce fatalism and to never give up: 'the capacity to always begin anew, to make, to reconstruct, and not to spoil, to refuse to bureaucratize the mind, to understand and to live as a process – live to become – is something that always accompanied me throughout my life. This is an indispensable quality of a good teacher' (1993, p 98).

On the journey towards a critical-creative pedagogy, discovery and discomfort are educators' constant companions. For HE in particular, such a pedagogy also demands a decentring of fundamental and often cherished assumptions: 'rethinking the meaning of the higher educator may require the unlearning of traditional approaches to theoretisation which privilege performativity over humble co-operation, abstraction over praxis, individual knowing over collective learning, and monological solution-giving over dialogical inquiry' (Amsler, 2014, p 279). Sharing one's work, resources and time and working collaboratively with colleagues and students in meaningful rather than tokenistic ways are forms of prefigurative politics within the academy, where educators can enact in the here and now the visions they have for the future.

This includes (publicly) reflecting on one's teaching experiences, as Wendy Harcourt (2017) has done for her critical-creative redesign of a flagship MA course at the International Institute of Social Studies (ISS), a well-known European postgraduate research institute in the Netherlands. The course centred on discussions of key postdevelopment[6] texts and incorporated creative activities such as videos, poetry, role play, photos and blogs. Teaching was carried out through interactive, often student-driven seminars, following a Freirean pedagogy that asked questions and posed problems rather than provide answers. Student reactions to the course varied widely, in keeping with the diversity of the students who took it, who came from 57 countries, mainly from the Global South. Some of these students, who as employees of governments, international non-governmental organizations or development organizations in their own countries were beneficiaries of the successes that the global development industry had brought for the rising middle classes, reacted to the course with confusion, disbelief or anger. They wanted practical information and solutions they could take back home: 'these students did not want to be part of an experiment. They wanted the teachers to tell them what development was about; they had not come to the ISS to problem-solve with other students' (p 2707).

Their criticism was partly directed against an unfamiliar teaching style and partly against the content of the course, which disrupted their notions of mainstream development. When one of these students asked Harcourt 'Why did you want us to see development in the same way that you were looking at it?' this also entailed a questioning of Harcourt's role as teacher. Her age, gender and ethnicity were not what some students had expected and her positionality as a feminist and former activist, which shaped her teaching, was seen as an exercise of power in the classroom. Harcourt reflects that 'maybe I embodied the confusion about what authority was; particularly my willingness to expose my doubts and concerns about the development process were questioned' (p 2713). Students who were critical of the course demanded that she reassert her pedagogical control, which felt safe and predictable.

Other students embraced the course wholeheartedly. They appreciated that there is no single story to development, that it is a contested and context-dependent process and that their assumptions, beliefs and privilege were being challenged. They liked the opportunities to work with others creatively, for example through producing a short video for one assessment. They also wanted to learn about possible spaces for transformation and change because 'unmaking development can only serve a purpose if we subsequently remake it somehow', as one student put it. Significantly, Harcourt also reflects on the critical reaction from her colleagues as one of the most difficult aspects of the redesign. While she understood their reactions in the context of possible financial cuts at ISS, an ongoing shift towards a more conservative and competitive teaching environment and a national right-wing, anti-immigration climate, she wonders whether their criticism of teaching postdevelopment 'was also unconsciously about the unsettling of their privileges as "experts" on development who see their job as providing a professional set of prescriptions to students' (p 2715). Transformative teaching can be perceived as a threat on multiple levels, and demands fortitude and commitment in the face of such resistances.

Harcourt's combination of teaching that is critical of mainstream development and creative exercises to explore alternatives is a good example of a critical-creative pedagogy. Her experiences also reveal the range of reactions to such a pedagogy, from enthusiastic embrace to outright rejection. Being aware of the possibility of such diverse responses as well as of student expectations of teaching styles and content delivery, and working out how to react to all of these, is an important part of educators' self-reflexivity. It calls for creating spaces in which honest comments can be made and for a preparedness to explain teaching methodologies. These processes can result in adjusting classroom practice; Harcourt changed to a partial lecture format in response to initial student feedback. Her experiences also show that teaching involves situated knowledge. Recognizing the partiality of educators' positions means 'displacing ourselves from the centre of the world; interrupting our desires to look, feel and "do" good; exposing the source and connections of our fears, desires and denial; letting go of our fantasies of certainty, comfort, security and control' (Andreotti et al, 2015, p 36). This is teaching without guarantees, grounded in unlearning educational practices and remaking academic subjectivities.

As Harcourt shows, there are potential openings for transformative teaching within universities. She had been given freedom and encouragement by ISS's teaching director to redesign the module, and used it to experiment and unsettle. Similarly, in Chapter 6 I describe how I redesigned a module on activism to combine theory and practice. Nevertheless, in an atmosphere of increasing 'pedagogical correctness' (Harding and Hale, 2007, p 1), there are institutional challenges to overcome in the design of a critical-creative pedagogy. These can include a prescribed curriculum that does not leave time for experimentation, rigid learning objectives that do not easily accommodate creative learning and assessment criteria that do not allow for open-ended exploration.

On the other hand, individual staff still have some freedom to design their own modules as I did with my Urban Futures module, with corresponding possibilities to provoke and subvert, although these activities are always circumscribed by multiple other demands on staff time. In a follow-up article, Harcourt describes how, two years after the original implementation, many of her colleagues now want to teach on the course, which continues to receive positive comments from students and external evaluators. One student thanked Harcourt for her teaching, adding that 'you can't imagine how students treasure the professors willing to take the kind of risks you take' (cited in Harcourt, 2018, p 2203). This comment sets the stage for the next sections, in which I draw on various critical-creative teaching activities at Sussex to examine students' experiences in the classroom more closely.

Whither saviourism

Students in the social sciences sometimes enter university with an 'under-scrutinized moral compulsion to help' (Cameron et al, 2013, p 356). This desire relates to the wider phenomenon of saviourism, in reference to individuals who want to alleviate the poverty and plight of faraway others. Saviourism can take the form of emotional reactions to representations of generic poor people, in response to which saviours click, buy, donate and volunteer. Their actions are often based on a limited understanding of the contexts that create particular situations and can therefore be short sighted, externally imposed and potentially harmful in the long run. Other students, by contrast, are brought to university precisely because they have experienced at first hand the shortcomings of helping, as I show in Chapter 6. One student recounted in her journey interview that before coming to Sussex she had spent three months working in a school in South Africa, where she came face to face with the problematic practices of voluntourism.[7] She felt that "coming to Sussex was like a breath of fresh air and quite therapeutic, because I could unpick what had gone wrong in South Africa".

Early on in their studies, students recognize the idealism and naivety that often bring them to studying global development in particular, together with wanting to work for the UN or other large organizations for which they think a degree in the field is necessary. While it is important to distinguish between the mainly young British undergraduate students and the older, often professional MA students from the Global South who, like in Harcourt's case, come to Northern universities for a year to get better credentials, a desire to work in mainstream institutions that manage and govern change is often shared. These institutions reproduce orthodox neoliberal and managerialist discourses, practices and systems of change couched in the language of modern development and technological progress. Studying in the critical social sciences stops this desire hard in its tracks, often beginning with dismantling saviourism.

Disrupting the saviour narrative starts with using critical pedagogies to discuss forms of privilege and the multiple ways in which they are experienced at the intersections of race, gender, class and other identities. Because privilege 'is a concept that has the potential to leave those who name it in a place of double comfort: the comfort of demonstrating that one is critically aware, and the comfort of not needing to act to undo privilege' (Heron, 2005, p 344), such discussions need to be linked to interrogations of power relations to ensure that students not only recognize their privilege but also work to unsettle and undo its operations. For this to happen, personal experience needs to become part of praxis by recognizing its embeddedness in relations of power. According to Freire, 'functionally, oppression is domesticating. To no longer be prey to its force, one must emerge from it and turn upon it. This can be done only by means of the praxis: reflection and action upon the world in order to transform it' (cited in Straubhaar, 2015, p 393).

This calls for politicizing students' encounters within racialized, gendered and class-based structures inside and outside university classrooms to develop their critical consciousness. Continual self-evaluation, together with questioning the structures into which individuals have been socialized, can lead to transformational personal insights, which can contradict not only cherished beliefs and aspirations but also lived experiences. To pursue and act on these insights is hard mental and emotional work, as many students experience themselves. For them, dismantling saviourism entails asking questions that do not have easy or indeed any answers and challenging themselves to consider their own prejudices, assumptions and certainties. Acknowledging personal complicity encompasses both banal complicity in reference to everyday practices and historical complicity in reference to individuals' situatedness in political-economic systems and socio-historical processes that have created current global inequalities and environmental emergencies. The resulting process of unlearning asks students to 'retrace the itinerary of [their] prejudices and learning habits ..., stop thinking of [themselves] as better and fitter and unlearn dominant systems of knowledge and representation' (Kapoor, 2004, p 641).

For all global development students at Sussex this process begins during a first term core module called Colonialism and After. Here, students learn about the impact of the British Empire on Africa and Asia, the oppression of indigenous peoples in Australia and North America, colonialism's influence on constructions of race and their continued importance for mainstream change projects. Students also learn that colonial discourses were not monolithic and provided spaces for subversion and resistance, such as the appropriation of colonial institutions by colonized groups. The module critically interrogates whose voices are excluded from the writing of colonial history, for example through alternative reading of the Haitian revolution and how it influenced abolitionist debates (Bhambra, 2016).

Especially for White British students, detailed critical attention to a history of which they might not have been aware can be eye opening, overwhelming and deeply unsettling. One student was "shocked that up until the age of 20 I could name more famous Tudors than countries in the former British empire". This is in large part due to the white-washed history curriculum in UK secondary schools; in Chapter 6 I discuss a student campaign to change that curriculum. Another student remarked that "learning how the world of colonialism has shaped Britain's position in the world was mind-blowing. How is it that I have not known about this?" While generally appreciating this new knowledge, for some students it provoked "an existential crisis, asking Why am I here?", as one of them put it. Students began to question their reasons for coming to university, alongside plans they had for what to do after leaving it. Teaching them about alternative histories is one way to nurture students' sense of possibilities when their old certainties are starting to crumble.

This happened in another first-year core module, taught by my former colleague Andrea Cornwall, who reflects on her teaching of development similar to Harcourt (Cornwall, 2020). Cornwall's module on Development Ideas and Actors was inspired by Walter Mignolo's concept of the pluriversal, as well as Critical Pedagogy and Cornwall's own experiences teaching in Zimbabwe and working with participatory methodologies. In one of the interactive exercises of the module, students groups were assigned a particular period in history, to research its events and processes, from crisis to conquests, discoveries to disasters, invasions to achievements. Students translated these research findings into visuals that were put up around the walls of the lecture hall in chronological order, creating a timeline of alternative and official histories. Moving around the room to study these histories they had co-created, students learned about the contributions that civilizations of India, Egypt, Zimbabwe and Peru have made to fields such as mathematics, medicine, engineering, philosophy and literature. In this way, achievements that are usually overlooked in a Eurocentric history of the world were made visible and the narrative of assumed Western universality was interrupted. In addition, students were able to start tracing the historical linkages between actions in one part of the world and suffering in another; linkages that are often hidden, indirect and non-linear.

What emerged were the devastating effects of slavery and empire and their continuities in Britain's development industry, trade practices and foreign policy. These insights were then connected to academic accounts of reframing aid as a form of reparation and of questioning its usefulness, drawing on voices from the Global South channelled through TED talks, YouTube videos and blogs. For the assessment, students wrote their own blogs, which 'led to an explosion of creativity' (Cornwall, 2020, p 43). Similarly, in the final class students were asked to think forward 30 years to what they would have achieved at the apex of their careers. Cornwall invited them 'to imagine the world around them, one that they might have played a part in changing. Some students were completely thrown by this: it was a task with no readings, no references, just imagination. But then they got into it. And the writings they produced were a mix of the dystopian and the visionary' (p 43). When given opportunities to be creative, most students find within them corresponding ideas and imaginaries. When nurtured in creative spaces, these can grow into visions of diverse alternative futures.

As a result of these modules, students finish their first term at Sussex with a profound sense of disorientation, which was tangible in the journey interviews. They talked about "stripping away preconceptions" and "learning to question everything, in a productive way". They also described becoming "quite cynical", "quite hopeless and depressed" and "being worn down" and "considering dropping out". Wanting to make the world a better place is recognized as far less straightforward than many imagine, as students realize that there are no easy solutions and that coming up with one course of action can have many, including negative and unintended, consequences. For one student, that was a profound paradox: she had come to study global development because she wanted to work in the field, but then her studies made her question whether development was even working. Such student reactions are rarely acknowledged by teachers. According to Ruth Barcan, writing about her experiences teaching critical theory in Australia: 'I have seen either an ignorance of the potentially life-changing impact of such teaching, a simplistic celebration of it, or a tendency to see it as a form of necessary initiation' (2016, p 153). When educators become aware of the effects of their teaching on students and take responsibility for them, these responses are recognized as insufficient. Conversely, finding better responses that support students through these experiential transformations does not mean abandoning critical teaching and learning.

In their journey interviews students themselves often articulated the need to gain more critical and informed knowledge. Comments such as "if we don't study that development projects can have negative outcomes, then we risk reproducing them" and "the critical aspects of teaching are important so we don't make the same mistakes" link these critiques to personal transformation. One student argued:

'I don't think Sussex should lose that spark which pushes us to be critical and question international development, even if that means being slightly disillusioned with it when we leave. That is a GOOD thing! It means we hopefully won't fall into any traps, where we are "helping" countries that don't need our help or volunteering in places when we know nothing about them.'

What students took away from their studies was not the toolkit to save the world they had initially hoped for, but critical knowledge and personal understandings to guide their future choices. These included the importance of local ownership of change projects and of decentring themselves and their desires "to be up front and centre", as one of them put it.

As I show in greater detail in Chapter 6, many students abandoned their desires to work for mainstream development organizations and some also talked about now wanting to work in the UK rather than abroad, becoming more aware not only of the magnitude of problems at home but also of their abilities to effect change here. Thus, working for transformative change was not written off. Instead, students also asked to learn about alternatives and for spaces to creatively apply their own ideas. Colleagues at Sussex have responded to these demands in various ways, and throughout the following chapters I describe many critical-creative teaching activities that nurture students' abilities to imagine alternatives and begin creating them. The first of these activities is body mapping, whose description opened this chapter.

Embodied learners

In his 1928 address to the New York Academy of Medicine, John Dewey observed that

I do not know of anything so disastrously affected by the habit of division [of mind and body] … the evils which we suffer in education, in religion, in the materialism of business and the aloofness of 'intellectuals' from life, in the whole separation of knowledge from practice – all testify to the necessity of seeing mind–body as an integral whole. (Cited in Bresler, 2013, p 8)

Dewey connected the mind–body dualism that has been foundational to Western thought to a range of social ills of the time. In education, this dualism is replicated in classrooms that place a premium on academicism and analytical reasoning and neglect other forms of knowing (Robinson, 2001). To move towards a pedagogical practice that acknowledges students as whole-person learners, educators often look towards arts-based methodologies, following the work of Maxine Greene and Augusto Boal, mentioned earlier. The body is central in processes of inquiry and learning based on the performative arts such as theatre and dance, while singing, painting and making enable embodied learning experiences, and creative writing also draws in the emotions. All arts-based pedagogies are grounded in phenomenological forms of experiential education, which centre on the subjectivities of bodies, selves and senses (Roberts, 2008). Such experiences start personal and become social through individuals' embeddedness in groups and networks inside and outside classrooms.

In the social sciences, creative forms of writing hold much potential for helping students to imagine alternative worlds. Incorporating fiction and poetry into reading lists has the potential to provide students with access to rich interior worlds that can foster emotional and intellectual capacities for transformation. This can be complemented by students' own creative writing, which deepens imaginative engagement. Craig Hammond, in his proposal for a utopian pedagogy based on the works of Roland Barthes, Guy Debord, Ernst Bloch and others, asks students to write a 'creative autobiography' as a 'non-linear, personal-creative work to recognize and reflect their unique voice and experience' (2017, p 111). Teaching in the media studies field, he centres these autobiographies on cultural productions, with students writing about their favourite pieces of art and the personal transformations these have brought about. For Hammond, incorporating creativity, spontaneity and adventure into education can challenge consumerized learning, through awakening in students 'active, militant and constructive hope' (p 107).

A more multidimensional activity is body mapping, which has been used by my colleague Beth Mills in a number of classes and workshops. Mills was involved in body mapping's initial activist use in South Africa with HIV-infected women, to counter the stigma attached to the disease and advocate for access to life-saving drugs (MacGregor and Mills, 2011). In its original version, the activity involves tracing a life-sized image of one's body on a large piece of paper or cloth and then filling out the shape, using colours, symbols and slogans (a good guide is Solomon, 2002). This usually takes place over several days, and involves working with a second person who draws the outline and who, in the South African context, became the support person through the patient's illness journey. Because of this social justice background, body mapping lends itself as a method for transformative teaching.

In the classroom, body mapping can be adapted to teaching sessions of three hours or longer. For shorter sessions or larger classes, rather than life-sized maps, students can fill smaller, body-shaped outlines with colours, craft materials, slogans or magazine cut-outs, guided by prompting questions that act as metaphors, as described in the opening vignette. For Mills, "working with colour in institutionalised settings can be liberating and transcending to more playful learning, which is one of the most powerful ways of knowing. Bringing the child out also makes us joyful." Playful exploration of different materials can stimulate imaginative learning, which Mills has used with students to explore a range of issues, from power and gender to participatory research methodologies.

Mills has incorporated body mapping into a third-year undergraduate module that focuses on the social life of aid through the reading of ethnographies. This module often cements students' disillusionment with the development industry that began in the first-year modules described earlier. In response, and to "balance hope and despair", Mills used body mapping to refocus students' attention inward, on their own lives and the capabilities, resources and connections they have within them. The emphasis is on "how they are as people in the world", which can support alternative narratives of self, others and society. In the course of creating their body maps, students reflect on the changes they have undergone during their studies, often foregrounding their involvement in campus groups or local and community projects, working at food cooperatives or joining environmental campaigns. According to Mills, "these activities might not be as glitzy and glamorous as the original development work they saw themselves doing when they first came to uni, but they recognize it as meaningful work".

In this way, body mapping and the whole-person learning it generates contribute to a decentring of mainstream development, in generative ways that allow for other possibilities to emerge and grow, rather than foreclosing alternatives through disillusioned or cynical retreat. Students interrogate their motivations for the work they wanted to do and have been doing, in the process extending theoretical discussions about privilege and saviourism that were started early on in their education in experiential ways. Countering the initial doubt these early discussions provoked with more affirmative practices helps to keep students' hope alive, because for Mills "hopes are precious in a dire, bleak world. They can easily be decimated but can also become sources of inspiration." The created body maps often serve students as visual reminders of their engaged and connected locations in the world. Through linking body mapping with vision mapping, Mills also invites students to think how they can take their personal journeys forward after they graduate.

For Mills, body mapping involves decolonizing knowledge production in several ways, beginning with student and teacher positions. Through creating their body maps, students become producers of knowledge about their experiences and situatedness in larger systems, bringing together inner life-worlds and outer journeys as well as giving meaning to individual experiences and connecting them to social structures. They are given the option to present their creations in front of the class, and once a few brave students volunteer, others usually follow. This can radically shift the classroom dynamic, as it establishes more equitable ways of learning together and counters practices of othering that are often recognized as institutional. Body mapping can produce powerful emotional reactions in students, which invite practices of listening and care from other students. To guide these, teacher-facilitators need emotional awareness and facilitation skills.

This is the case for whole-person learning in general, which accesses students' emotional and physical worlds in addition to their intellectual ones and demands extra awareness, care and support from critical-creative educators. In body mapping, teacher-facilitators also model the activity through creating their own map, which is an important part of critical-creative teaching in general. As bell hooks wrote, 'engaged pedagogy does not simply seem to empower students. Any classroom that employs a holistic model of learning is also a place where teachers grow, and are empowered by the process. That empowerment cannot happen if we refuse to be vulnerable while encouraging students to take risks' (1994, p 21). Educators participating in creative learning is crucial to this dual empowerment; for Mills there is a shared physicality because "all of us are sitting on the floor, getting dirty". In addition, in body mapping teacher-facilitators encourage those students who feel overwhelmed because "I can't draw", provide technical assistance and build a general atmosphere of trust, kindness and listening. While this has the potential to flatten power relations, it is essential that teachers establish boundaries and provide structure. They are also mindful of the emotional labour students are asked to perform and willing to redirect reluctant students towards more conceptual work.

A second aspect of decolonized knowledge production lies in body mapping's embodied knowledge making, which counters the usual subordination and neglect of the body in learning and instead asserts the importance of bodily forms of knowing. Feminist scholars have shown that this subordination is often connected to the devaluation of feminine forms of knowing and being in the world (Lugones, 2010). Being a visual activity, body mapping also decentres linear ways of knowing and can evoke knowledge that might not be accessible through verbal or written means. As I show in the next chapter on design, learning through the use of one's hands can lead to deeper reflections, especially when using materials that stimulate not only sight but also smell and touch and therefore involve multiple senses.

Such embodied forms of learning have been analysed in various ways. James and Brookfield (2014) draw on Howard Gardener's concept of multiple intelligences that are combined in different ways within each individual.[8] Gardener himself advocated for a broad vision of education that took these multiple intelligences into account, with the aim 'to create a world in which a great variety of people will want to live' (Gardener, 2006, p 40). James and Brookfield, who in their own HE work use creative practice to stimulate more reflective learning, also show that creativity is often visceral, drawing on feelings, instincts and intuitions, and that engaging these multiple forms of knowing can help learning to 'stick' better. Similarly, Guy Claxton's work on embodied cognition shows that 'the body, not just the brain, is the centre of higher learning' (cited in Staley, 2019, p 143). Multi-sensorial cognition adds depth and complexity to learning that are absent from reading and writing activities.

According to Mills, body mapping is literally "fleshing out the body" through creative practice and making critical connections between personal experiences and larger contexts, from gendered relations to power structures within and without university classrooms to systems of privilege, authority and expertise in social change projects. To create a classroom atmosphere where students feel comfortable to participate in such whole-person learning, activities should have a 'trans-creative and non-prescriptive openness and invitational format' that can hold in place diverse and multiple identities, experiences and forms of learning and expression (Hammond, 2017, p 111). All of these are also shaped by students' locations outside the classroom, and the next learning activity connects the classroom with these locations. For most third-year students at Sussex, they include Brighton and the university campus. While the campus will take centre stage in Chapters 5 and 6, in the next section I show how students have explored their physical, emotional and material connections with their places of dwelling through writing an urban manifesto for Brighton.

Locating the personal

The Brighton Manifesto is part of a specialist undergraduate module on Urban Futures that I designed and taught for the first time towards the end of my research for this book. The weekly three-hour workshops are structured as a combination of mini-lectures, seminar discussions of readings and creative activities. During the first class I told the students about my research project and its links to the creative activities of the class, all of which were non-assessed. I also devised different feedback mechanisms besides the standard module evaluation to collect research data, such as weekly online surveys and a short reflective section in the final assessment. Once students' grades for the module were finalized, I obtained their permission to use excerpts from these reflections and some of the artefacts they had created in class, and also invited them for follow-up interviews. This resulted in rich information, on which I draw in this and subsequent descriptions of activities from the module. Another source of data is the reflective teaching journal I kept throughout the term to record my own thinking behind the design of the module and to chronicle the various activities as they unfolded in class as well as students' reactions to them.

The journal reveals the mixed emotions I experienced throughout the term: excitement and trepidation before the first class, as I did not know how students would react to – especially – its creative aspects; nervousness and doubt before individual sessions when I was experimenting with new things; frustration when the students were less energetic or enthusiastic than I thought they should be; disappointment when classes didn't go as well as I had hoped; and joy and elation when an exercise had gone to plan and I had received positive comments. I also wrote about becoming more creative myself as the term went on and enjoying designing the exercises and establishing their pedagogical elements; I repeatedly reflected that this was not about students being creative just for the sake of it but for learning in a different mode. A few times, after particularly challenging classes, I wondered about the necessary personal attributes of educators who want to encourage students to be more open ended, less easily stuck on details and less quick to discard ideas. Does wanting to nurture creativity need particular traits in educators, besides being comfortable with ceding control, being able to handle discomfort and being flexible and open to different classroom interactions, challenges or silences? More than anything, pushing my students out of their comfort zones started with testing out and stretching my own.

I also wrote several times about the need to provide students with clear structures, through templates, guidelines, instruction sheets or examples, for them to be able to carry out the more open-ended exercises that were unfamiliar to them. Successful informal learning needs formal preparations and guidance, also to allow students to bridge the analytical and creative parts of teaching (Boys, 2010). One student commented in their final reflections that

> one needs to learn how to be creative. It is an adjustment for the brain to go from reading 30 pages to building houses out of Play-Doh or Lego. It takes time to teach the brain how to get out of its own comfort zone, to above all, build confidence in one's own creativity, to be able to induce the discussion needed to meet the full potential of creative activities. It also takes time to truly learn and understand the objectives of every activity, as the university-taught brains are not geared towards creativity first and foremost.

This student's reflections were spot on, as creative activity does not come easily to students who have gone through UK secondary education, and therefore needs time and practice to flourish (Robinson, 2001). They resonate with many passages in my teaching journal that show the intellectual and emotional demands of a critical-creative pedagogy on both teachers and students, and of the risks and rewards that flow from its praxis.

In the Urban Futures module, students writing an urban manifesto was a two-part activity that took place early in the term. The first part was a homework assignment set at the end of the very first class. I asked students to pay more attention to their daily routines, travels and interactions in Brighton throughout the upcoming week and create an artefact that would reflect their lives in the city. The following class began with a mini-lecture and seminar discussion of Lefebvre's theory of rights to the city, which complemented an article students had read for the previous class on what makes a good city. In addition, students read and discussed two policy documents that used the right to the city, from UN-Habitat and the World Social Forum, to understand how academic and theoretical concepts are translated into policy and actionable language.

The students then self-organized into small groups for the in-class part of the activity. As this was only the second class of the term, I asked them to reintroduce themselves to each other, this time as Brighton residents, with the help of their artefacts. These included lots of photos displayed on phone screens – of places of work, shopping or entertainment, of a view from a room, of a group of friends hiking in the South Downs. Several students had created maps tracing their daily routines (Image 2.1). There were a home-made T-shirt, a pack of playing cards, bus tickets and (imaginary because the student had not actually built them) scales attempting to balance academic and leisure life. Students' efforts in making these artefacts had ranged from high to non-existent; the ones that had been made showed an amazing variety.

When I taught the module in the spring of 2021, for the second time and in virtual mode, I realized that I needed to make space for students to express the upheaval that COVID has created in their lives. I set up a padlet and invited students to upload images and stories of what they missed most about their pre-COVID lives in Brighton. I suggested that the students should explore and document these changes and pay attention to the emotions to which they had given rise – inviting students to remember, reminisce or grieve. In this way, I opened the door for whole-person learning that encompassed not only students' intellects but also their bodies, emotions and experiences. Their contributions on the padlet speak of sociality and conviviality, created by everyday encounters and togetherness that were impossible in the early months of 2021 and much missed and mourned. But they also show what students drew strength from in these trying times as they continued to live and learn: the sea front and its murmurations, a pair of sneakers, the check-out line at the local supermarket.[9]

On the basis of their increased awareness of how they had been inhabiting the urban spaces of Brighton, together with the academic articles and policy reports, students then drafted a manifesto for how to make Brighton a more

Image 2.1: Map created by student for Brighton Manifesto exercise

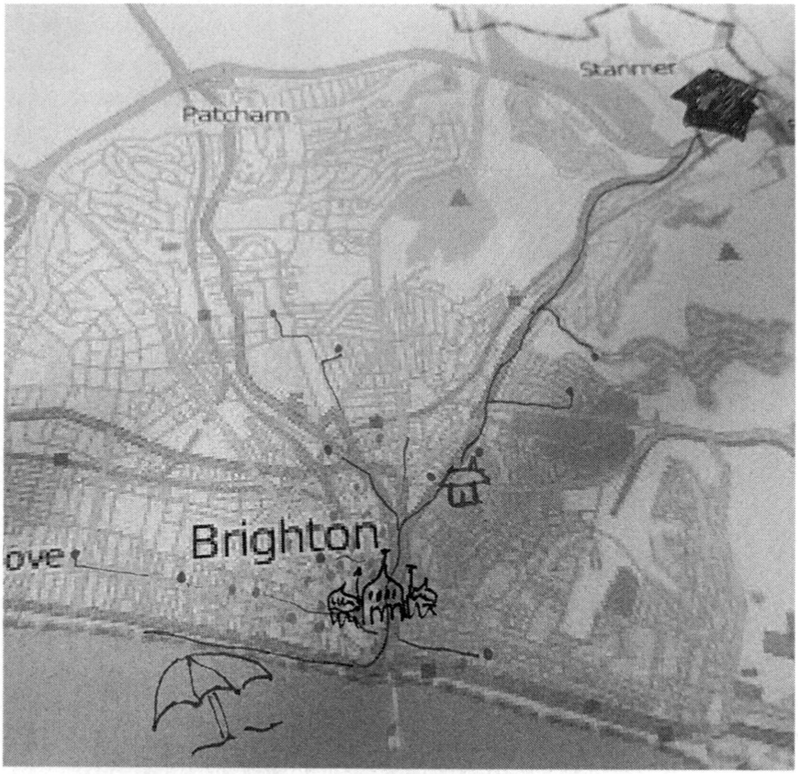

Photo: Author, used with permission.

liveable, inclusive and equitable city. I had written a general description of a manifesto as 'a statement of ideals and intentions that sets out beliefs, visions and policies, to make the reader feel hope, excitement, curiosity and to invite them to join you in making your vision a reality'. I had also provided three sample manifestos and a template of statements – we believe, we envision, we are committed to – that the students could begin to work with. Lastly, I let each group pick a sheet of coloured paper on which to write their manifesto, giving material shape to my expectation that they would need to produce something by the end of class. Because we ran out of time, students completed their creations at home, and the final manifestos I received were of varying states of completion and quality but showed that each group had creatively engaged with the activity (Image 2.2). In general, having enough time for these activities was a constant challenge, as they usually took place in the second half of the three-hour class, when I thought students would enjoy more creative and less analytical work. While that made pedagogical sense, I wondered if I was unconsciously implying that these activities were

Image 2.2: Brighton Manifesto created by students

Photo: Author, used with permission.

less important than more formal lectures and discussions. Or was I running up against an institutional constraint of needing to prioritize teaching core knowledge in more conventional ways?

Rather than being a fun add-on, the urban manifesto activity combined a number of pedagogical elements. By asking students to apply their theoretical knowledge about liveable cities to a concrete situation with which they were familiar, it encouraged learning by doing. Instead of discussing in the abstract how cities could be transformed, students worked through how this could happen in the specific case of Brighton. For this, they also drew on their own knowledge about the city, thereby activating whole-person learning. In their artefacts, some students had traced their physical movements in their maps, while others had incorporated emotive elements into the images they presented, such as feeling safe hiking with friends or feeling happy while pursuing leisure activities. The 2021 padlet in particular provided a space for students to share their sense of loss and sadness, but also of what kept them grounded and going in difficult times. The activity therefore made use of various strands of experiential learning (Roberts, 2008).

Using their own experiences as Brighton residents drew in phenomenological elements of situating themselves in the city.[10] Several students commented on how the first half of the activity had made them more aware of their daily habits in Brighton and of what they had previously taken for granted. Reflecting on their interactions with others within the social spaces of the city and then discussing their artefacts with fellow classmates incorporated interactive aspects of experiential learning. Lastly, connecting these personal experiences to broader questions around rights of the city and how they are experienced intersectionally, a praxis notion of experience was activated that asked how different groups of residents have different kinds of access to Brighton and how these urban experiences are enabled or disabled by power relations. Applying such whole-person learning to an urban transformative project put theoretical knowledge into practice, opening up the classroom to the outside world and imagining how to enact transformative change in it.

Furthermore, students drew together various sources of knowledge, complementing standard academic texts with policy papers and their own knowledge as expressed in the artefacts. These, as well as the production of the written manifesto, asked students to externalize their personal reflections. 'Incubat[ing] inspirations and then materializing them' enables students to not only think but also create and act in alternative ways (Hammond, 2017, p 111). The manifestos were exhibited during the last class of term, when I placed all of the students' creations around the room for a gallery walk that showed them the knowledge they had co-produced throughout the module and its varied creative expressions. I asked students to jot down on index cards words that came to their minds while viewing their works, which included visionary, surprisingly valuable, care and community, eye-opening, people power and activism. The urban manifesto was thus the first of several activities that connected students' everyday lives and study experiences to the places in which they unfolded, manifesting students as situated learners. As a result, students became more aware of their own and other people's locations within the city and made that knowledge actionable by imagining concrete ways in which Brighton could become a more hospitable city. Lastly, they began to work towards that change by collectively writing a manifesto that invited others to join their vision. In the next chapter I show how students continued this work through a design activity that gave material shape to the manifestos.

Conclusion

In this chapter I have explored critical-creative pedagogy's potential to transform educators and students alike. Such a pedagogy calls for the remaking of academic identities through questioning privileges and positionalities, through uncovering assumptions and unlearning knowledge and through letting go of ambitions and aspirations. These processes can be uncomfortable, disorienting and painful, and, as educators, 'we must think carefully about what it means to change the inner worlds of those we see in our classrooms each week' (Barcan, 2016, p 158). For students, emphasizing that being critical is not the same as being cynical or negative might not be enough when they feel disillusioned and question their own moral projects and identities. A critical-creative pedagogy provides a way forward that combines critical analysis with nurturing students' imagination, creativity and hope. This calls for open, inviting and safe classrooms and for educators to participate in creative practices, to show their own courage to experiment and to share the initial unease that comes with being pushed out of one's comfort zones. The challenges that such a pedagogy has to overcome are not to be underestimated, particularly in the neoliberal HE context in the UK and beyond. Throughout this chapter I have presented some of the transformative responses to these challenges, from Critical Pedagogy to decolonizing universities. I have explored how situated forms of teaching can invite students as whole-person learners located in complex worlds, in order to enable them to imagine alternative futures for the places in which they live and learn. In the next chapter I show how these imaginings can be materialized through the introduction of design methods and practices into social sciences classrooms.

3

Designing Futures

I grew up in a small town in former East Germany, located about 20 km from Weimar. A historical home to thinkers and artists such as Johan Wolfgang Goethe, Friedrich Nietzsche and Rudolf Steiner, Weimar was also where the Bauhaus was founded. This design school opened its doors here a little over 100 years ago, as a radical experiment in arts and design education. Walter Gropius, its first Director, had chosen the name Bauhaus in a modern reference to the medieval guilds of craftspeople, called Bauhütten, and a combination of theoretical studio work, practical workshop application and communal living became the school's signature characteristic. Its vision was of 'an open, experimental structure to give students a wide-ranging character-building education' (Friedewald, 2009, p 35). This vision was shaped by Gropius' experiences on the Somme during the First World War, from which he emerged believing in radical social reform in which creative people played a central role. The Bauhaus attracted some of the most avant garde artists of the time, from Paul Klee to Vassili Kandinsky, Laslo Moholy-Nagy and Lionel Feininger. A Swiss educator called Johannes Itten developed the Vorkurs, the precursor of today's arts and design schools' foundation year, which focused on the development of students' creative capabilities through cultivating their minds, bodies and souls.

Education at the Bauhaus was characterized by collaborative work and the combination of previously separate disciplines and media, by a general rejection of academicism and by forging links with industry to give students practical experiences and to complement the school's meagre public funds. Although not always able to live up to its ideals, the Bauhaus envisioned a new union of arts, crafts and industry, above all maintaining human and artistic elements under the onslaught of mass production, standardization and industrialization at the beginning of the 20th century. There are important parallels between Germany in the 1920s and the world today. The former was a time of intense political, economic and social upheaval. In the year of the Bauhaus' founding, the Weimar Republic, Germany's first foray into democracy, was declared in the National Theatre across town from the Bauhaus, against a background of pitched street battles in many German cities between communist and socialist workers and reactionary vigilante groups. This increasing political polarization went along with a rejection of foreign people and ideas that culminated in the rise of Hitler, with deep economic inequalities resulting from post-war deprivation, the Great Depression and subsequent hyper-inflation, and with intense debates about how technologies were changing society and work. Within this context, the Bauhaus experiment can be seen as a historical inspiration for the contributions that an arts-and-design-informed education can make to imagining and creating alternative futures.[1]

During the 14 years of its existence, 1,300 students studied at the Bauhaus. Similar to Gropius, many of them had experienced at first hand the ravages of the First World War and subsequent turmoil and hardship. They shared his radical ideas about the role of art and design in social change and brought them to life with youthful enthusiasm and creative drive, declaring that 'we do not want to become artists, but human beings, and intensify our looking, experiencing and sensing',[2] and that 'the value is not in what is taught but in how it is taught, that one first trains and educates people who think and act for themselves before one conveys the necessary knowledge to them'. Another student spoke for many when saying that 'most people come with the genuinely serious intention of entering a community which differs fundamentally from the contradictory world around them, where they can develop new points of view for the systematic creation of a new society'. This community included students growing their own food and cooking, eating and living together. Students were conscious that they were participating in a history-making educational experiment, aiming 'to model a democratic creative community [and] proving by their own example that a better world does exist' (Forgács, 1991, p 4). They were to some extent prefiguring the society they were trying to build, where creative people had a key role to play in creating an alternative future with deeply communal values. This vision did not sit well with Weimar's deeply conservative burghers, who had protested against Bauhaus faculty and students, with their gender-bending ideas, indecent clothes, wild parties and generally un-German behaviour, from the beginning. When they succeeded in having public funding cut, the Bauhaus relocated the Dessau and then to Berlin. There, branded as Bolshevik and degenerate, it was closed in April 1932 following one of the first decrees issued after the Nazis came to power.

I am aware that I am painting a simplified and idealistic picture of the Bauhaus, which for all its intentions could not escape institutional hierarchies, necessary trade-offs between professional, pedagogic and economic demands and traditional gender norms, which replicate existing male biases in the design field. Still, the Bauhaus provides a generative opening to this chapter, which focuses on the role of design in the challenge-focused social sciences, because of its experimental and whole-person teaching methods. While today design is integral to teaching in arts, design, architecture and engineering departments, and increasingly in business schools, its concepts and methods are largely absent from social science teaching. However, there is much that critical and socially engaged design can offer to these disciplines. Design provides students with knowledge about contemporary challenges as wicked problems, due to their complex, indeterminate and multifaceted nature, and about design thinking as an open-ended, iterative approach to addressing these challenges. Design can also foster in students orientations of becoming more comfortable with ambiguity in their learning and of embracing humility and empathy in their interactions with others. These orientations give students capabilities to hold open spaces for reflection, discussion and action and to explore different questions before settling on answers and ways forward. Lastly, because of its fundamentally material nature, design raises questions of resource politics that can help students to navigate questions of power, privilege and positionality from a material perspective. It also highlights the material dimension of teaching that is often missing from more theory-focused classrooms.

I begin the chapter with a general introduction to what design is and what its methods can offer the social sciences and then explore the relationship between design and educational futures. Analysing the role of space and materials in a design-inspired education allows me to then connect resource politics to specific university contexts and funding models. In the second half of the chapter I describe two teaching activities: in the first, students imagine and build scenarios of urban futures, while the second is an individual student's experiments around future food systems.

What design? Why design?

Design is a broad and dynamic field, which is being repositioned as 'a key space for thinking about life and its defense from increasingly devastating anthropogenic forces ... a decisive world-making practice, even if often found wanting' (Escobar, 2018, p 139). Most generally, design 'defines the specifications, plans, parameters, costs, activities, processes and how and what to do within legal, political, social, environmental, safety and economic constraints in achieving an objective' (Kumaragamage, cited in Schwittay, 2014, p 30). While mention of design often invokes product, graphic or fashion design, the practice also encompasses the creation of novel services, systems, experiences and environments. Design can best be thought of as 'an integrative discipline that connects knowledge from the arts and the sciences and applies it to the problems of the present, with a forward-looking orientation' (Buchanan, 1992, p 11). Its multidimensional character encompasses material, cultural, epistemic, political and ontological elements.

Within the field, a broad distinction can be drawn between commercial and socially engaged design. The former is often deeply implicated in unsustainable production and consumption practices, partly contributing to the current era of the Anthropocene, where the global environment has become a product of human activity. Since the first half of the 19th century, through educational institutions such as the Bauhaus, design has been codified and become a professional field, with trained experts often proclaiming themselves to be revolutionary change makers (Suchman, 2011). While from a commercial perspective design is regarded as a neutral tool to transform the world, design scholars, anthropologists studying humanitarian design and others have shown that it is deeply embedded in broader structures that impact on how and by whom design is used and what its effects are (Schwittay, 2014). Their work shows that design's destructive resource politics contribute to the field's central involvement in contemporary practices of 'defuturing', through making ever-new things whose production necessarily involves the depletion of resources and whose uptake reframes the old as obsolete and worthless by design (Fry, 2018).

Because of design's complicity in defuturing, more critically oriented designers are recognizing their responsibilities to redesign the world in response to anthropogenic damage and are 'embrac[ing] the vital normative questions of the day ... from out-of-box perspectives' (Escobar, 2017, p 45). Socially engaged design is contributing to this redesign by addressing social, ecological and economic issues as design problems (Nieusma, 2004). Many of these critical and emancipatory approaches are feeding into the emerging field of transition design, which recognizes itself as a fundamentally ethical and political activity rather than a market-driven and consumption-oriented one (Yelavich and Adams, 2014). Design also has a singular dimension, expressed in the concept of everyday design as 'the human ability to prefigure what we create before the act of creation, [which] defines one of the fundamental characteristics that makes us human' (Fry, 2018, p 2). Design shapes every human's engagement with the material world, with other beings, things, institutions and systems. As such, each act of design incorporates both intellectual and material activities, conceptualizing something and then giving it material shape. As a result, design has the potential to bridge or at least narrow the mind–body gap, a fundamental dichotomy that is put into question by many of the alternatives explored in this book (Gatt and Ingold, 2013).

Design is also intimately connected to narratives of modernization and progress that have shaped the post-Second World War world; international development in particular has been called a 'daring, albeit utterly arrogant, design vision' (Escobar, 2017, p 6). In response, designers in the Global South are problematizing design's embeddedness in histories of colonialism, empire and other forms of domination and its continuing functioning within various matrixes of power (for a good summary, see Escobar, 2018). By contrast, their practices of autonomous design harness its potential for liberatory struggles. Similarly, in *Designs for the Pluriverse* Escobar seeks to reclaim design for the making of alternative futures. Following his lead, I believe that design has much to offer a critical-creative pedagogy, beginning with its open and experimental methods and the ethical orientations they can foster in students.

Design uses an open-ended process, sometimes called design thinking, to understand challenges and develop responses to them (New and Kimbell, 2013). Rather than taking a solution to a problem from a pre-existing list, designers work through an iterative process of continuous testing and adjustment to co-evolve solutions, often with future users. This process involves the making of prototypes, which are rough material manifestations of ideas to test assumptions and elicit reactions. It also involves asking 'what if' questions that disrupt taken-for-granted understandings and call for imaginative answers. Another critical design concept is that of wicked problems, defined as 'social system problems which are ill-formulated, where the information is confusing, where there are many clients and decision-makers with conflicting values, and where the ramifications in the whole system are thoroughly confusing' (Rittel quoted in Buchanan, 1992, p 15). In contrast to problems that follow more linear processes to precise solutions, wicked problems are indeterminate because they have no clearly defined limits and more than one possible explanation. They are also symptomatic of higher-level problems, and many contemporary challenges are wicked problems because of their complexity and interconnectedness with other problems.

This calls for different disciplines to work together in formulating responses, and design can enable collaborative environments through its 'new integrations of signs, things, actions and environments that address the concrete needs and values of human beings in diverse circumstances' (Buchanan, 1992, p 21). At the same time, design has been called the art of the possible because of its inherently optimistic approach. Transition design in particular harnesses design's potential for alternative futures and, like the generative theory informing this book, 'transcends the limits of deconstructive and discursive analysis by venturing into the positive project of how the world can be – and be understood – otherwise' (Escobar, 2017, p 96). It is an explicit example of socially engaged design whose methods can inform social science teaching.

Learning by design

Currently, design joins arts and media education in being seen as paradigmatic for new learning modes that involve creativity, learning by doing and an intersection with activities beyond campus (Boys, 2010). The connection of these fields with the creative industries shows their affinity to instrumental forms of creativity I critiqued in Chapter 1, and mainstream design education is largely formulated around the needs and expectations of commercial employers (Light, 2018). This necessitates the redeployment of design education for more emancipatory purposes, where its active and three-dimensional character, which incorporates experimentation and collaboration, embraces ambiguity and question posing and fosters empathy and humility, holds much potential for challenge-focused social science education.

Firstly, experimentation is integral to design education and can range from structured scientific experiments to testing ideas and experiences to open-ended playful exploration (Lyons, 2011). Experimentation involves risk taking and boundary crossing, which can result in divergent or unexpected outcomes. Experiments can also fail, and design helps students to reframe failures as learning opportunities that invite reworking rather than resignation. Experimentation and iteration emphasize the openness and emergent qualities of things, and can encourage students to explore different avenues before settling on a specific course of action. Design's experimentation is cautious, as 'the creativity of design is found not in the novelty of prefigured solutions to perceived environmental problems but in the capacity of inhabitants to respond with precision to the ever-changing circumstances of their lives' (Gatt and Ingold, 2013, p 145).

Design is also collaborative, and not only because designers always work in teams. Informed by Jean Lave and Etienne Wenger's (1991) work on communities of practice, where craft skills are acquired through situated learning incorporating practice and participation, there is a growing field of participatory design for learning that looks at how collaboration and co-design can be harnessed for pedagogical purposes (DiSalvo et al, 2017). Of particular importance is the progressive tradition of co-design developed in Scandinavia around workers' participation in workplace decisions (Ehn, 1993), which can provide insights and tools for students to negotiate differences and co-create visions of alternative futures with diverse groups.

Secondly, design education fosters students' tolerance for ambiguity, defined as being open to more than one possible meaning or interpretation. The ability to be comfortable with ambiguity is one of the key markers of creative problem solving, which contains ambiguous periods during which different responses to problems are considered. For this, 'it is necessary to withstand the uncertainty and chaos that result when the problem is not clearly defined or when it is unclear how the pieces of the solution are going to come together' (Harding and Hale, 2007, p 3). Ambiguity can create discomfort and anxiety, but because complex challenges as wicked problems do not have easy, fast or definite solutions, being able to consider more than one course of action is important. Design methods can help students to embrace ambiguity by enabling them to look at various angles of a problem or situation, to suspend judgement and to shift emphasis from looking for a solution to considering various responses. Giving students purposely puzzling instructions for a learning activity and then resisting demands for clarification and instead explaining that their experiences of discomfort or frustration are part of the learning experience is a concrete example of fostering tolerance for ambiguity that can be used in diverse classroom situations. Ambiguity can also fortify educators working in the belly of the neoliberal university beast with stamina to persist in the increasing 'pedagogical correctness' of the current HE system: 'if we can tolerate the ambiguity of the (insoluble?) problem of working within systems that often seem to function as anti-creative forces, this approach may offer strategies that could help us live within the discomfort of a situation' (p 9).

A tolerance for ambiguity is closely connected to the ability to continuously pose questions. Many students I interviewed described critical thinking as 'questioning everything'; design can push them to consider whether they are even asking the right questions. This supports unlearning as a letting go of certainties and confidences and is reminiscent of Freire's education as problem posing, which he himself connected to creativity (Darder et al, 2009). Focusing on asking questions also avoids 'ideological thinking [as] a state of mind in which the answers are known before the questions have been asked' (Staley, 2019, p 205). Ideological thinking introduces biases into information gathering and analysis, narrows students' vision and excludes the exploration of some possibilities from the outset. Becoming comfortable with ambiguity and questions, rather than yearning for certainty and solutions, can therefore prepare students for tackling wicked problems.

Thirdly, a designerly attitude has also been linked to empathy and humility. Empathy, broadly defined as the ability to imagine other people's feelings or to emotionally identify with another person – to put ourselves in their shoes – is usually connected to the education of doctors, social workers and other care professionals. In design, empathy is central to especially user-centred design, which takes the perspective of end-users into account throughout the design process. New and Kimbell (2013) differentiate designerly empathy from a more rational managerialist empathy that isolates and simplifies problems and then draws on familiar prescriptions to solve them. By contrast, designers take a 'creative leap into the experience of another' in more affective, immersive and holistic ways (p 5). This involves cognitive processes of understanding, and affective processes of emotional and embodied labour. To achieve this, students can be introduced to designers' tools such as visualizations, the construction of personas, role-plays and co-immersions. Empathy in university classrooms can encourage whole-person learning that is embodied, emotive and experiential. As I showed in the previous chapter, this needs to be guided by educators in caring and aware ways, especially in the context of rising student mental health and emotional well-being needs. Empathy and compassion are important orientations for educators to respond to these needs.

When used by students, empathetic understanding must be grounded in qualitative, ideally ethnographic, research with or about those affected by particular challenges, and must be informed by an open orientation that does not judge or rush to solutions based on emotionalized reactions. Asking students to put themselves into others' shoes without understanding their situations can lead to students projecting their own emotions or experiences onto others and to patronizing assumptions or misrecognition (Schwittay and Boocock, 2015). Instead, design can provide students with knowledge and orientations to put themselves, literally and metaphorically, into situations where they encounter, learn about and interact with difference. Understanding privilege and discrimination on a more experiential level can then become another form of embodied learning. However, empathy can also become parochial, instrumentalized and lead to short-sighted policy decisions (Bloom, 2017). In spite of these dangers, when used in an aware, ethical way, developing empathetic understanding can be a pedagogical tool that increases students' capacity not only to learn about the world but also to engage in it with care.

This is best done from a position of humility. Although, especially, commercial design is often associated with hubris (Suchman, 2011), Bruno Latour argues that 'designing is the anti-dote to founding, colonizing, establishing, or breaking with the past. It is an antidote to hubris and to the search for absolute certainty, absolute beginnings and radical departures' (2008, p 5). For Latour, design is humble and modest. Designers proceed with caution because they realize the complexities and interlinkages of wicked problems and the unintended consequences of all possible actions. A critical-creative pedagogy informed by design practices can therefore teach students how to approach contemporary challenges from a design-thinking perspective, can help them to become more comfortable with ambiguity and open-ended questions and can encourage them to practise empathy and humility. In the next section I explore how such knowledge and capabilities can contribute to students' imagining alternative futures.

Educational futuring by design

According to Tony Fry, 'design futures or defutures – it rides the line between bringing things into being that sustain the conditions upon which viable futures depend and taking the possibility of such futures away' (2018, p 211). Which of these potentials comes to pass depends in part on what came beforehand. Walter Benjamin's Angel of History, who is blown into the future by the storm of progress while looking backwards over the debris of history piling up in front of it, is an apt visual metaphor for the ways in which the past opens or forecloses future possibilities. While Benjamin was writing in the context of Nazi Germany, today's social and environmental challenges pose similarly grave, if different, problems. Any talk of the future must therefore be informed by an understanding of the past. As design anthropologists have shown, this is not a straightforward process, as 'to design is to imagine, and imaginings are necessarily complex articulations of unknown futures and selectively recalled histories' (Berglund, 2015, p 35).[3] These articulations are also political and power laden, even when seemingly neutral.

In education, visions of the future are often dominated by economic mandates of participation in national economic projects and wrapped up in the use of technologies, where 'the digital is used as a proxy for transformation [resulting in a] monocultural and economically dogmatic account of educational futures' (Facer, 2018b, p 199). As laid out in Chapter 1, Facer shows how these dominant visions disconnect education from its social moorings. Based on her research of the historical development of different university models, Facer posits five possible educational futures.

Modelling can encourage students to create models of potential futures, be they artistic, mathematical or scientific. Stewardship fosters practices of care and restores diversity through the humanities and ecological sciences. Reflexivity, as taught by the social sciences and statistics, enables students to critically interrogate narratives of the future. Disciplinarity teaches students the different ways in which disciplines make sense of new information, also with an eye to encouraging transdisciplinarity. And finally, experimentation allows students to imagine and create different futures, using the arts and design, engineering or computing and the social sciences. All of these practices are relevant for critical-creative pedagogy. The futures they help to create are unknown and stand in complex and non-linear relationships with the past and present. To enact these potentialities, universities must become accountable to the publics whose futures are being shaped by academic work and think more clearly about what kind of students they want to educate. A final educational future therefore is centred on public participation and institutional reflection on the role of universities in future making. For students, this results in a form of engaged learning that moves from theoretical analysis of futuring to active future making in their own lives and communities, which I explore in greater detail in Chapter 6.

David Staley's Future University concept presents several ideas for realizing educational futures, centred on students' creation of future-oriented design fictions. This university focuses on both pure futuring, through a liberal arts–type education where students explore the future 'as a possibility space', and applied futuring, through more vocationally oriented teaching where students are 'making the future happen' (2019, p 193). Teaching would encompass systems thinking, dystopian and utopian science fiction reading and writing and the incubation of new social forms within the university. It would also include the making of objects that materialize students' visions of the future. Such critical-creative learning fosters students' curiosity, introspection, imagination and situational awareness. Studying at the Future University culminates with a capstone project that could include enacting particular scenarios within the university, which becomes a prefigurative living laboratory. Staley gives the example of universal basic income as an experiment with redistributive justice that would allow students to viscerally experience future-making forms. Critical reflection on students' personal experiences would be an important part of the learning process. So would scenario building.

Scenarios are stories about a possible future as one among several options (Manzini, 2015). Anchored in understandings of the past and present, the development of scenarios is shaped by different ideologies, while their building is infused with relations of power over who can say what count as preferable futures. Scenarios have been created for mainstream and alternative ends. They were first used in the 1950s for US military planning in the context of the growing nuclear war threat. The practice was taken up by large corporations, most notably Shell, which in the 1970s began to build energy scenarios to inform its evolving business practices. In 1995, the Global Scenario Group, convened by the Tellus Institute and the Stockholm Environment Institute, started developing multiple planetary scenarios.[4] The group also identified values, practices and strategies that have informed the Great Transition Initiative, which is an international network of citizens, scholars and activists that incubates transition experiments, also feeding into the field of transition design (Escobar, 2017). It has become a global citizen movement that unites diverse local initiatives and shows that scenario building can be harnessed for social activism, transformative change and heterodox alternatives. The emphasis is on multiplicity, best expressed in the image of an

archipelago of futures [that] deviates dramatically from the future colonized by the technological frontrunners and the innovation centers of the world ... There is no single future arriving first and fastest, only multiple, heterogeneous, and controversial futures that are in the making, composed through the networking, the many entanglements, the ongoing thinging and infrastructuring, the patchworking and collision of intersecting rhizomes, and quite mundane design and innovation activities. (Ehn et al, 2014, p 10)

Imagining multiple and diverse futures has been connected to ideas of the pluriverse, which posits a world encompassing a multitude of interconnected worlds with different ways of thinking, being and doing. In the design space, this has given rise to autonomous design practices emerging from Latin America which centre on 'questions of care and repair', draw on multiple temporalities and worldviews and can support subaltern struggles (Escobar, 2018, p 140). Buen Vivir, which I present in Chapter 5 on repairing ecologies, is one example of these practices.

How can socially engaged, transition and autonomous design thinking and methods be used in social science classrooms? While I describe two teaching activities in detail later, here are some initial ideas. One possibility is to introduce students to 'prefigurative criticism', which associates emerging products or practices with negative values through placing them into undesirable contexts, which would decrease demand for them and thereby eliminate the need for future production (Fry, 2018). Students could explore recoding the value of things through creative alterations of brands, adverts or billboards, following the work of organizations like Adbusters. They could also examine their own consumption habits and the values underlying them and then experiment with recoding. Other activities could involve reclaiming past practices and knowledges, which connects to decolonizing moves that (re)valorize previously marginalized, including indigenous, creative traditions that might be very different from Western-based models and provide pluriversal alternative visions (Tunstall, 2013). Lastly, crafting alternative futures through collaborative design can become an end in itself, rather than working to replace materialistic products and aspirations (Light, 2018). Here, the process of students working with others to imagine and design alternative futures is as important as the outcomes. Such learning activities can be enhanced through providing engaging spaces and materials.

Spaces matter

In Chapter 1 I describe the brutal-modernist architecture of Sussex University, which can be traced back, via a number of detours, to the modern style that the Bauhaus helped bring into existence. The built environment of Sussex also makes visible the contested nature of space for teaching and learning experiences. Most generally, educational spaces are seen as important for promoting learning, motivating students and creating inclusive environments (Boys, 2010). Learning spaces need to accommodate different activities, ranging from the private thinking and incubating of ideas, to the collective sharing of information, to discussions and collaborations on projects. Spaces express historically specific learning philosophies, from the rooms of medieval universities where the enlightened scholar's elevated position showed his authority in the delivery of original knowledge, to modern lecture halls efficiently accommodating increasing numbers of students arranged in immovable rows of seats facing a lectern occupied by the expert professor, to seminar rooms with their horseshoe-shaped table layout that allows students to face and interact with each other, to flexible spaces with chairs and tables that can be clustered in any configuration to foster active, workshop-style and student-centred teaching (Beichner, 2014). Technology labs that incorporate digital learning technologies have become central in today's universities, although during the COVID-19 pandemic they were mostly replaced by students accessing learning from private spaces via their laptops.

Educational spaces are deeply entangled with resource politics, which raise questions of the public, private or philanthrocapitalist financing of universities and corresponding possibilities or foreclosures. This was brought home to me during a visit to the Hasso Plattner Institute of Design at Stanford University in California, commonly referred to as the d.school. Its space is large, open and light filled, full of whimsical invitations to be creative, such as a van lined with cushions to crawl into and jot down thoughts on sticky notes; working spaces in different configurations; colourful provocations and manifestos; photos of all the students who have ever taken a d.school course and their endorsements of the school's work, and lots and lots of materials and tools. I have to admit that I loved the place, feeling like a kid in a candy store and imagining what it would be like if Sussex had a space like this. Alas, it does not. The d.school was established with a large donation from a corporate donor, who was undoubtedly attracted by the university's elite status as well as its long history of corporate collaborations,[5] and is being supported by Stanford's own resources, including the building. Such spatial and material possibilities are firmly out of the reach of most universities the world over. At Sussex, an admittedly very small design programme has little studio space, while a general space crunch sometimes means that workshops are not taught in spaces where tables and chairs can be moved around. When I visited a number of public universities in Bolivia, the neglected state of many teaching spaces showed financial and material limitations even more starkly.

Current discussions about the connection between educational spaces and learning often rest on behaviourist assumptions of an automatic relationship between spaces and the activities and interactions taking place in them (Boys, 2010). However, space is not a neutral container waiting to be filled with learning activities, and learning spaces are not just physical but also emotional, biological, metaphorical and conversational. Most importantly, how different groups of students experience and use space cannot be assumed:

> for some [students], beanbags may imply informality, for others childishness. For a student who has had bad experiences in education

Image 3.1: Purpose-built creativity space at the University of Sussex (unused during COVID)

Photo: Author.

before, the conventions of a lecture theatre might feel safer than the 'unknown' of an unrecognisable learning space; or an informal space might be preferred because it helps to relieve previous anxieties. (p 129)

Ethnographic studies of teaching spaces, such as the one exploring perceptions around a purpose-built creativity space at Sussex, show that what some students – and teachers – find stimulating and liberating others might find intimidating or unsettling (Melhuish, 2010).[6] Informal spaces can lead to students feeling pressured to be creative, which shows the norms and values expressed in the design of learning spaces but also in the teaching that takes place in them (Image 3.1).

In design education, the predominant spatial form is the studio.[7] Studios combine skills acquisition with critical reflection and provide a material infrastructure for the realization of creative projects through experimental, often collaborative, practice. Design anthropologists have explored the application of a studio mode to social science teaching, where the seminar room becomes a space for creative practice with peers, teachers and maybe community members, focused on emerging ideas, concepts and objects (Halse, 2013). Keith Murphy and George Marcus characterize studio work as 'spaces of intervention, an active role in producing occasions for experimental, and indeed speculative thinking and the collective and material making of concepts' (2013, p 255). Recognizing that creativity is not explicitly valued or infrastructurally afforded within the social sciences, they nevertheless invited a cohort of anthropology PhD students to rearticulate their ethnographic material through a design studio process. One of the most crucial differences to emerge from this was that design studio pedagogy includes public critique as a component of learning in ways that are absent in the social sciences.

During so-called crits, positive and negative critique comes from instructors and peers, who query the choices students have made in their creative practice. 'These moments of criticism, in which instructors identify the problems in a student's work (as well as the positive details), are where a great deal of the pedagogical work is accomplished in design education' (p 266). Were negative assessment not forthcoming, students would feel short-changed in their opportunities to defend their work and learn from their mistakes. During her journey interview for my book, a student who had undertaken an arts foundation year prior to studying at Sussex explained it to me in the following way:

'A design course allows the individual time to prototype, to tangent and circle back, to learn from failures and use them to continuously develop a project. At each stage projects are discussed with fellow students openly, and critique is often welcomed over compliment. This is where the learning itself comes from, and the main thing I think the social sciences could learn from a design school is the ability to learn *through* creativity. Creative students from day one are almost forced to share their thoughts and processes with fellow students, something which continues throughout a module, teaching them to use and take critique. The culture in a social science degree, meanwhile, is not about sharing. Pressure to produce a grade from one or two essays results in a fear of critique, despite this being fundamental to learning effectively. Leaning away from the assessment of a final result and more toward ongoing critique of processes and ideas might help remove the vulnerability and timidness that is often felt in students toward their own work and encourage greater contribution within the classroom.'

For this student, assessment through a final essay or exam, which is still the norm in the social sciences, does not encourage ongoing experimentation or an openness towards sharing ideas in progress with others.

In the social sciences, negative critique does not come publicly, but in private comments on written work or during office hours or in the small circle of a PhD viva. When students experience more open forms of critique, it can evoke a range of reactions (AAA, 2018). Anthropology student participating in a conference panel on the pedagogical intersections between a seminar classroom and a design studio described how they felt pushed out of their comfort zones when instead of only sharing finished pieces they had to continuously show their work in progress. This created vulnerabilities in some students, but was perceived as liberating by others because it resulted in ceding some control over and applying less filters to their work. Input from fellow students and instructors at earlier stages of work was particularly generative in developing novel ideas; it also "kept churning things in a more productive way" and made knowledge creation a more public process.[8] A design studio process helped some students "to break free from their disciplinary straight jacket" and break down boundaries between different domains. These experiences show how physical and conceptual spaces can open up creative learning opportunities, while at the same time maintaining elements of critical reflection. Generous learning spaces can invite partial connections, experimental stances, emerging creations and collaborative endeavours, through their physical design and the shared work of educators and students as co-creators of learning within them. This works best when spaces contain materials stimulating students' creativity and imagination.

Material making

Alongside space, learning materials also matter for critical-creative pedagogy. A distinction can be made between thinking materials, which are physical items that enable students to visualize their ideas, and making materials, which are things that afford building, from low-tech craft materials to higher-end raw and recycled materials and the tools to manipulate them. In today's social science classrooms, both types of materials remain secondary to written media. Universities were born during the rise of books, and written texts are still the predominant teaching material, with several implications. Information acquisition through the written format, whether on paper or screens, is reduced to the movements of eyes and fingers. Information is confined to what is suitable for the page, and 'the logic of the academic book as a sequential and sustained [written] argument is seen to both represent and reinforce the authority of the expert' (Boys, 2010, p 146). Written texts therefore materialize linear arguments by a single or collective authoritative source. This dynamic has been opened up somewhat by the shift towards online materials, especially when containing hyperlinks and incorporating other media, where more open-ended and multiconnected formats can lead to a decentring of authoritative knowledge. In addition, visual materials can convey various ideas and layers of meaning simultaneously and better express thoughts that do not fit the linear structure of words (Robinson, 2001).

A shift away from written materials also 'de-center[s] written texts as the only source of legitimate knowledge within the academy' (Laing, 2020, p

12). Such critiques of librocentrism have been incorporated into decolonial analyses, with important implications for experiential learning. Writing about Bolivia, Anders Burman has contrasted government-sponsored indigenous universities that are part of top-down decolonizing agendas with more radical, activist-led institutions that practise 'epistemic disobedience'. The latter is anchored in an Aymara worldview that regards humans as 'relational subjects thinking and producing knowledge from within and with the world' (2012, p 115). Such knowledge cannot be gained from books that reproduce other people's understanding, but from experiences in the world that involve bodily and ritual practices. While the context is obviously very different from UK universities, Burman draws on design anthropologist Tim Ingold's 'epistemology of engagement', which is grounded in authentic experiences of the world (Ingold, 2000, p 216). Here, the Carthusian autonomous rational subject, who knows the world without being part of it, is replaced with a relational subject who knows itself in the world. This includes an engagement with the world's materiality, not as inert matter but as 'performative objects with agency [that] have pedagogical effect' (Mäkelä and Löytönoen, 2017, p 254). In the classroom, these effects are created through the quality and presentation of materials and tools.

For both thinking and making materials, multi-use objects are preferable to single-use ones, as they provide students with base materials that can be manipulated to express ideas. Thinking materials include the ubiquitous multicoloured sticky notes, marker pens, stickers and large sheets of paper as well as representational prompts in the form of photos, quotes, icons or other visuals, all of which enable students to give visual shape to their thoughts. Making materials range from crafty stuff to Play-Doh, pipe cleaners and string to Lego and wooden blocks. Especially important are materials that are found in or sourced from natural environments and those that are reusable and recyclable, connecting design's resource politics to environmental sustainability. Making materials allow for more multidimensional and multisensorial creations than thinking materials, and how both are presented shapes how inviting or intimidating they seem to students. According to Joachim Halse, a design anthropologist, 'instead of smooth-looking visuals, demonstrations of new technologies, or authoritarian statements of what goals to reach, ... [a] large amount of local photographs and quotations by project participants, rough sketches of design ideas, and materials for tinkering scattered over the tables, along with utensils to transform them' can better stimulate imaginative uses (2013, p 186). These materials can be deployed to visualize ideas, create stories or build scenes, which could be followed up by role-play or enactments. Materials can also help to create 'what if' situations through which educators can encourage students to imagine and reflect, rather than trying to convince or indoctrinate them. This speaks to the performativity of material things that can play an active role in teaching and make unexpected and surprising contributions to learning through their open-ended nature (Mäkelä and Löytönoen, 2017). In addition, handling and manipulating materials 'prompts physical, intellectual and emotional responses' through a form of hand knowledge, where students' hands become translators between words and materials (Blakey and McFadyen, 2015, p 134).

Materials call for making.[9] This form of learning is often new to social science students, who, sometimes after initial hesitancy, often come to appreciate it. One student of my Urban Futures module told me that the emphasis on making in some of the creative activities made her come alive, which is an evocative description, especially when juxtaposed to conventional seminar discussions in which students can seem passive and uninvolved. The student's comment also shows that creative making is a whole-person activity, as it requires not only intellectual reflection and analysis but also embodied knowledge and emotional interpretation (Shreeve and Austerlitz, 2008). Often this is tacit knowledge that can best be accessed through experiential learning rather than literal articulation or teacher instructions. Making is also a multisensorial activity with visual, tactile and olfactory dimensions. It is experimental when presented in a way that allows students to play around, try out, take apart and rebuild, to find out what is meaningful for them and the task at hand; 'deeply engaged in active process, the maker is alert to possibility: vibrant, responsive and improvisational' (Blakey and McFadyen, 2015, p 134). Making involves deep situatedness, active participation and real-time connection, a coming together of mind, body and material that Ingold calls 'animacy' (2013, p 100). While social science students might not experience this as intensely as art and design students, the newness of making activities for them can open up spaces in which thinking can happen differently and learning can stick better (Image 3.2). Making also brings students together in ways that can be more interactive and fun than discussing an article or preparing a presentation.

In design, making takes the particular form of prototyping. Prototypes are physical manifestations of experimentation, giving material form to ideas in rough, unfinished mock-ups using whatever materials are at hand. For students, they can become 'a technology of the imagination [that] allows [them] to specify details of something otherwise only partially visible on the imaginative horizon'; details that can show the potentials and limitations of their ideas and elicit conversations with others (Halse, 2013, p 190). Prototyping is the material enactment of possible futures in the present; a future-making practice that extends the boundaries of the present through projections of hopes and dreams unto artefacts that are in the making. It is precisely the combination of collaborative experimentation and intrinsic futurity that makes prototyping a potent mode of engagement in the current moment: 'here is an epistemic culture built on collaboration, provisionality, recycling, experimentation and creativity, which seems as

Image 3.2: Students building urban scenarios

Photo: Author, used with permission.

much oriented to the production of technological artefacts as it is to the social engineering of hope' (Corsín Jiménez, 2014, p 382). Prototyping also allows students to shift back and forth between immersion in making and commentary on created objects, and makes this process available for collective learning. It is therefore a good example of how creativity is not disengaged from critical reflection, but how the two are intrinsically connected. The next section presents thick descriptions of two teaching activities that incorporate design thinking and methods are exemplary of this entanglement and the potential that design-informed teaching holds for challenge-focused social sciences.

Designing back from the (urban) future

Between 2017 and 2019, I organized a series of design activities in which students collectively imagined and built scenarios of alternative futures. These consisted of two half-day extracurricular workshops, attended by 70 under- and postgraduate students from Global Studies, and a two-hour in-class 'big build' activity towards the end of my Urban Futures module.[10] The workshops focused on the creative exploration of the Sustainable Development Goals (SDGs), with student groups choosing one goal and developing a future scenario for it. In both workshops, at least one group chose SDG 11, which aims to 'make cities and human settlements inclusive, safe, resilient and sustainable'. The big build focused on the future of Brighton, connecting it back to the urban manifestos presented in Chapter 2, which the students had written at the beginning of the term. In between manifesto and big build, students had read and discussed critical urban theories and learned about a range of topics, from urban citizenship, informality, infrastructures and work to processes of planning, building and governing. They were therefore familiar with urban debates, had explored various case studies and also undertaken a series of creative activities throughout the term, of which the big build was a culmination. By contrast, the workshop participants did not have such specialist knowledge and many also had not encountered creative design activities in the university context before. Drawing on both the workshops and the big build therefore allows me to show the creative potential of building scenarios in different learning contexts and how the activity can be tailored for those. While both activities focused on the challenges of future cities, scenario building can be applied to other social, ecological and economic challenges.

I structured the scenarios around an exercise called 'designing back from the future', following Anne-Marie Willis' (2014) account of her class at the German University in Cairo, where design students developed scenarios for Egypt 2060. For Willis, scenarios are the projection of likely futures, opening them up for reflection, including on the actions that need to be taken to achieve these futures. She distinguishes between negative scenarios exploring undesirable futures and positive scenarios that focus on preferred futures, which was the case for my activities. They were also proactive scenarios that focused on what might be possible to achieve through asking 'what if' and 'how' questions. Willis explains that, to work best, scenarios should be set in a specific place and time horizon. To stop scenarios from being fantasies, they need to be based on research to enable a thorough understanding of historical contexts, present situations and future challenges. To this end, Willis had conducted her scenario exercise over a whole semester, with several weeks allocated for students to undertake research. This is a challenge for scenario learning activities that are shorter and therefore might not have allocated research time, as was the case for the SDG workshops. Here I explained the importance of research to the participants, who drew on their own prior knowledge and used laptops to access basic information around their chosen topic. In the Urban Futures class, students had learned about general urban issues and different case studies throughout the term, were living in Brighton and had undertaken creative work in relation to the city already, therefore occupying a middle ground in terms of research.

Both the workshops and the big build took place in spacious rooms with movable tables and chairs. Prior to the students arriving, clusters of tables fitting six to eight students had been set up and covered with colourful thinking and making materials. I had also developed visuals to remind students of the open-ended and out-of-the-box nature of the exercise.[11] These included a prompt to see the activities as 'rapid experiments that help you question your assumptions and tackle unknowns' and another one to 'be experimental – this is about generating new ideas even if they might be unrealistic. Don't get stuck in the details or focus on limitations.' A visual on ambiguity explained it as exploring multiple ideas and ways forward simultaneously and encouraged students to suspend their inclinations to want to find answers or solutions quickly. Such visual reminders can surreptitiously foster open-ended and exploratory student orientations. Each table also had a random object, borrowed from my children's toy box, including a wooden carrot, a knight and a small plush animal, which groups needed to incorporate into their scenarios. These objects acted as material expressions of ambiguity, as they could take on multiple meanings or become metaphors for students to play with. There was also a common resources table where groups could get material refills and access bigger items and tools, as well as a snack and drink table. All of this was enabled by having access to an appropriate space and a departmental budget for such activities, which is not always the case for resource-constrained universities, especially in the HE world impacted upon by COVID-19.

This overall set-up communicated to the students entering the room that they would be allowed and indeed expected to be creative and to make something, but also to have a good time. Background music contributed to creating an informal atmosphere that was clearly distinct from a regular classroom setting. Students were excited as they settled into the space and many of them immediately began to play with their hands, opening cans of Play-Doh and commenting how its distinct smell brought back childhood memories, or bending pipe cleaners into whimsical shapes. Clearly setting the scene for a period of free creativity and playful exploration is important to communicate expectations of more open-ended learning. This needs to be complemented with structured guidelines to ensure that such learning can take place. Each table therefore also had sheets with general activity guidelines akin to a design brief, together with an approximate timetable, and I verbally explained the activity to the whole group in the beginning. Both the workshops and the big build were framed around the questions of 'What do we want the future to look like? How can we get there? Who will participate and in what ways?' I concluded my introduction by reminding students that there were no right or wrong answers or bad ideas and that the activities were about engaging in a creative process with fellow students to imagine, in hands-on and fun ways, possible actions towards more liveable, equitable and inclusive futures.

The big build in the Urban Futures class was preceded by a warm-up exercise in which students used Lego blocks to build their ideal house of the future.[12] Many of their models had environmental features such as oars for hydroelectric power, wind turbines and solar panels, which one student combined with a rotating mechanism so that his house would always face the sun. Other models explored social issues through the regeneration of old buildings and the maximization of communal areas. For the actual big build, I had pre-developed a normative scenario in the interest of time: 'Brighton in 2050 is a self-sustaining, hospitable and generous city. Its environmental footprint is minimal, it is welcoming of diversity and provides all of its residents with a decent quality of life.' I had set up tables around three more specific topics that corresponded to themes we had covered in previous lessons – sustainable infrastructures, deep governance and radical conviviality – and asked students to self-select into groups.

Each group had their own guideline brief, further specifying their vision through 'what if' questions and providing examples as starting points for their scenario journeys. Ideally these would be developed by the students themselves, but because the activity was only two hours long, more initial guidance was needed, since I wanted to make sure that students had enough time for the actual building part. Instructions included mapping the institutions that already exist by drawing on their own knowledge of Brighton and using their computers, which constituted a short, scoping-only research phase. Next they designed mechanisms through which their visions would be realized, and considered what their implications might be for particular groups of people. Most importantly, they had to build a rough prototype of their ideas with the materials at hand. Groups were soon busy at work and created visions that incorporated what was familiar and dear to students. In the spring of 2021, all of this took place on Zoom, jam boards and padlets. This did not stop students creating compelling visions of alternative future urban spaces. The infrastructure group created a virtual mock-up that connected Brighton and Sussex campus via a chain of new allotments and ponds, culminating in a reimagined university village (Image 3.3).

In the physical classroom a year earlier, the conviviality group took Brighton's well-known status as a City of Sanctuary as a point of departure to create spaces where refugees could obtain homes, food and skills and be integrated with fellow urban residents. Ideas ranged from the more conventional, such as housing refugees with families and giving them jobs in cafes and shops so that they could interact with residents on a daily basis, to the more out-of-the-box, such as repurposing Brighton's famous Royal Pavilion as a communal food hall. The governance group focused

Image 3.3: Student mock-up of reimagined urban spaces in Brighton

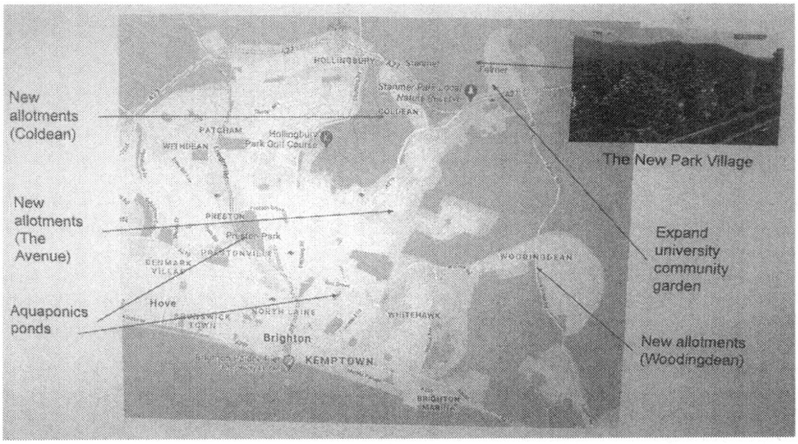

Photo: Author, used with permission.

on creating mechanisms to enable homeless people to participate in urban decision making, by creating spaces where they could tell representatives what they wanted and be part of participatory budgeting activities. A Brighton citizenship card would get them access to free food and transport, with the overall goal to incorporate a group of residents that usually self-excludes from decision making and to ultimately write a more informed and inclusive Brighton manifesto. This focus on refugees and the homeless is not surprising, as students are often engaged with community work focusing on these two groups, the latter of which is also very visible in Brighton.

Both groups are raising the question of empathy as a recognition of difference and challenged students to think through what welcoming difference might mean for their imagined future: what if the integration of refugees is a part of that vision – how can situations be created where meaningful interactions with other Brighton residents happen that respect and celebrate what refugees bring to Brighton? What if an urban manifesto that includes the perspective of all Brighton residents is important for a truly inclusive city – how can participation in the process be afforded for homeless people who have historically not been part of the process, often by choice? What are the normative assumptions of these scenarios? And how might students themselves be implicated in exclusionary practices or help to address them? Such questions can also be asked in post-building discussions which highlight the critical element of creativity. None of the ideas the students developed was radically new, but that was not the point of the exercise, as its process was more important than its outcome. What was remarkable was how the students brought together different domains in their scenario creation: drawing on their own experiences, theoretical knowledge gained in class discussions, inspirations from previous activities as well as practical making. Collectively, they had built plausible scenarios that were materializing alternative urban futures and were desirable to students while considering the rights and needs of diverse groups.

For the afternoon-long SDG workshop, which I conducted together with Paul Braund, a design-trained colleague and the help of student coordinators, I used a more open-ended approach. The overall question was 'In relation to your group's chosen SDG, what would you like the world to look like in 2050?' The first task was for groups to develop a concrete vision and action plan for their preferred future, supported by several starting questions such as: what things will have been achieved; what new institutions, laws, norms and behaviours will have been created; who would be affected and how? This led to intense discussions in some groups as students from very diverse backgrounds negotiated a collective idea. To compensate for the lack of a research phase, I invited students to localize their scenarios in a place that was familiar to at least one person in the group, and both groups working on SDG 11 selected Brighton. While the workshop scenarios remained more speculative than those created in the Urban Futures class, students again incorporated their own knowledge of living in or near Brighton. Once students had developed their visions, they were prompted to think about concrete ways in which these could be realized. In parallel, students started building, materializing their ideas of a future sustainable and inclusive city (Image 3.4). These visions often included tried and tested components such as community buildings and

Image 3.4: Urban futures scenario created by students

Photo: Author, used with permission.

gardens, solar panels, bike stands and public assembly places, but also mega greenhouses and a free tram line as more far-reaching proposals. Although because of time restrictions students did not reach the final stage of the exercise, which would have involved thinking through the specific actors, institutions and practices necessary to realize their alternative future, it was clear that they saw value in the creative process of the activity. This was evident in student comments provided during a follow-on survey and in-person conversations with some participants.

In response to the question of 'What did you like most about the workshop?' students overwhelmingly commented on its creative, practical and hands-on way of bringing students together. The collective process was especially enjoyable; one student wrote, 'I was enlightened by my peers' perspectives and ideas', while several others liked this more informal way of interacting with each other. Design-inspired workshops therefore can create conviviality in unique ways. The question 'Did you learn anything new from the workshop?' elicited some comments on learning more about the SDGs, but also on 'a new way to think (not just words)', 'how to involve different backgrounds into development', 'a more open way of thinking outside the modules' and 'that there are 100 ways to work'. These comments show that students brought together knowledge from formal instructions, personal experiences and the workshop activities in a format that was new to them.

This in turn resulted in novel insights that connected back to learning, such as the realization that development thinking is not as rigid as often presented in theoretical discussion and that change projects can be more personal and allow students to apply their learning to their local areas. Comments such as 'the workshop highlighted the complexity of designing and implementing solutions and the contradictions and huge interlinked challenges' show that ideas about change and how to engage with it were broadened as well. As I show in Chapter 5 on ecological challenges, developing complex systems thinking is an important way for students to understand how global challenges call for non-linear and divergent ways of thinking, which design methods can foster. Lastly, a question about how the workshop could be improved resulted in suggestions for clearer directions, instructions and time limits, confirming that informal learning needs to be supported by structured guidelines to enable students to find their way through the myriad possibilities that such open-ended and creative learning afford.

One of the workshop student coordinators was the aforementioned student who had undertaken an arts foundation year before her studies at Sussex. While supporting different groups with their creative work, she noticed that students preferred discussing and writing out ideas rather than drawing or otherwise visually presenting them. She had developed these visual skills during her foundation year and realized that most students who do not have her training need much more support and encouragement. As

I wrote in the body mapping activity in Chapter 2, comments such as 'I can't draw' express students' fear of not being creative enough and anxiety about having to step out of personal comfort zones – emotions that call on educators' awareness, care and flexibility to foster such orientations. The student also made a distinction between creatively presenting new knowledge and actually learning through creativity, which shows varying degrees of pedagogical creativity that can be adjusted to different students' needs and abilities. Finally, one student wrote in their survey that 'the workshop has re-established hope and encouragement for the future [through] more hands-on learning, not just [learning about] theory not working'. This comment speaks to the potential of creative learning that goes beyond theoretical critique by incorporating an open-ended, experimental and collaborative approach based on asking questions, developing possible responses and building prototypes. Such an approach can reanimate critical hope in students who seek to understand how their learning can help them enact transformational change in the world. This was also the case for the second learning activity, which describes an individual student project that explored the future of food.

Future food

Food systems pose wicked problems because of their complex and interconnected nature, including highly polluting commercial food production that is contributing to climate emergencies, a reliance on chemicals that are depleting biodiversity, unequal national and global food policies that institutionalize food insecurity and poverty in many marginalized places and the role of food marketing in multiple adverse public health crises. Food connects personal and collective politics, and studying 'the production of food is actually one of the most direct ways to gain an understanding of sustain-ability; it is a very direct and powerful way to communicate the connection between the care of the bio-physical environment and care of the self' (Fry, 2018, p 88). For all these reasons, learning about food challenges lends itself to critical-creative pedagogy.

The work undertaken by Diana Garduño Jiménez, a Sussex graduate in geography who became a member of the founding cohort of the MA in Design for Social Change at the University of Edinburgh, is a powerful example of how this potential can be realized. According to its website, the MA aims 'to foster a new breed of designers for the 21st century [who] can address the complex, real world challenges communities face through design-led interventions driven by tactical, critical, strategic and creative approaches'.[13] For one of her modules, Garduño Jiménez undertook a personal experiment and a scenario-building exercise to explore alternative food practices. Complementing the urban futures group workshops with the learning activities of one student shows the potential of combining critical analysis, experiential learning and making to create powerful collective and individual learning experiences. My analysis draws on multiple conversations and e-mail exchanges with Garduño Jiménez as well as two written assessments (Garduño Jiménez, 2019a, 2019b).

During a personal three-day experiment, Garduño Jiménez attempted to reduce to zero all of her food consumption emissions, including transport, packaging, cooking and disposal. Her point of departure was a critical analysis of the global agro-industry as a major emitter of greenhouse gases and as a promoter of increasingly fast-paced life-styles that shape how people buy, prepare and eat food. Garduño Jiménez connected these problems to Escobar's decolonial critique of Eurocentric ontologies and to Victor Papanek's calls for socially responsible design,[14] arguing that moving towards a zero-emission future 'is not just a question of developing new technologies but also of considering the ethical and value systems that underpin them' (2019a, p 27). Through her experiment Garduño Jiménez explored several dimensions of food by engaging in whole-person learning. This can be seen in the story board she created for the assessment, where she visualized how she cycled, walked or foraged to procure local seasonal food, stored it without a fridge and composted any leftovers. Sourcing local food during a cold Scottish February became a major research, logistical and time-consuming challenge. It tested her physical capabilities and made her intensely aware of the various emotions she experienced, ranging from determination, regret, exhaustion, fear, anxiety, happiness and relief to accomplishment. Such emotions are usually absent from convenient trips to the supermarket and have also been sidelined by the emotional distancing resulting from the commercial production and consumption of food, where 'a weaker affective connection works to hide any ramifications my consumption choices have on the broader living world system' (2019b, p 2).

Another dimension of the experiment centred on food subjectivities. Garduño Jiménez' Mexican identity led her to critically reflect on how taste can be manipulated by corporations, with cultural aspects of eating complicating environmental concerns. She also established new social relationships as she became more reliant on others to help her source the right kinds of food, as a result changing from an individualistic consumer to becoming part of a web of foragers, producers and vendors. Building a composter added a making element to the experiment, for which she repurposed materials to move towards cradle-to-cradle design.[15] Summing up her experiment, Garduño Jiménez reflected that 'the phenomenological experience of food opens up avenues through which design could begin to address the high-emission food system we prop up three or more times a day' (2019a, p 22). Through a literally embodied learning experience, Garduño Jiménez was able to critically and creatively explore an alternative way of procuring and consuming food. Combining her own experiences with academic readings and conceptual discussions about food systems, decolonial critiques and design theories, Garduño Jiménez' experiment shows how a critical-creative pedagogy can open up spaces of possibility in which other ways of thinking, being and doing can germinate.

A second element of her activity was the development of a future scenario, 'to render visible the importance of considering alternatives and how these alternatives can easily become silenced through historical narrative' (2019b, p 26–7). By building a series of objects Garduño Jiménez wanted to challenge mainstream narratives that simplify complex histories and to materialize the subjective experiences of historical actors. The scenario's departure point was an international ban on greenhouse gas emissions for food production, consumption and disposal coming into effect in 2030. In response, a multinational corporation called POWdER introduced a zero-emission food powder. By 2060 POWdER, which came only in three 'ancestral' flavours, had become the only form of nutrition; all other foods had become either socially unacceptable or illegal. As an extreme form of convenience food, POWdER concealed how food establishes relationships between people and their environments, as well as alternative modes of food that also reduce greenhouse gas emissions.

One hundred years later, an archaeological discovery, reported in the form of a video clip, unearthed artefacts that queried the mainstream narrative around POWdER's dominance by identifying four main groups of eaters: Only POWdER eaters (O.P.s); Emotional Eaters (E.E.s), who, after coming into contact with plant-based food, began to question their food choices and identities; POWdER Plant Inventors (P.P.I.s), who combined POWdER and plant-based food; and Zero POWdER eaters (Z.P.s), who obtained their food from foraging and hidden gardens. Garduño Jiménez designed a number of artefacts, including a POWdER container, diary entries from E.E.s showing their struggles with food and a P.P.I.s machine mixing POWdER and plant-based ingredients. In addition to these material eating technologies, other exhibits showed ongoing communal relations that had gone underground: an invitation to a secret dinner party, a foraging map and secret letters revealing a clandestine network of seed exchanges. These artefacts were informed by her own experiences of relying on others during her personal experiment, and showed identity struggles connected to food choices and the crucial importance of communal relations for food production. Through her creative speculative objects, Garduño Jiménez gave material expression to ideas around food consumption, incorporating the insights she had gained from her research and personal experiment.

Throughout the whole activity, learning took place on multiple critical-creative levels. Conceptually, developing a critical perspective on the current high-emission food industry and connecting this to decolonial debates was combined with creative ways of exploring how to move beyond reliance on this industry. Garduño Jiménez conducted a personal experiment that centred on experiential learning, visualized this learning through a story board and a scenario that materialized her ideas and extended them into the future. In this way she was able to express in written and material form the manifold ways in which current food production and consumption is severing connections to living systems in which humans are embedded. She imagined and experienced alternatives, for example of how foraging develops practices of care with other humans and surrounding environments. To extend these relationships of stewardship and responsibility, Garduño Jiménez asked how emotional relationships to food could be redesigned, thereby moving from imagining alternatives to beginning to create them.

During the studio crit of her scenario, a fellow student suggested to incorporate a participatory component, inviting the audience to imagine themselves in the year 2160 and what that future would look like for them. This led Garduño Jiménez to reflect that

> giving the audience an opportunity to design their own objects from the future which support, counteract or present alternative narratives … could highlight how such a future might be dystopic for some and utopic for others, rendering visible the different ways in which we value our relation to food and opening them up for discussion. (2019b, pp 28–9)

Her comments show that alternative (food) futures are contested and entangled in normative assumptions. Garduño Jiménez took these ideas further in her final dissertation project, for which she used a decolonial approach to design a workshop toolkit for a national food justice organization. As I am writing this, she is working for the organization to implement her ideas. This clearly shows how a critical-creative pedagogy, articulating decolonial perspectives, personal experiences, experimental projects and material making, can lead to students' imaging and creating alternative futures, in this case connected to food. As deeply personal and collective practices, growing, procuring, cooking and eating food can provide powerful research, reflection and action opportunities for students to ask big, open-ended questions and experiment with multiple responses.

Conclusion

This chapter has explored how design concepts and methods inform a critical-creative pedagogy. I have shown how design's open-ended questioning, iterative processes, embrace of ambiguity, empathy and humility and its use of space and materials can provide potent ways for students to learn about contemporary challenges as wicked problems and understand their resource-politics implications. My description of two learning activities, focusing on the future of urban spaces and food systems, highlights various aspects of creative design activities that can be used for experiential and hands-on learning. These include the need to provide structure, in the form of guidelines, templates, prompts and examples, to facilitate open-ended learning; the playful raising of expectations about designing and making that invites rather than intimidates students; and the emphasis on everyday creativity and collaborative experimentation through low-tech thinking and making materials that can reactivate childhood creativity. In these manifold ways, design concepts and methods contribute to all strands of critical-creative pedagogy: whole-person learning through emotional, embodied and experiential engagements; creative and imaginative modes of learning; praxis through practical, hands-on activities informed by theoretical and conceptual discussions; and critical hope through enabling students to imagine and begin creating alternative futures.

4

Reclaiming Economies

On 2 November 2011 about 70 students walked out of Economics 10, Harvard University's introductory economics class taught by Gregory Mankiw. The students, who were inspired by the Occupy Wall Street movement that had begun in New York's Zucotti Park two months earlier, published their reasons for the walk-out in an open letter to Mankiw. They wrote that: 'since the biased nature of Economics 10 contributes to and symbolizes the increasing economic inequality in America, we are walking out of your class today both to protest your inadequate discussion of basic economic theory and to lend our support to a movement that is changing American discourse on economic injustice'.[1] The letter went on to question Mankiw's class for its teaching of conservative economic theories and for an overreliance on his own macroeconomic textbook. Principles of Economics *has sold over one million copies since its first publication in 1997; according to the Open Syllabus Project, Mankiw is the most frequently cited author on college economics course syllabi. He is therefore an authoritative source for many economics students, some of whom are beginning to question his teachings and the orthodox economics they underpin.*

This chapter is not about teaching economics students per se, as it considers how teaching about economic alternatives can help social science students to better address challenges resulting from economic inequality. It nevertheless takes its inspiration from the activism of economics students described here, who, through protests, creative interventions and global student associations, are demanding that economics courses embrace more theoretical and methodological diversity and include the perspectives of feminist and Global South scholars. Because 'economics is the mother tongue of public policy, and the tool used to tackle global poverty and manage our planetary home' (Raworth, 2017, p 217), such diversity is important not only for theoretical reasons.

Economic thinking occupies a central place in interventions to global challenges, both mainstream and alternative, because 'the task of reclaiming and reshaping our economies is central to any project of societal transformation' (St Martin et al, 2015, p 1). Conversely, many ideas that transform economic thinking come from other social science disciplines. Located at this intersection, this chapter shows that introducing students to knowledge about diverse and embedded economies can open up their conceptual thinking beyond the capitalist status quo. Embracing heterodoxy and resituating themselves as alternative economic subjects are orientations that can help students to enact this knowledge. Both new knowledge and orientations can support a politics that re-embeds the economy in social relations and political structures. Showing students the close links between economic academic work and policy interventions reinforces the importance of such a political shift.

The chapter begins by presenting the neoclassical orthodoxies against which demands for more pluralist and heterodox teaching have been made. In particular, I examine how these alternative approaches can help students to understand the rethinking of mainstream economic principles forced by the COVID-19 pandemic. Increased attention to inequality and the inclusion of historically marginalized voices are additional examples of heterodox teaching. I then turn to Bolivia's pluralist and solidarity economies to explore how ethnographic accounts that ground economic theories in specific contexts can lead to experiential teaching. To extend this discussion to the imagining and building of diverse community economies, I draw on J.K. Gibson-Graham's work of making visible, including in university classrooms, alter- and non-capitalist economies. The final part of the chapter describes two teaching activities: in the first, students create personal diverse economy portfolios to resituate themselves as diverse economic subjects; the second is a collective exercise to design the plans for a recycling cooperative.

(Development) economic orthodoxies

In her book *Doughnut Economics: Seven Ways to Think like a 21st Century Economist*, Kate Raworth argues that 'today's economics students will be among the influential citizens and policy makers shaping human society in 2050. But the economic mindset that they are being taught is rooted in the textbooks of 1950, which, in turn, are grounded in the theories of 1850. Given the challenges of the 21st century this is shaping up to be a disaster' (2017, p 8).

Conventional neoclassical economics teaching presents itself to students as instilling them with a timeless understanding of 'economies as markets separated from the rest of the societies in which they are embedded and heavy reliance on methodological individualism and quantitative modeling'

(Alves and Kvangraven, 2020, p 147). Orthodox economic principles include rational decision making by autonomous individuals, demand and supply equilibria, firm and market competition and utility and profit maximization, all of which are regulated by limited but enabling government functions. Mathematical modelling is used to support the discipline's claims to scientific objectivity, neutrality and universality.

Students imbibe these principles through popular textbooks such as Mankiw's. This reliance on authoritative texts, written by upper-/middle-class White men usually working at elite universities in the UK or US, has a longer history, stretching from J.S. Mills' *Principles of Political Economy* (1848), Alfred Marshall's *Principles of Economics* (1890) and Paul Samuelson's *Economics*. The latter was first published in 1948 and, now in its 17th edition and co-authored by William Nordhaus, is still used by students today. Over the years, the neoclassical theories expounded in these texts have been critiqued for internal and conceptual inconsistencies, methodological problems and lacking relevance for contemporary challenges. However, 'it is the continued unquestioning commitment to that orthodoxy in the face of these critiques that is so frustrating for the dissidents' (Stilwell, 2006, p 46).

The field of development economics, which I briefly want to consider here because of its focus on economic processes in Global South countries, presents a more complex picture worth examining. Raworth recounts that when she studied economics at Oxford University she took a second-year course on the economics of developing countries, for which she had to write an essay on the best way to measure successful development. This was the first time that the purpose of economics had been raised in her studies and an eye-opener for her. The field of development economics, although still male dominated, exhibits a more diverse history of thinkers, beginning with its founding by Arthur Lewis.

Born in the then British colony of St Lucia, in 1933 Lewis was the first-ever Black student to be admitted to the London School of Economics (Tignor, 2006). During his studies there, Lewis met many anti-colonial advocates who shaped his economic thinking, together with his studies of the British empire and 19th-century England. He became Britain's first Black professor when he was appointed at the University of Manchester, where he developed his well-known dual economy model, for which he was awarded the Nobel Prize in 1979. Like so many academic economists, Lewis was also a policy advisor, first for the British Colonial Office and then to several newly independent governments in Africa and the Caribbean. There he also served as Vice-Chancellor of the University of the West Indies, before taking up a professorship at Princeton. Teaching students about the life and work of this founding figure shows how, in economics, theory/academia and practice/policy as well as empire and post-colony are entangled in complex ways that defy easy categorization and ideological pigeon-holing. While this is true for all social sciences, it is particularly pronounced in economics because of the policy uptake of the discipline's ideas.

This is equally true for Walt Rostow, whose five stages of economic growth, developed in the 1950s, are the most significant example of modernization theory. This theory posits a shared development pathway from traditional to modern societies, driven by progress in science and technology that will bring economic growth and social development. Rostow's worked was shaped by the Cold War, as shown by the subtitle of his seminal book *The Stages of Economic Growth: A Non-Communist Manifesto* (1960). An avowed anti-Marxist, he saw the location of Cold War politics shifting from Europe to the Global South, which led him to advocate for US foreign aid expansion (Gilman, 2003). This aid was to support countries embarking on their journey through the five stages, moving towards mature economies that would use their surplus resources to pursue social welfare, mass consumption and external influence.

For Rostow, the goal was to build a democratic welfare state in the US and for 'underdeveloped' countries to successfully resist Communist temptations. As the 1960s progressed, however, civil and political upheaval in the US and abroad, as well as growing levels of unemployment and resulting material deprivations, cast doubt on his theory that economic maturation would bring social harmony and stability (Pupavac, 2010). Furthermore, Rostow's active support, as the US national security advisor, of the Vietnam War also undermined claims that his model would lead to more humane policies and that the US was a benign country. This, together with persistent academic critiques, has led to modernization theory having generally been abandoned, although it did shape development policies in some South-East Asian countries and has remained a metanarrative that lends legitimacy to popular development imaginaries (Gilman, 2003).

Critiques of modernization theory have included E.F. Schumacher's ideas that materialism can lead to spiritual corruption and his resulting advocacy of appropriate, local technologies (Pupavac, 2010). Underdevelopment and dependency theories were advanced by Latin American economists, who showed that the region's underdevelopment was actively produced by its incorporation into the capitalist world system (Gudynas, 2009). Another significant shift in development economics thinking has come from the work of Indian economist Amartya Sen, who argues that 'poverty is a deprivation of basic capabilities, rather than merely low income' and that development is about the freedom of individuals to make choices they have reason to value (1999, p 20). Economic advancement is only one among these choices, and material well-being is often an enabler of other areas of wealth. Sen's ideas, for which he received the Nobel Prize in 1998, have led to the UN's Human Development Index, which ranks countries according to per capita income, but also life expectancy and educational attainments.

Feminist economists such as Diane Elson, Ruth Pearson and Naila Kabeer have made visible the important economic contributions of women through the care economy and are arguing for an expansion of economic domains to include households. Ha Joon Chang critiques neoclassical assumptions about developing countries' economic trajectories, while Esther Duflo and Abhijit Banerjee's work on poor economics and randomized control trials has shaped World Bank thinking. Teaching students not only the main theories of development economics but also how they have arisen from personal biographies and institutional locations shows a dynamic field shaped by diverse voices, many of which are located at elite US or UK universities but maintain strong ties to Latin America, the Caribbean and India. Students can therefore understand the development of economic theories and policies as situated and contested knowledge, which has become even more pronounced with the gradual shift towards non-orthodox economics teaching in some universities.

Pluralist and heterodox teachings

Critiques of orthodox economics teaching have been advanced for several decades, but accelerated at the turn of the 21st century, especially after the 2008 global financial crisis, and have been renewed in the context of the COVID-19 pandemic. Earliest efforts were made by proponents of a 'pluralist pedagogy, i.e. a teaching practice that explores a plurality of different ways of understanding how the economy works ... [as] the principal antidote to the reproduction of a narrow orthodoxy in the discipline' (Stilwell, 2006, p 43). Such pluralist teaching exists at a few universities worldwide, although it is often strongly resisted by mainstream faculty members. It includes, among others, institutional, Marxian, feminist and, increasingly, environmentalist economics. Pluralist teaching asks students to consider how these different theories interact with each other, converging around a set of principles that include recognizing the role that history, ethics and power play in economic discourse, policy and practice, understanding the complexity of economic systems and acknowledging that situated knowledge, value judgements and political ideologies shape economic decision making (Fischer et al, 2017).

More recently, Kate Raworth's (2017) doughnut economics articulates seven principles for how a 21st-century economy must be reshaped to enable humans to fulfil basic needs while living within planetary boundaries. These principles range from changing fundamental economic goals, to redesigning economic systems, to remaking their basic assumptions. Similarly, the degrowth movement, which was launched at the turn of the 20th century by activists challenging economic growth imperatives, advocates for 'voluntary societal shrinking of production and consumption aimed at social and ecological sustainability' (Demaria et al, 2013, p 192).

The latter examples show that in response to critiques of liberal pluralism, which argue that the simple addition of other economic schools leaves neoclassical assumptions untouched and does not sufficiently decentre orthodox norms, heterodox economics takes a more critical approach. It 'is concerned with the study of production and distribution of economic surplus, including the role of power relations in determining economic relationships [and] the study of economic systems beyond market relations' (Alves and Kvangraven, 2020, p 168). The potential of this critical perspective for understanding contemporary challenges has been revealed during the COVID-19 pandemic, which forced a rethinking of mainstream economic principles and practices.

Foremost among these orthodox principles is a view of the economy as disembedded from and independent of society, evident in mainstream economists initially trying to treat the pandemic as an external shock, another externality preventing the effective functioning of markets. Instead, the pandemic forced policy makers, economists and everybody else to 'see the big picture' by changing their perspectives from that of self-contained, efficient markets as the mainstay of the economy to markets embedded in society and nature (Raworth, 2017). Similarly, economic responses to the pandemic have highlighted the usually more implicit and hidden value judgements made by economic policy makers, such as trade-offs between public and economic health. These forced many governments to institute far-reaching measures such as income guarantee, self-employed worker and small business support schemes, some of which approximate universal basic income programmes (Baker, 2020). The latter guarantee all citizens of a country a minimum amount of money to cover basic needs and recognize the responsibility of governments to enable citizens' fundamental material well-being.[2]

Another heterodox call came for revalorizing the commons, especially public health systems and their key workers. For many years these have been ravaged by fiscal austerity, which the pandemic has shown to be 'a political choice rather than a necessity' (Alves and Kvangraven, 2020, p 171).[3] Related demands have been made for opening up the knowledge commons to ensure that reliable information leads to informed debates that take local values, priorities and needs into account (Callahan, 2020). Against dominant claims of 'the' science driving government decisions, it has become clear that difficult ethical decisions need to be made by policy makers, who, rather than relying on narrow, medically focused forms of expertise as has been the case in the UK, should also include philosophers, sociologists and historians of science in key advisory groups.[4] An informed public also needs to be involved in these deliberations. The latter show the importance of considering alternative views of human behaviour that do not subscribe to rational, self-optimizing individuals.

Feminist economists have long drawn attention to the importance of social reproduction and social relations for the economy. Especially during the most strict lockdown periods, when schools and workplaces were closed, 'society has been forced to grapple with the importance of social reproduction as a core activity that keeps the economy going' (Alves and Kvangraven, 2020, p 169). Such a resocialization of the economy was also visible in self-organizing neighbourhood groups operating according to principles of mutual aid, which show the interdependence of human beings. As the pandemic is continuing, what has emerged most strongly is the complicated relationship between individual and collective desires for autonomy and the need for connectedness, between personal liberties and group solidarities. However, lest problematic assumptions about women's and other groups' obligation to and endless capacity for providing care and nurture are reinforced, heterodox economists also study inequalities related to social categories such as gender, class and race. This structural attention counters narratives of the pandemic as the great leveller, as its uneven impacts along lines of existing inequalities are emerging ever more clearly.

Increased attention to inequality, popularized by Thomas Piketty's *Capital in the 21st Century*, is therefore a central component of heterodox teaching. My Sussex colleague Paul Gilbert has developed a third-year specialist module on Wealth, Inequality and Development, which interrogates the drivers and consequences of inequality and uneven wealth accumulation. The module focuses on issues such as taxation, land inequality and international law, which situates economic questions in broader contexts and debates. It pays particular attention to the work of advocacy, campaigning and research groups, following a problem-focused pedagogy where theoretical discussions are linked to specific challenges. This lends itself to critical-creative pedagogy that combines critical reading of academic, policy and activism texts with creative activities. In a class on the privatization and financialization of infrastructures, for example, students research their local water provider, trying to find out about its ownership structures, profit and dividend amounts as well as leakage rates, information that then feeds into a class discussion about the politics of nationalization.

During a class on tax justice, students explore questions of tax avoidance, capital flight and illicit fund flows to global financial centres, to counter standard narratives of development investments from the Global North and government corruption in the Global South. Gilbert introduces interesting data sets such as the Panama Papers to get students thinking about how different actors use and manipulate figures and data. Students then learn the basics of practical skills used by non-governmental organizations (NGOs) and investigative journalists to read corporate accounts to detect tax avoidance and evasion, thereby developing a hands-on understanding of these practices, seeing them in action and thinking through their implications. Subverting the Economics 101 skill of reading financial statements for the financial health of companies, students learn to read them 'for difference' to destabilize mainstream ideas and uncover what is unseen and possible (Gibson-Graham, 2008). The whole module is built around a post-colonial perspective by, for example, focusing on colonial drain and reparations and the colonial origins of contemporary corporate dispute-resolution mechanisms (Gilbert, 2018). Gilbert also uses the work of the Southern Centre for Inequality at Wits University in South Africa to complement the Piketty debates. The latter raises the question of how to include scholarship from the Global South and marginalized voices more generally in economics-focused social science teaching.

Calls for the inclusion of undervalued economic perspectives have been linked to broader efforts to decolonize economics, by showing that the discipline's claims to universality mask its Eurocentric origins and continue to exclude work by women and scholars from the Global South. Jonathan Langdon provides a critical-creative example of the inclusion of historically invisible voices by asking students to read historical texts against each other, in order to 'destabilize the foundational authority of economics to vision of progress' (2013, p 293). Students read excerpts from Adam Smith's *The Wealth of Nations* alongside the autobiography of Olaudah Equiano, published 12 years after Smith's book, in which Equiano describes his experiences of enslavement, the middle passage, slave labour and eventual freedom.

For Langdon, such a reading does not only reveal the gulf between Smith's rational, self-centred mentality and the human experiences of slavery, but also how Equiano himself used Smith's writings to advocate for the efficiency of wage over slave labour. This shows how (former) slaves were able to appropriate Western arguments for the abolitionist cause; discussing more generally how both texts were used by proponents and opponents of the slave trade prompts students to ask why they have heard of Smith before but not of Equiano. Langdon argues that 'it is only by bringing in the voice of those impacted by [the slave] system that the immorality of the economic arrangements stands out in sharp relief' (p 393). Situating both books during the emergence of capitalism provides a fuller historical context and allows for an ontological reframing of capitalism from a structural given to a system produced by particular discourses and practices and therefore changeable (Gibson-Graham, 2008).

All of these examples show that heterodox teaching emphasizes how different streams of economic thought have arisen from particular historical positions, interact with each other, inform policy making and provide spaces for alternatives to take root. While they have been presented here at a fairly general level, as an anthropologist I am also aware that pluralism, economic or otherwise, operates in particular contexts. The work of economic anthropologists such as Stephen Gudeman (1986), who often draw on the foundational thinking of Karl Polyani (1944), is particularly apt at analysing how locally grounded understandings about the economy, values and markets negate abstract economic concepts.[5] Rather than theorizing universal models, learning about economic pluralism therefore must also encompass an understanding of such localization. To show how this can be done in university classrooms I return to Bolivia.

Pluralism *in situ*

Bolivia has a long tradition of economic pluralism, defined as the co-existence of economic units with different aims, labour relations, ownership models and governance structures; these units include private and state-owned enterprises, social cooperatives and indigenous-communitarian organizations (Wanderley, 2019). Economic pluralism was officially recognized in the country's 2009 constitution, within a broader agenda of plurinationalism and decolonization resulting from the ascent to power of Evo Morales and the MAS party in 2006. Taking an ethnographic focus to understand economic pluralism in practice can show students the opportunities, complexities and productive tensions that accompany any search for (economic) alternatives. In this section I draw on writings by and interviews with academics in La Paz to explore some aspects of Bolivia's economic pluralism and how it is being taught, particularly at a local public postgraduate institution where my research was based.

Over the last decade, cooperative and indigenous-communitarian enterprises in Bolivia have come together under the banner of *movimiento de economía solidaria y comercio justo* (solidarity economy and fair trade movement), which connects them to the Latin American solidarity economy. This economy can be situated within the global movement of Social and Solidarity Economies (SSE), which also encompasses social entrepreneurship in the US and UK and the social economy of Canada and Europe. SSE is an 'economy of hope', built of grassroots initiatives coming together around the values of economic cooperation, environmental sustainability and democratic self-management (North and Scott Cato, 2017, p 1). Within SSE, there is a tension between reformist approaches that aim to economically integrate those who have been excluded by the capitalist system and radical approaches that aim to reclaim the economy in non-capitalist ways. For the latter, a 'convivial low-carbon economy is seen as preferable to a low-carbon version of exploitative capitalism' (p 9). Alternative accounts in Latin America include the Zapatistas revolution that in 1994 began to build a 'post-capitalist indigenous communalism' in the Mexican state of Chiapas (Gibson-Graham, 2006, p xx). This ongoing experiment encompasses struggles for territorial autonomy and economic self-sufficiency, rethinking power through creative practices as well as experimenting with alternative education such as the Universidad de la Tierra[6] (Santos, 2017).

As in Chiapas, in Bolivia indigenous peoples have played an important role in forging social and economic alternatives. From the 1980s onward, in response to the country becoming ground zero for a neoliberal shock doctrine that led to massive unemployment, declining public subsidies and increasing informality, a popular economy emerged as the basis for social movements to come together around shared experiences of insecurity, deprivation and precarity (Wanderley et al, 2015). Importantly, within this movement previous class references that had been anchored in mining work and union activities were replaced with a revived indigenous identity, forged around the recuperation of ancestral memories, indigenous cultural and organizational practices and the emergence of indigenous peoples as political subjects advancing demands for territorial autonomy and self-determination. This resurgence was supported by academic and activist research, for example by the Taller de Historia Oral Andina en Bolivia, and resulted in the assertion of values such as reciprocity and interdependence in economic practices. Today, the solidarity economy has become 'the most organized part of the popular economy' in respect to membership and institutional capacity (Hillenkamp, 2014, p 63).

The official recognition of economic pluralism went along with the establishment of various government departments and para-statal organizations, but over time the relationship between the MAS government and grassroots economic groups has become fraught (Wanderley et al, 2015). These conflicts have been caused by the deep gaps between Morales' rhetoric of environmental protection and practice of neo-extractivism, by legislation to support the solidarity economy not being implemented or associated government departments being sidelined, and by large, state-owned cooperatives undermining small local co-ops. These difficult circumstances have caused some co-optation and fragmentation within the solidarity economy. From a generative theory perspective, these challenges do not condemn the movement to failure but provide openings for new possibilities.

Ana Dinerstein (2017) argues that the full integration of the solidarity economy's alternative visions into government policies could lead to deep social, economic and political transformations that would also reframe public policy. Drawing on de Sousa Santos' sociology of absences and emergences, as a practice not just of looking back to what has become marginalized or delegitimated but also of looking forward to the not-yet and in-formation, Dinerstein proposes a policy of 'prefigurative translation'. Because it is located in a zone beyond current government legibility, such a policy 'needs also to be prefigurative, that is, it must be directed to render visible what is already being proposed and experienced by the SSE movements' (p 67). By incorporating the experiential critique of hegemonic capitalism advanced through the everyday practices of SSE members, government policy can be pushed to join SSE alternative visions that ask 'what if we ...' questions to open up spaces of possibility. Operating in this beyond zone requires a tolerance for not knowing, for being open to a reality that is emergent and as yet undisclosed and for being comfortable with ambiguity — all orientations that can be fostered through design thinking and practices, as I showed in the previous chapter.

Given the close relationship between, especially, public universities and public debate in Bolivia that was highlighted by some of my interviewees, Bolivian academics play important roles in articulating and strengthening the country's solidarity economy. This includes research, publications (many of which are available for free on institutional websites) and public talks, as well as teaching. The latter is done through postgraduate programmes such an MA in Social and Solidarity Economies, as well as diplomas and short courses offered by universities to community activists, NGO practitioners and government employees who want to learn about topics such as the care economy or fair trade in more practical ways. All of these programmes bring together a great diversity of students in the classroom, which one interviewee described as "becoming an experimental space". Educators try to connect theoretical teaching to students' diverse life and work experiences, for example by encouraging them to undertake thesis research in their neighbourhoods or workplaces.

Many students at public universities are of Aymara descent, often living in El Alto, the large Aymara city at the outskirts of La Paz. El Alto's economic landscape contains elements of the solidarity economy which draw on Aymara principles of reciprocity, well-being and cooperation within and among families, communities and economic associations (Hillenkamp, 2014). These principles are based on a recognition of interdependence among humans and humans and nature, and result in forms of mutuality such as labour exchanges, practices of care and redistributive rituals. All of these activities are changing under the influence of urbanization, commodification and evangelization; they are also fraught with tensions and conflict. These dynamics can be explored through experiential learning that incorporates students' and their families' economic practices in various ways, of which I highlight three.

Firstly, students in El Alto are sometimes participating in their families' petty commodity activities such as small manufacturing and trading. This can bring an understanding of domestic economic solidarity as not always based on equal relationships within the family, and instead involving the (self-)exploitation of women and children (Hillenkamp, 2014). Secondly, many families in El Alto and other urban areas maintain or re-establish ties with their rural places of origin, which means that students regularly return to *el campo* where their families keep homes and plots of land. These are worked through reciprocal labour relations with rural family members, who share the proceeds from the harvest in return for their labour. These relations are embedded within wider redistributive practices that are necessary for urban-based families to ensure continued rural membership. Symbolic and material exchanges include participation in local politics, engagement in communal working projects and sponsorship of social events and ritual celebrations (Tassi and Canedo, 2019).

Thirdly, one student talked to me about her work for an NGO aiming to bring economic development to El Alto, and how it was some of her doubts about local women's preferences for commercial over subsistence activities that led her to pursue postgraduate studies, to be able to interrogate these processes more critically. But she also talked about the NGO's support for local producer and artisan cooperatives that are formed, often by women, to get better access to markets. These associations highlight members' rural origins and refer to Andean cultural traditions to articulate their principles of equity, solidarity and reciprocity (Hillenkamp, 2014). Their operations are based on horizontal interdependence among producers, democratic self-management through rotating board membership and weekly meetings, collective investments and the pooling and sharing of technical knowledge and tools. Relations with fair-trade organizations, often abroad, help associations to sell their products for better prices.

It is through accessing this experiential knowledge, and articulating it with theoretical readings of Bolivian, Latin American and Western academics and critical discussions in the classroom, that students learn how the solidarity economy works, in concrete and sometimes contradictory ways, in the diverse settings of families, neighbourhoods and communities. For Bolivian students and their counterparts in universities in the Global North, understanding how individuals and organizations face everyday constraints, how tensions between collective ideals and norms and individual aspirations and subsistence struggles can complicate or even derail solidarity, and how cooperatives negotiate their values in the broader market economy, shows that solidarity practices are dynamic, can reinforce or create unequal relationships and should not be idealized or romanticized. The same holds true for other alternative economic forms.

Diverse community economies

Gibson-Graham's project of diverse economies searches for, makes visible and sometimes brings into being alternative-to-capitalist economic practices and subjects. In their book *A Postcapitalist Politics*, Gibson-Graham define diverse economies as 'economic experimentation[s] in which collective actions are taken to transform difficult or dire (or merely distasteful) situations by enhancing well-being, instituting different (class) relations of surplus appropriation and distribution, promoting community and environmental sustainability, recognizing and building on economic interdependence, and adopting an ethic of care of the other' (2006, pp xxxvi–ii).

Most fundamentally, diverse economies decentre capitalocentric discourses that naturalize capitalism and assign positive value to capitalist economic activities, while devaluing all others activities (Gibson-Graham and Dombroski, 2020). Capitalocentrism is based on structuralist and essentialist concepts of the economy, which deny economic diversity by condensing different practices, such as economic exchanges, into 'a single unity ... that is in turn conflated with capitalist economy' (p 56). Similarly, all economic behaviour is read through the singular lens of calculative, self-interested rationality, which displaces the importance of other forms of behaviour guided by different motivations. Drawing on de Sousa Santos, Gibson-Graham show that the effect of this conflation and displacement is to deny visibility and credibility to, and thereby strangle, existing non-capitalist alternatives. This in turn forecloses economic experimentation.

The task of diverse economies is to work against this foreclosure by retheorizing, reframing and reclaiming the economy to make alter- and non-capitalist practices count. The authors introduce the image of the economic iceberg, where the small, visible tip represents standard capitalist activities of wage labour in a capitalist firm producing commodities for market exchange (Image 4.1). This tip rests on an invisible body of a multitude of economic activities, sites and people through which humans produce, exchange and distribute value. These range from spaces such as families, neighbourhoods and places of worship, to practices including barter, moonlighting and self-provisioning, to institutions like cooperatives. Representing this diversity can help to produce an anti-capitalocentric reading that focuses on the multiplicity, openness and potentiality of economic activities. Importantly, this implies generative theorizing to nurture economic experiments and allow them space to germinate and grow.

Under the diverse economies umbrella, Gibson-Graham develop the concept of diverse community economies which, 'unlike the structurally configured Economy with its regularities and lawful relationships ... is an acknowledged space of social interdependence and self-formation ... an unmapped and uncertain terrain that calls forth exploratory conversations and political/ethical acts of decision' (2006, p 166). Diverse community economies are contingent on local conditions and built around the resocialization of economic relations. This is achieved through making explicit the sociality of all economic activities and the interdependence of economic actors, both of which are obscured by capitalocentrism but have come to the fore during the COVID-19 pandemic. The diverse community economies space is open for reflection, debate and negotiations, which often focus on its community aspect.

Like other thinkers such as Raymond Williams, Gibson-Graham are suspicious of moralistic notions of community that centre on 'normative ideals of the community as a fullness and a positivity' (2006, p 87). They

Image 4.1: Diverse Economies Iceberg

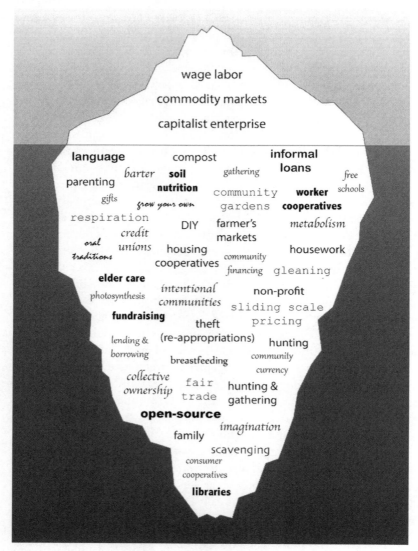

argue against notions of unity, harmony and sameness that are mobilized in the name of community to suppress economic differences. Getting students to interrogate the concept of community is particularly important because of its cherished status in fields such as anthropology and global development, where it is often romanticized as an idealized state of communal strength or instrumentalized as a set of social resources to legitimize the roll-back of public services and investments. In both cases, community can activate problematic traditional hierarchies based on patriarchal or gerontocratic norms. Similarly, invocations of community can rely on dichotomies that positively value everything small-scale, participatory, local, collective and common, while negatively valuing the large-scale, global, individual and impersonal. As I show throughout this book, alternatives are more complex, contested and contradictory than these black-and-white representations allow for, which in itself is an important insight for students.

Instead of subscribing to normative harmony or localism, diverse community economies recognize and celebrate multiplicity, and work through amplifying, connecting and negotiating diverse initiatives within the frame of interdependence. This does not exclude contested activities, which can challenge students' notions of right and wrong in unsettling ways. Gibson-Graham present the example of theft, reframed as 'a mode of transaction ... in which the sociality and interdependence of economic relations is ... violently and coercively present' (2006, p 98). Rather than judging theft as falling short of the norms of community, it can be seen as a '(problematic) resource for projects of becoming, a place from which to build something more desirable in the future' (p 98). Taking this generative stance, participants in a diverse community economy initiative 'might decide that theft is a legitimate mode of redistribution when it involves reclaiming a commons that has been unlawfully taken, as in land, resources or intellectual property' (p 98).

Calling such a reframing 'ethical praxis', Gibson-Graham echo Freire's circle of reflection, discussion and action on the world and show that economic decisions are political at their heart. Diverse (community) economies aim to imagine and enact other economies and, by extension, other worlds (St Martin et al, 2015). This not only situates the project within the global transition movement but also links it to pluriversal politics that centre on the relocalization of economic activities (Escobar, 2020). Connecting up through meshworks of local initiatives and working with generative theorizing and against capitalocentric domination, diverse community economies make alternatives credible and viable and generate practices that can bring alter-capitalist activities, subjects and spaces into being.

How can diverse community economies be used in university classrooms to reframe orthodox economics-focused teaching? One possibility could be to follow Gibson-Graham's lead in finding projects – their book contains case studies from India, Mexico, Kiribati and the US – that show the different ways in which diverse community economies have been defined and enacted. Students would firstly undertake a strong theory analysis of their chosen example, using their well-honed critical thinking skills to find instances of limitations, co-optation, undermining or takeover that might invalidate such projects from a capitalocentric perspective. The next part of the exercise would then ask students to re-read the material for difference to uncover alternative possibilities (Gibson-Graham, 2008). Aided by representations such as the economic iceberg, students would undertake generative theorizing towards a more hopeful analysis, by searching for non-capitalist elements, mapping alternative practices and investigating how different economic subjects are nurtured.

Such an exercise would challenge students to read the same material from multiple perspectives, pushing them against their own academic instincts in order to be less critical and more generous in their analysis and to explore the different possibilities this would open up. Rather than producing concise and complete analytical accounts, students can be encouraged to produce a 'laundry list' of characteristics and traits that makes visible alternative practices in inclusive and open-ended ways. Alongside this, rather than trying to determine whether an economic experiment is successful or not, students could better understand the continuum of success and failure. They could also develop nuanced understandings of the multifaceted and sometimes contradictory motivations of economic actors, which can be in conflict with idealized assumptions of collective or communal solidarity. Through such a theoretical reading-against-the-grain, students can open up their thinking and push themselves out of their analytical comfort zones. While this includes creative elements, in the next part of the chapter I describe two teaching activities that put even more emphasis on creativity, in order to think through, in theoretical and practical ways, alter- and non-capitalist alternatives.

Personal portfolios

Creating personal diverse economy portfolios invites students to shift from 'the paralyzing question of what is to be done' to the more productive one of 'what is already being done', with a focus on their own practices (Gibson-Graham and Roelvink, 2010, p 331).[7] Departing from theoretical readings and case studies of alternative economic arrangements, students create personal portfolios by researching, reflecting on and analysing their economic activities. The aim is for students to recognize the diversity of these activities, including capitalist, alter-capitalist and non-capitalist ones, to resocialize them and to realize themselves as interdependent and ethical economic subjects. Because this activity has not yet been carried out, my reflections remain more speculative but are still able to show its potential to combine whole-person learning with critical analysis and creative visualization, and to inform praxis.

The activity consists of four steps (diary, inventory, reflection and creation) that could be undertaken as an independent project over the course of a term or as a two-week more intensive exercise. Since it mainly involves students working on their own, it could be done remotely and the final portfolios shared and discussed virtually. The activity begins with students becoming more aware of their economic lives by keeping a diary over the course of week, recording all of their economic transactions and exchanges, where they took place and whom they involved. Next to each entry they are asked to characterize their activities, for example noting whether money was involved or if the exchange was a market or non-market transaction. To do so they draw on relevant class readings, which will also help them with the second step of drawing up an economic inventory.

This inventory consists of three parts in which students record their transactional exchanges, economic organizations and labour practices.[8] Transactional exchanges are likely to comprise standard market transactions, but also alternative ones such as swapping, barter or buying a vegetable box from a local farmer, as well as non-market transactions such as sharing household labour, free-cycling, gifting, couch surfing or gardening. The second part registers the diverse economic organizations with which students interact, beginning with conventional stores such as supermarkets or department stores, but likely also encompassing alternative capitalist enterprises such as op-shops, fair trade stores, non-profits, cooperative and community enterprises, food-waste apps and shared ownership schemes. Non-capitalist organizations could include communal and household groups or independent businesses that might be supported by friends, children or other family members giving their labour for free.

The final part of the inventory includes diverse labour practices, beginning with wage work that many students have to engage in to make ends meet. Then there are alternatively paid labour activities such as under-the-table tutoring, self-employed gig work or maybe swapping childcare with other student parents or final thesis drafts with fellow students. Unpaid labour includes housework, household or family physical and emotional care, and maybe volunteer work or self-provisioning through gardening or foraging. All of these elements might have been altered in response to COVID-19 restrictions, leading to new economic practices that put longer-established ones into sharper relief. Beginning the sub-inventories with standard capitalist entries does not mean that these have primacy, but they are likely the most familiar ones to students and thus provide an easier starting point for students to build on as they develop their inventories. The emphasis of the inventories is not on completeness or correctness but, rather, on externalizing and thereby making explicit the multiple forms of economic activities students engage in. Incompleteness also implies an openness to change or new activities that show the emergent nature of economic activities.

In the third step students are asked to reflect on two overarching questions: on what basis are they making economic decisions and what kinds of social relationships are they entering or creating in their economic lives? The first question is likely to show multiple reasonings, including affordability, convenience and ethical concerns such as fair trade, animal treatment or food miles. Recognizing the plurality of their choices and calculations shows students the limited application of neoclassical theories of self-interested, utility-maximizing individuals. It reveals (most) students as ethical consumers who complement their financial calculations with non-financial questions about how their economic activities might be impacting on other human beings, animals or the environment. Similarly, students can identify ambivalent and contradictory motivations that show that alternatives are hybrid rather than pure. Establishing this awareness also includes folding the economic into the ethical and re-evaluating economic activities through multifaceted prisms.

The second question builds on these reflections and goes to the heart of resocializing economic relations as it makes students realize the diversity of relationships on which their economic activities are based. These can range from a consumer relationship to parent/child or other kin connections, neighbour, flatmate, tutor or mentor and friend. Becoming aware of this economic relationality and interdependence also undermines orthodox notions of autonomous, self-maximizing individuals and shows the economy as embedded within social systems. The final step of the activity involves students creating a visual representation of their diverse economy portfolios in the form of their own icebergs or other creative, potentially multimedia, formats. The intention of this final step is to move students from the linearity of writing to experimenting with other creative forms of expressing themselves as diverse economic subjects.

This activity can result in learning 'not in the sense of increasing a store of knowledge but in the sense of becoming other, creating connections and encountering possibilities that render us newly constituted beings in a newly constituted world' (Gibson-Graham and Roelvink, 2010, p 322). It does not forego analytical thinking, which students will need to map their own activities onto the categories established from the readings and to critically reflect on their practices. But the end goal is for students to imagine themselves as diverse economic subjects and to experientially understand the limits of capitalocentric thinking about the economy. When students realize that standard capitalist practices constitute only a small part of their economic lives, with alter- and non-capitalist ones adding richness and diversity, they can use this to imagine what the implications might be for the economy at large.

Thinking of themselves and others as diverse economic subjects can also result in practical efforts to strengthen alternative and non-capitalist forms by growing, amplifying and potentially connecting them into larger meshworks or movements. Beginning with an understanding of what students are already doing, and asking what else they could do differently allows for new possibilities to emerge. Rather than remaining at the level of theoretical understanding, grounding this thinking in praxis is important, as these are 'ontological changes that establish the self as change agent ... entertaining a leap of imagination and an overturning of existing economic wisdom, as opposed to simply trying to extend existing economic theory' (Fry, 2018, pp 136, 213). To move from imagining to practising economic alternatives also involves the development of new capabilities and tools, as suggested in the next activity.

Cooperative designs

This activity, during which students are imagining what it would take to set up a cooperative enterprise, was developed by my colleague Demet Dinler, in the context of a course on Utopia and Alternatives in Development. She conceived the activity as a series of six workshops to run alongside weekly lectures and seminar discussions. The overall objective is to think through how to design, sustain and scale a recycling cooperative as a local alternative-economy initiative that provides collective sources of income for waste pickers, tackles intersectional inequities and creates a broader social and political movement around the values of cooperation and mutuality. The cooperative, located in a specified urban neighbourhood in a country in the Global South,[9] would give individual waste pickers the opportunity to bring, sort and sell their waste to the organization, which would then sell it directly to recycling plants. As an alternative to individuals selling to middlemen, this would cut out exploitative intermediaries and make possible collective negotiations for better prices.

The activity is the outcome of Dinler's own theoretical interests in alternative economies, empirical research with Turkish recycling cooperatives (Dinler, 2016) and her work as a labour activist with Turkish unions and co-ops. Aiming to show students the possibility of 'combining utopian desires with the constraints of everyday life', the activity teaches students not to focus on identifying failure but to consider under what conditions alternatives can work. Like Dinler's teaching more broadly, the activity is thus a powerful example of critical-creative pedagogy, whereby 'students will be invited to push the boundaries of what is possible/impossible, to release their imaginative powers [and] to analyze and design change as something that can happen here and now, by examining and working within structural constraints' (Dinler, n.d., p 1).

Each weekly workshop is structured around an objective, a number of challenges that need to be overcome to achieve the objective and several tasks that clearly spell out what students need to think about in order to address the challenges. This structure ensures the clear guidance that is necessary for students to successfully engage in more open-ended and creative teaching. For Dinler, it is practice and structures that can unleash everyday creativity in students. Because they might not yet be familiar with economic alternatives, background literature as well as sufficient contextual information about the location of the co-op are also necessary to engage students meaningfully in the activity.

Providing a script also allows for the designing-in of specific elements. These could include an emphasis on the constraints that many organizations encounter as they try to enact alternatives – constraints of which Dinler is acutely aware from her own activist work. Such constraints range from mundane things like gossip, envy and competition to more structural inequalities around gender, class and ethnicity, to macroeconomic policies and crises. References to such constraints are scant in the literature, but students need to understand that they exist and that alternatives can reinforce existing unequal power relations or create new problems. Finding ways to address and overcome these constraints is also a useful capability for students to apply to other settings. Over the course of the six weeks, as students become more familiar and confident with the workshop format and process, the tasks increase in scope and complexity. Developing this confidence can also result in students making more open-ended connections and generating more experimental and bolder ideas.

The first workshop begins with setting up the cooperative and focuses on recruiting financial and other supporters, overcoming resistance from middlemen and the vested interests of established recycling plants, as well as addressing ethnic and gender hierarchies that discriminate against the equal participation of women. Tasks include establishing the general principles that govern the co-op, arranging house visits to talk to families about women's participation, setting a list of prices and determining how waste pickers will be paid. Subsequent workshops aim to make the cooperative sustainable in the face of a world economic crisis that depresses prices for recyclable commodities, the formation of a rival cooperative that is luring members away and newcomers not subscribing to the founding values of the cooperative. Here, tasks range from holding meetings to work out dispute-resolution mechanisms, to curating a ritual to reinforce the bonds among co-op members, to developing training and retirement schemes. The next workshops aim to expand the cooperative through new investments in a recycling plant and a regional recycling auction using an alternative currency, which calls for finding new equipment, people with different skills, more strategic thinking and the building of broader alliances. Finally, students are challenged to use the cooperative as a progressive space to discuss social issues around intersectional inequality and to build a network of cooperatives that can shape a national economic platform in the run-up to a general election. This raises a host of new issues from finding ways to work together across difference to entering the formal political domain.

I adopted this activity for a two-hour exercise in my Urban Futures class. It took place during a week when students explored whether urban waste constituted garbage or resources. To get ideas and context for the activity, students had read a case study about a recycling cooperative and trade union in Pune, India, written by two activists who had participated in setting it up (Chikarmane and Narayan, 2005). Given the much shorter duration, I adjusted the objectives of the workshop to students designing a plan to set up a recycling cooperative and also formulated new challenges that connected the activity with some of the module's other topics. For example, in addition to overcoming the resistance of middlemen to the new co-op, students had to contend with rumours that the municipal government was planning to outsource garbage collection to a private company, which would displace waste pickers altogether. This connected to previous class discussions around the privatization of urban services and challenged students to develop plans to prevent the outsourcing, including lobbying the municipality and building local political alliances. Another set of challenges focused on the unequal use of urban spaces, which had been the topic of several classes on rights to the city and the production of informality. It asked students to think about how to design economic equality among all co-op members against ethnic cleavages that mapped onto differentiated access to higher-value collection points or different possibilities to use street spaces to sort recycled materials.

The first task was for the whole class to decide where they wanted to locate their co-op. I had pre-organized four groups, focusing on governance, external support, economic mechanisms and social issues, into which students self-selected. Each group worked for an hour according to a task sheet, and then everybody came together into a large group to negotiate a master plan incorporating the groups' suggestions and design a poster as a final creative output. As always, time was too short for the final step to be carried out fully, which shows the importance of making such activities an integral part of a class rather than an add-on. Students' suggestions were diverse, including a membership card, for which they had designed a logo, with a nominal fee charged that was redirected into social services for members; alliance building with existing diverse urban movements on the basis of rights as urban citizens; various communication strategies such as street theatre and local radio stations; and working with a national environmental and human rights organization to demand access to a public piece of land where the co-op could build a permanent sorting station and meeting place.

Should this request be refused, students proposed the insurgent occupation of roadsides or a strike to show the general population how important their work is. The co-op therefore was seen not only as an economic institution but also as a political platform for members to voice their grievances and demand their rights.

These proposals show that students used ideas from the theoretical readings, especially around rights to the city and the production of informality, to apply to the situation at hand. As one student commented, the activity "really allowed us to put what we've learned over the last weeks into quite a specific context and just really exercising our ability to apply knowledge in a practical, albeit hypothetical way". According to another student, "often just having lectures and readings can produce a tendency to overthink and overtheorise certain issues which actually may just require 'common' sense and basic necessities". For me, rather than calling for a simplification of complex ideas, this comment shows that the student had complemented his theoretical understanding with practical knowledge to carry out the project work.

During the group work, I sat with each group to provide feedback on ideas. Such facilitation is essential to support students' creative activities; it also allowed me to observe how some students got stuck on details, for example how much to pay an accountant. This struggle 'to make things up', as students have described it to me numerous times, relates to an in-built tension in practical exercises that remain hypothetical and ask students to take imaginative leaps. To work best, these activities should be based on research and contextual knowledge, but there is always an element of imaginary work that students need to undertake. As pointed out in previous chapters, many students feel ill-equipped to do so, given their journey through secondary education systems and induction into a 'question everything mode' in initial undergraduate modules. Ideally, these early modules would contain light-touch critical-creative activities for students to become familiar and more confident with creative modes of working, which then allows specialist modules to tackle more complex creative learning.

In the reflective journal I kept while teaching the Urban Futures module, I wondered whether the 'stuckness' I observed was due to students not being used to such exercises, needing more structure and time, or my own inability to inspire students' creativity sufficiently. These reflections speak to educators' personal doubts and discomforts that I have explored in Chapter 2, which call for honesty, courage and persistence. The support of colleagues is equally important, and, in the case of the co-op activity, conversations with Dinler proved invaluable to carrying out the exercise. For her, the activity enables students to 'feel' some of the issues of waste cooperatives through their own experimental designing that bridges different domains, through negotiations with other students during group work and through the in-built possibility of failure and frustration, which can themselves be great sources of creativity. Using existing and emerging skills in the new context of planning a recycling cooperative, practically applying theoretical knowledge and understanding as well as overcoming constraints all help students to develop new mental skills and an ethics of care that can be taken out of university classrooms into their engagements with the world.

Conclusion

This chapter has explored what a critical-creative pedagogical approach to teaching social science students about economic challenges could look like. Departing from the shortcomings of orthodox economic theories, I have argued for pluralist and heterodox teaching that introduces students to different economic schools of thought that incorporate history, power and ethics into their analysis of economic activities. These insights can be applied to understandings of how the COVID-19 pandemic has been forcing a rethinking of economic principles, to the teaching of economic inequality and the inclusion of marginalized voices that link economics-focused teaching to broader decolonial debates. I then introduced Bolivia's solidarity economy to show how local histories, cultures and politics matter and how students could use their own experiences of economic activities across different sites to develop a nuanced contextual understanding of the solidarity economy. More broadly, Gibson-Graham's diverse economies project can introduce students to the limits of capitalocentric thought, the possibilities of alter-capitalist economic practices and the contested dynamics of community economies. This set the stage for the description of two teaching activities, where students create a personal diverse economy portfolio and design a recycling cooperative, which articulate theoretical and practical work. Throughout the chapter, this interplay of theory and practice has shown how the critical-creative teaching of economic alternatives can deepen students' understanding of the social and political embeddedness of the economy, with the overall aim to enable them to 'retheorize capitalism and reclaim the economy here and now in myriad projects of alternative economic activism' (Gibson-Graham, 2006, p xxi).

5

Repairing Ecologies

I have joined a group of final year undergraduate students taking a module about climate change and development; we are waiting expectantly to play an educational game called Sendai that has been designed by some of their classmates around the Sendai Framework for Disaster Risk Reduction that the students have studied in class.[1] When the game starts, students split into three groups representing Japan, Mexico or Myanmar and their first task is to answer a series of questions about their respective countries to show their knowledge. The Japan team has the least amount of questions, reflecting the country's better-resourced and disaster-prepared state, and therefore finishes way ahead of the other groups. In the next task, the students use chairs to move across the room without touching the floor. Laughter and shouts fill the classroom as they lift, pull and push each other, in an experiential approximation of collaboration to strengthen disaster-risk governance, which is a central pillar of the Sendai Framework. Once again, Japan has the advantage by being able to use four chairs between the five players, while the Myanmar team has only two. This makes getting to the other side of the room impossible, and so the players have to ask Japan for help; it gives them two chairs but only in return for one of the resource cards each group was given at the beginning of the game. This shows Japan's heavy involvement in development aid, especially for other Asian countries, but also the fact that aid always comes with strings attached.

The third task focuses on another Sendai pillar, investments in disaster-risk reduction. Each group picks an investment card out of a hat, which tells Myanmar to prepare for a tsunami. After briefly consulting the Sendai Framework, the players decide that with the limited resources they have been given, they can invest in high sea walls and education, which earns them almost full points as it covers many of the Sendai targets. It also allows them to take ten blocks for their final task, which is to build a tsunami structure to manifest their disaster preparedness.

They have only two minutes for their build and loud, heavy metal music now fills the air, heightening an already tense atmosphere. As the tsunami arrives, their structure gets drenched with water from a bottle and barely survives. The other groups are not faring much better, the Mexico team experiencing an earthquake that violently shakes the table and topples their block structure, while the Japan team has to contend with a tornado in the form of a hairdryer furiously blowing air unto theirs. The structure holds up, and, not surprisingly, the Japan team wins by point count, reinforcing its already advantageous condition. There is more laughter, but also sighs of relief as the groups come together to reflect on their experiences of playing the game and what they learned from it: the persistent inequality among countries, the uncertainty and chance that came with picking random cards, the pressure under which the students operated and how that affected their actions and the way they were forced to collaborate in their teams. They agreed that it was a different and fun, if at times stressful, way to learn experientially about an otherwise abstract and remote policy framework.

Serious educational games combine student research about particular concepts, frameworks or events with designing and playing games to enact learning in experiential ways. They are a good example of critical-creative pedagogy that can help students better understand and address complex ecological challenges. I use the term ecologies in a dual sense, encompassing both its narrower environmental meaning and its broader reference to interconnections, especially in relation to the embeddedness of humans in the 'web of life' (Capra, 1996). The chapter also takes a reparative stance that is 'receptive and hospitable, animated by care for the world and its inhabitants' (Gibson-Graham and Roelvink, 2010, p 324). Such a stance is particularly conducive to learning, and in this chapter I show how teaching about ecological challenges can impart new knowledge about alternative ecological understandings, such as the Latin American concept of Buen Vivir and complex systems thinking, both of which highlight the relationality between humans and the natural environment. Critical-creative learning also has the potential to foster student orientations towards working with, rather than being immobilized by, uncertainty and embracing transdisciplinary learning. These knowledge and orientations inform a politics of shifting from anthropocentrism to eco-centrism, which recognizes and respects the intrinsic value of the natural world. This is also a politics of sustain-ability, a term I borrow from Tony Fry (2018), for whom the hyphen makes visible human responsibility to sustain life in its interdependent wholeness.

The chapter begins by critically interrogating the dominant discourse of sustainable development that prioritizes economic growth over environmental sustainability, and then introduces eco-centrism as an alternative. This leads into a discussion of Education for Sustainable Development as a global educational programme advanced by the UN. The next two sections explore two alternative approaches to understanding ecological challenges. Buen Vivir has emerged from South American indigenous thought to influence global environmental debates, while complex systems thinking introduces students to ideas of ecological webs, emergence and interdependence to better understand the uncertain and complex nature of ecological challenges. The chapter concludes with two learning activities, the first describing the use of serious games to teach students about climate change uncertainty, and the second showing how mapping campus infrastructures can help students to think about the sustainability of their learning environments.[2]

Decentring sustainable development

Sustainable development is a widely used concept in relation to environmental issues, but has severe shortcomings in its application to environmental crises. Within the long history of the general notion of sustainability, its use for environmental purposes began during the 1960s and came to prominence following the first-ever Earth Day in the US in 1970 (Amsler, 2009). Significantly, that event was originally conceived as a college and university teach-in inspired by anti-war protests, but in the end involved millions of Americans whose environmental consciousness had been raised by the publication of Rachel Carson's *Silent Spring* and the iconic Earth Rise photograph taken by Apollo 8 astronauts. In these early days, talk of sustainability showed a growing recognition of the effects of population and economic growth on the environment, public realization of ecological destruction and a loss of faith in technological and scientific solutions. This was reinforced by the publication of *Limits to Growth*, a report written by a group of systems thinkers who used computer simulations to model exponential growth within a finite supply of resources. The report posited three possible future scenarios and concluded that

> if the present growth trends in world population, industrialization, pollution, food production, and resource depletion continue unchanged, the limits to growth on this planet will be reached sometime within the next one hundred years. The most probable result will be a rather sudden and uncontrollable decline in both population and industrial capacity. (Meadows et al, 1972, p 23)

Limits to Growth, and its proposed zero-growth model, started a serious debate about whether continued economic growth was possible or desirable, as well as a discussion about other ways forward.[3]

The most prominent of these ways has been sustainable development, a term that emerged from the work of the World Commission on Environment and Development, an international group of political, economic and scientific experts convened by former Norwegian Prime Minister Gro Harlem Brundtland on behalf of the UN. They were tasked with identifying long-term environmental strategies that would also ensure human needs and interests being met. The result was the 1987 report *Our Common Future*, better known as the Brundtland report, which famously defined sustainable development as 'development that meets the needs of the present without compromising the ability of future generations to meet their own needs' (World Commission on Environment and Development, 1987, p 43). Without clearly spelling out whose development and needs were to be considered and how these were to be determined, the report was a compromise between the formerly antagonistic ideas of conservation as the protection of natural resources, and economic development as their exploitation (Du Pisani, 2006).

More specifically, environmental protection was subsumed under economic growth, which was legitimized and reaffirmed as necessary to the solution of environmental problems, via the detour of poverty alleviation in developing countries. This also links sustainable development to the mainstream development industry, wherein both people and nature are managed through top-down technocratic policy approaches driven by actors in the Global North (Escobar, 1995). The primacy of economic growth was reinforced at the 1992 UN Conference on Environment and Development. Commonly referred to as the Rio Earth Summit, it promoted the idea of 'sustained, inclusive and equitable economic growth'. The rise of the green economy and environmental economics operationalized the belief that economic growth and environmental sustainability are compatible, made possible by scientific and technological progress bringing about improvements in efficiency, productivity and pollution control (Kothari et al, 2014).

Together with voluntary business actions, free trade regimes and market mechanisms, this reliance on science and technology has become a central focus of mainstream sustainable development interventions. The language of natural capital and environmental resource management signals the instrumental use of nature for human and economic ends, while practices such as species banking, biodiversity derivatives and carbon trading show that market interventions have become preferred solutions to environmental problems (Kopnina and Gjerris, 2015). The SDGs, as the most recent UN global framework, continue to prioritize economic growth over ecological concerns and seek voluntary implementation mainly by those institutions that are responsible for unsustainable resource use, foremost among them the private sector (Eisenmenger et al, 2020). Many activist and academic critics have pointed out the anthropocentrism at the heart of sustainable development, which is neither sustainable nor developmental (Kopnina and Gjerris, 2015).

More radical approaches demand a shift from anthropocentrism to eco-centrism, which recognizes that nature and non-human species have intrinsic value, independent from their utility for humans. Eco-centrism emerged in the 1950s from Aldo Leopold's land ethic, which redefined human beings as symbiotically living in an interdependent community that also includes soil, water, plants and animals. The ethical dimension meant that for Leopold 'a thing is right when it tends to preserve the integrity, stability, and beauty of the biotic community. It is wrong when it tends otherwise' (cited in Meadows, 2008, p 182). Leopold's ideas were further developed in the early 1970s by Norwegian philosopher Arne Naess, who contrasted a 'shallow ecology' fighting pollution and resource depletion in the service of human development with a 'deep ecology' built around the radical interrelationship of all systems of life (Naess, 1973). Deep ecology encompasses respect for the integrity of the environment, a moral obligation to accord nature and ecosystems an independent place in ethical reflections and a duty to protect the environment through consistent attitudes, policies and actions. Naess's ideas have influenced many contemporary eco-centric approaches, for example those that argue for the rights of nature and animal species (Spannring, 2019). Degrowth is another proposal that calls for the abolition of growth as an economic, social and political objective, in order to achieve environmental sustainability. In all of these approaches, sustainability is seen not as 'a technical problem of rationalizing the distribution and use of resources, but as a normative position which is accomplished through political and cultural struggles to assert certain values' (Amsler, 2009, p 123). How has education contributed to these debates?

From education for sustainable development to sustain-ability education

In parallel to the rise of the environmental movement, and drawing on nature studies and conservation education, the field of environmental education emerged in the late 1960s. It was centred on an understanding of humans as an integral part of a system consisting of humans, culture and the biophysical environment and a recognition that human action could alter this system in fundamental ways. Drawing mainly on the natural sciences, environmental education aimed to make students aware of ecological damage caused by human activity and the importance of environmental protection. When environmental education began to be taught in the Global South, it became clear that the economic and social impacts of environmental destruction and mitigating actions on people's livelihoods needed greater attention (Kopnina, 2012). This precipitated the incorporation of economic growth as a central concern within environmental teaching, which, together with the general shift towards sustainable development, led to the emergence of the UN's Education for Sustainable Development initiative, commonly referred to as ESD and defined as

> a vision of education that seeks to balance human and economic well-being with cultural tradition and respect for the earth's natural resources. ESD applies transdisciplinary educational methods and approaches to develop an ethic for lifelong learning, fosters respect for human needs that are compatible with sustainable use of natural resources and the needs of the planet and nurtures a sense of global solidarity. (UNESCO 2002, cited in Bessant et al, 2015, p 418)[4]

Within this educational vision, HE is seen to play a central role in developing new knowledge, shaping policy and educating future leaders and citizens (Bessant et al, 2015). The Rio Earth Summit called on HE institutions to incorporate ESD in their curricula; in response, and also driven by student interest, ESD has become part of the global HE landscape. Universities the world over are developing sustainability-focused teaching and research programmes, adjusting campus operations around environmental management directives and engaging with communities on sustainability issues.[5] This operationalization has not been without criticisms, focusing on ESD's market-driven nature, the sidelining of ethical and moral questions and its purportedly global character.

It should come as no surprise that ESD reproduces the limitations and contradictions of sustainable development, mainly through developing students' competencies to participate in the green economy (Kopnina and Meijers, 2014). This is clearly visible in the UK, where the title of a 2012 report for the Higher Education Academy – *Universities and the Green Economy: Graduates for the Future* – clearly shows that 'a significantly growing discourse area in the ESD world involves drawing direct linkages and synergies between ESD and the student employability, skills and consumer rhetoric' (Bessant et al, 2015, p 424). Being shaped, promoted and funded by mainstream development organizations and their corporate partners, ESD is instrumentalized according to mainstream notions of sustainable development and implicated in the neoliberal HE regime described in Chapter 2. This is reinforced through a discourse of developing students' competencies.

Many of these competencies include orientations that are also fostered by critical-creative pedagogy: systemic and holistic thinking; interdisciplinary and heterogeneous group work skills; dealing with complexity, uncertainty and ambiguity, and anticipatory and future-oriented thinking to be able to 'hold multiple futures in one's frame of reference, preparing oneself for discontinuity and surprise' (Gardiner and Rieckmann, 2015, p 10560).

However, framing these orientations as competencies situates them squarely within the neoliberal education system rather than supporting a vision of education as broad human development.[6] Specifically, the competencies approach allows for testing, standardization and ranking, achieving specified learning outcomes and acquiring predetermined knowledge and skills in accordance with indicators and benchmarks (Lozano et al, 2012).

Competencies do not neglect questions of ethics, rights and values, but approach these from a primarily functional and utilitarian point of view and as tools enabling participation in the market economy. By contrast, a values-based environmental education can strengthen emancipatory educational goals (Molina-Motos, 2019). Such an education is based on deep ecology, and includes ecofeminist understandings of the role of patriarchy and androcentrism in the construction of hierarchical binaries between men/women, culture/nature, mind/body and reason/emotion. Ecofeminists argue for transcending these binaries in the search for an inclusive and relational ethic based on the values of care and compassion, while at the same time cautioning against essentialist identifications of women and nature. Political and social ecology interrogate the role of capitalism in the human domination and exploitation of nature, show the historical and ongoing unequal distribution of environmental resources and impacts, and propose the values of solidarity and respect. This values-based education also rejects authoritarian and elitist approaches that sideline the needs of, especially, marginalized people in the Global South in a quest for natural purity.

It is in the Global South that the global ambitions of ESD have been questioned most forcefully, by connecting them to larger decolonizing debates that highlight the marginalization of non-scientific and other subaltern knowledges (González-Gaudiano, 2016). ESD also neglects local economic and social contexts, ignores institutional and cultural specificities in its places of implementation and undermines pluriversal ways of relating to other humans as well as to plants and animals (Kopnina and Meijers, 2014). In response, some countries have resisted the adoption of ESD and made only cosmetic changes to institutional discourses (González-Gaudiano, 2016). Additionally, social and indigenous struggles against large-scale extractivist and other environmentally damaging policies provide important sources of alternative ideas about ecological sustain-ability. These perspectives are part of a larger movement towards Global South practices of sustain-ability education, which take into account the effects of historical resource flows and loss of commons as well as contemporary issues of climate colonialism and environmental justice. They embrace a 'commitment to generativity and emergence as principle, to open process dialogical, yet critical, aspirational and emancipatory principles for education and learning' (Lotz-Sisitka, 2017, p 55). These pedagogical practices are among a number of educational sustain-ability approaches that inform critical-creative pedagogy.

Its critical dimension draws on eco-pedagogies and eco-literacies, as an extension of Critical Pedagogy introduced in Chapter 2 to environmental concerns. Informed by Freirean popular education, eco-pedagogies encompass formal education and activist practices to develop students' 'planetary consciousness' through programmes that help them interrogate the intersection of social, political, economic and environmental systems, question the patriarchal, classist and racist constructions of mainstream representations of nature and incorporate praxis to connect learning to public discourse and social movements (Khan, 2009). In addition, the creative dimension of a sustain-ability education recognizes that creativity and imagination are necessary to imagine an ecological future drastically different from the status quo, which is deeply implicated in the current environmental crisis (Sandri, 2013).

Creative modes of thinking can also help students to 'unlearn unsustainability' (Wals, 2010), a process similar to unlearning privilege described in Chapter 2. It entails letting go of cherished assumptions and certainties that can be fundamental to students' (and teachers') understandings of progress and development, the value of the environment and their own personal, professional and political place in this complex ensemble. Sandri argues that 'certainty is lethal to two of our most redeeming and humane qualities, imagination and empathy. If the right answers are there to be learned by students, then there is no space for being wrong, experimenting, imagining alternatives or seeing issues from multiple perspectives and frameworks' (2013, p 774). This unlearning can be deeply unsettling for students, especially those who expect their university education to be a transmission of knowledge about the correct understanding of the world. Instead, understanding ecological crisis is about acknowledging uncertainty, while imagining ways forward requires divergent thinking in creative spaces.

Both are introduced into sustain-ability education by drawing on emotions, the arts and experiential, localized encounters with nature. Judson (2015) recognizes learning as an emotional and epistemological process and proposes an imaginative ecological education predicated on fostering an immersive relationship with nature and a sense of stewardship. This links directly to hope as an emotion that is of particular importance for sustain-ability education. Incorporating a sense of hope in teaching can address (some) students' pessimism or fear of environmental futures by providing positive ways forward (Ojala, 2017). However, such hope needs to be critical so as not to result in unrealistic optimism or wishful thinking, denial of the seriousness of environmental crisis or disengagement and distancing from it. Ultimately, 'hope is a positive emotion and an existential must that needs to be cultivated, by showing [students] that another way of being is possible, by encouraging trustful relationships [in the classroom] and by giving young people the opportunity to concretely work together for change' (p 83). Critical hope is also one strand of critical-creative pedagogy, and in the next chapter I show how it has motivated climate change activism among Sussex students. Critical hope can be cultivated through artful teaching practices, from creative science fiction writing to outdoor journaling to the making of artworks by students.

Another important component of creative sustain-ability education is attention to one's immediate physical location. Places such as university campuses can become co-teachers through fostering students' practices of place-making that avoid problematic assumptions of wilderness or superficial edu-tainment (Judson, 2015). Decolonial and indigenous scholars have argued that such place-based education must include attention to how human relations to land have been shaped by historical and ongoing effects of colonialism with their resulting violence, extraction and dispossession (Tuck et al, 2014). Indigenous cosmologies, to which land is often central, shape distinct practices of learning from the land and incorporate environmental, physical, intellectual and spiritual dimensions into collective visions. These often clash with dominant narratives and practices of modernization and progress and raise crucial questions about whose ecological futures become desirable. At the same time, these visions resist romanticized notions of indigenous peoples as 'ecological natives' that deny them possibilities of change and agency. Indigenous cosmologies give rise to 'radical well-being notions' that break with anthropocentric and capitalocentric logics, such as the South African concept of Ubuntu, with its emphasis on human mutuality, and the Indian concept of Swaraj, which focuses on self-reliance and self-governance (Kothari et al, 2014, p 372). In the next section I explore the Latin American concept of Buen Vivir, usually translated as good living or living well, which has taken centre stage in debates around environmental sustainability and education.

Buen Vivir

The concept of Buen Vivir emerged at the turn of the 20th century among various indigenous peoples in Latin America as a pluriversal alternative to Western anthropocentric worldviews and mainstream development interventions.[7] It centres on living in harmony with oneself, society and nature, pluriculturalism and the inseparability of all elements of life (Revello, 2018). As a deeply place-based notion linked to specific territories as the material and spiritual basis for life, Buen Vivir is enacted within socio-ecological communities that closely interlink humans and non-human beings. It is also a dynamic and open concept that does not discount technological advances or contributions from other cultures. From its indigenous origins, Buen Vivir has now become a 'plural endeavour', acting as an umbrella term that is amplifying and connecting various critical traditions searching for alternatives to development (Gudynas, 2011, p 445).

This broader uptake has a complex genealogy, forged by diverse actors in the context of broader political shifts in Latin America, global crises and social movement responses, which has resulted in contestations especially around activist and elite uses of the term (Hidalgo-Capitán and Cubillo-Guevara, 2017). While I was in Bolivia I had many conversations about Buen Vivir and its changing politics, and how Bolivian academics were engaging with these changes. These discussions were frequently connected to broader decolonial knowledge politics focusing on the relationship between Eurocentric knowledge and Bolivian academic and indigenous scholarship. A critical-creative exploration of Buen Vivir as part of a decolonizing curriculum can therefore introduce students to an alternative vision that has originated in the Global South and is becoming part of the global development discourse, in complex and sometimes contradictory ways.

The alternative posed by Buen Vivir presents a radical break with modernist traditions. Modernity here is conceptualized as 'a particular ontology that in the last centuries determined the division between nature and society, a colonial distinction between modern and non-modern indigenous peoples, the myth of progress as a unidirectional linear path and a strong confidence in Cartesian science' (Gudynas, 2011, p 447). Since the 1970s, the supposed universality of the nature/culture divide, and related ones such as mind/body and subject/object, has been 'provincialized' by scholars in the humanities, social and biological sciences, who have shown that it is the expression of a Euro-modern epistemic regime that emerged during the Enlightenment (Cadena, 2012). In the Americas, this divide was part of colonizing missions that superimposed themselves onto and thereby made invisible other, indigenous worlds.

While these dynamics persist under the current regime of coloniality, including an environmental ethics that problematically positions indigenous peoples as the eternal guardians of ancient ecological wisdom, other worlds are reasserting themselves through activist movements for social and environmental justice. Buen Vivir is an enactment of some of these other worlds and a manifestation of the pluriverse, shaped by epistemic and ontological multiplicity that includes a relational conception of the world and deeply experiential ways of knowing it (Burman, 2016). As I showed in Chapter 3, Buen Vivir's key ideas of autonomy and communality are contributing to designing new forms of life, in response to current crises that cannot be addressed with conventional modern practices (Escobar, 2018). These forms can nevertheless remain entangled in modernist aspirations, and while Buen Vivir therefore has the potential to counter mainstream development interventions, its complex local instantiations disrupt grand narratives (Killick, 2020). Bolivian government policies further complicate this picture.

In Bolivia, Buen Vivir's prominence began during a national citizen consultation in 2001, which was co-organized by the German development agency GTZ and led by Bolivian philosopher Javier Medina and Aymara sociologist Simon Yampara (Beling et al, 2018). Indigenous leaders then introduced the concept into the campaign programme of Evo Morales. When Morales was elected as Bolivia's first indigenous president in 2006, Buen Vivir became incorporated into government policy to decolonize Bolivian society. This inclusion resulted in a struggle over its interpretation and use by different government factions and their grassroots supporters. The 2009 Bolivian constitution adopted Buen Vivir as one of the 'ethical and moral principles describing the values, ends and objectives of the pluri-national Bolivian state' (Gudynas, 2011, p 443). Subsequent laws officially recognized the rights of Madre Tierra, the Spanish term for (mother) nature, but these have remained largely symbolic.

This has become especially obvious with the widening gap between government rhetoric around environmental protection and climate justice, and neo-extractivist policies that have pursued large-scale hydrocarbon exploitation and often involve the dispossession of indigenous lands and resources. These contradictions have to be understood in the context of Bolivia's history of resource extraction which began with the Spanish conquest and of contemporary demands for the redistribution of resource wealth through social programmes (Postero, 2013). Still, in light of the increasing human and environmental costs of continuing mega-projects, many indigenous groups argued that laws were more about "legitimizing the Morales government's developmentalist agenda rather than about rethinking the extractivist model and transitioning towards alternative, more ecological, modes of development" (indigenous representative, cited in Achtenberg, 2017). They and other critics accused Morales of appropriating indigenous ideas to mask economic practices that are damaging to the environment and directly contradict government agreements with indigenous peoples (Svampa, 2013). Morales was forced to leave office in 2019. A year later the MAS party returned to power; at the time of this writing it remains to be seen how the new government's policies will be unfolding.

Buen Vivir's wider uptake in Latin America began with an international seminar on indigenous development models, again organized by GTZ in Bolivia. From there, via the work of Latin American intellectuals, the term has gained greater purchase in international academic and development policy circles. This process has not been without critics. They argue that the indigenous creators of the worldviews subsumed under Buen Vivir have been sidelined and once again invisibilized as political actors (Altmann, 2019). This is an example of epistemic extractivism where indigenous concepts are taken 'out of the contexts where they were produced in order to depoliticise and resignify them from Western-centric logics' (Grosfoguel, cited in Altmann, 2019, p 93). As a result, Buen Vivir has become a Northern abstraction emptied of original content, a local variant of a global project and one among many alternative ideas. This appropriation has also meant that the concept has lost (some of) its radical potential; a 2013 UN Environment Programme report posited essential similarities between Buen Vivir and the green economy, based on how some governments, such as Bolivia's, have deployed the concept, but also because Buen Vivir itself has been institutionalized and tamed (Kothari et al, 2014).[8]

Morales was an important part of this internationalization, as he successfully promoted himself as a defender of environmental rights on the global stage. After the UN General Assembly declared him a 'World Hero of Mother Earth' in 2009, he convened the Global People's Summit on Climate Change and the Rights of Mother Earth the following year in response to the Copenhagen Climate Change Conference ending without a new global agreement (Postero, 2013). The summit brought together activists, scientists and policy makers from 140 countries in the Bolivian town of Cochabamba and provided a platform for Morales to expound his long-held opposition to Western consumption-driven capitalism. It concluded with a People's Agreement calling for limiting global warming to one degree Celsius and the passage of a Universal Declaration of the Rights of Mother Earth. Alongside the government-sanctioned summit, a counter-summit was held by various indigenous groups to expose environmental problems within Bolivia.

These contestations around Buen Vivir, within Bolivia and beyond, can inform critical-creative teaching about environmental alternatives. They can show students the complex articulations of local creations with national, regional and international actors, events and discourses, which lead to tensions, appropriations and resistances. Resulting discussions about knowledge creation and extraction can nuance idealistic and simplistic assumptions about alternative visions and deconstruct romanticized views of indigenous peoples. A critical exploration of the concept also includes reading a wide variety of sources, including Western and Bolivian academic texts, policy documents and activist and indigenous declarations. Such diversity is crucial to ensure that the plurality of actors involved in the politics around Buen Vivir are heard. Research into Bolivia's historical and current geopolitical and socio-cultural contexts also needs to be part of a critical analysis of Buen Vivir.

Creative teaching activities could include reading the Cochabamba People's Agreement against comparable UN declarations, to show students how different policy documents engage activist and academic ideas. Students could then write a UN response to the Cochabamba declaration and vice versa, and could also creatively enact a meeting space where both documents would be presented and discussed. This could include imagining the meeting's location, scripting its format, rituals and performances and role-playing the various actors that would come together. Such an activity would be based on in-depth research rather than speculation, while also engaging students' imagination and creativity. It would not only sharpen students' critical awareness of the complexities of formulating and enacting alternative visions within local and global contexts, but would also allow them to explore these dynamics in creative ways that can generate multidimensional insights into the difficult social and political lives of alternative visions. As an example of a decolonial alternative, Buen Vivir is a relational ontology that highlights the radical interrelationship between humans and the natural world. This connects Buen Vivir to current ecological thinking about the systemic and complex nature of the environment, and developing students' basic understanding of complex system thinking is another part of sustainability teaching.

Complex sustain-able systems

Issues like human-triggered climate change make painfully clear that the present major environmental, social, financial, economic and ecological disruptions (both acute and chronic) are interconnected and characterized by high levels of uncertainty and complexity. We live in a 'systemic world' characterized by multiple causation, interactions, complex feedback loops and the inevitable uncertainty, and unpredictability. Old mechanisms, coordination points, problem solving strategies, modes of scientific inquiry and forms of teaching and learning, seem inadequate in addressing the present global sustainability challenge. (Wals, 2010, p 90)

There are many reasons why knowing about systems and complexity can help students better understand ecological challenges. As Arjen Wals shows, current, more linear, ways of thinking and teaching about these challenges are ill-equipped to do so. In addition, overwhelming amounts of sometimes contradictory information from diverse sources, persistent questions about ecological impacts and trade-offs with no (easy) answers but enormous implications, and undeniable evidence of the increasing destruction wrought by human activity on the earth are all contributing to a loss of confidence in established interventions. In de Sousa Santos's words, 'we are facing modern problems for which there are no longer modern solutions' (cited in Escobar, 2020, p 69). Modern here refers to the reductionist and mechanistic worldview stemming from Cartesian science, which is beginning to be replaced with holistic, ecological understandings of the world that take seriously its systemic and complex nature. Within this shifting context, students are often passionate about environmental issues, and learning about ecological challenges as complex, wicked problems can contribute to a better understanding of these issues.

Several fields of research grapple with this complex world, including living systems theory, complex systems science, non-linear dynamics and chaos theory. In spite of the differences among these fields, all agree on a set of core elements that characterize complex systems. These include interdependence,[9] self-organization,[10] emergence[11] and non-linearity.[12] In this section, I draw on Donella Meadows' introduction to systems thinking, Fritjof Capra's writings on a systems view of life and transdisciplinary education to show how students' understanding of these elements and their implications for thinking about ecological challenges can be developed.[13] Such a pedagogical approach runs up against the prevailing educational paradigm with its disciplinary compartmentalization, standardized assessment and education for employability and career readiness (Steele, 2016). Paradigms are 'the shared ideas in the minds of society, the great, big, unstated assumptions [that] constitute that society's deepest set of beliefs about how the world works' (Meadows, 2008, p 162–3). Shifting them is not easy but can provide important leverage points, where small changes can bring about systems-level transformations. In sustain-ability education, that starts by educating the educators.

Being able to teach students about complex systems thinking often falters because educators themselves are not well versed in this area. To develop the necessary capabilities, educators can engage in various processes, including asking 'hard-to-answer questions [that] seem to instil in systems literate individuals a capacity to embrace ambiguity, uncertainty, and continual change'; broadening their reference points by considering multiple perspectives and the connections between them, and integrating insights from different, preferably conflicting, fields by adopting and/also instead of either/or perspectives (Steele, 2016, p 111). These processes, many of which I have explored in Chapter 3, can be complemented with immersion in key complexity concepts and issues to help educators develop an overall systems lens. This can be achieved in different ways, since 'from a systems view, emphasizing diversity, experimentation, and emergent solution making to redesign education systems holds greater promise than applying pre-established solutions' (p 113).

How can this general systems lens be useful for sustain-ability education? According to Capra, such an education needs to move from the current Cartesian mechanistic worldview to an ecological one that 'recognizes the fundamental interdependence of all phenomena and the fact that, as individuals and societies, we are all embedded in (and ultimately dependent on) the cyclical processes of nature' (1996, p 6). Teaching students to

Table 5.1: Shifts in sustain-ability education and teaching applications

Pedagogical shift	Teaching examples
From objects to relationships	Food webs and their implications for individual and collective food consumption
From contents to patterns	Ecosystems' zero-waste cycles and their applications in cradle-to-grave design or circular economies
From linearity to non-linearity	Climate tipping points (for example Amazon rain forest, Greenland ice sheet) and their connection to human activities
From parts to whole	Pollution as an example of externalities, where the costs of human activities affect third parties and are hidden in mainstream economic accounts

Source: Author, incorporating Capra, 1996 and 2005.

understand the fundamental importance of this ecological perspective calls for several shifts (Table 5.1).

The first shift, from *objects to relationships*, means studying networks, webs and their interrelations, rather than discrete entities. The latter are too often the focus of learning because parts are the most visible system elements, while their interconnections are harder to detect. Shifting from one to the other directs students' attention to interdependencies, cooperation and conservation. A second shift, from *contents to patterns*, includes moving from measuring matter to mapping forms. This foregrounds visual methods that can develop students' abilities to recognize and represent patterns, which make overall systems visible at a single glance. Patterns also reveal long-term cycles in ecosystems that have renewed themselves for millions of years, providing important lessons for sustain-ability by cautioning against single-focus, short-term solutionism. The third shift, from *linearity to non-linearity*, is one of the most challenging because of prevailing linear assumptions that 'when something works, more of the same will always be better' (Capra, 2005, p 20). This is not the case for non-linear systems, where the outcomes of change cannot be predicted or controlled and can lead to irreversible tipping points. The final shift, from *parts to whole*, helps students to see living systems as integrated wholes. Under the mechanistic paradigm, complex systems are deconstructed to analyse the properties of their parts, without then being reconstructed to consider the whole. This is still the basis of much university learning. In the holistic paradigm, parts can be understood only within the context of the larger whole, which also enables students to better see connections and to recognize sustain-ability as the property of an entire network. These four shifts are best achieved through disciplinary diversity.

This diversity moves beyond interdisciplinarity, where participants merely communicate across discipline-specific boundaries, and multidisciplinarity, which includes disciplinary cooperation among participants who nevertheless remain within their respective disciplines. Instead, complex systems thinking calls for transdisciplinarity, which 'involves learners sharing their disciplinary-specific skills and experiences (via cross-training) so they can produce new knowledge, together. Because the traditional boundaries between disciplines are intentionally broken down during transdisciplinary engagements, it is possible for learners to create new, integrated intellectual frameworks and not just draw disciplinary concepts together' (McGregor, 2015, p 81).

Transdisciplinarity is necessary because 'the right boundary for thinking about a [system] problem rarely coincides with the boundaries of an academic discipline' (Meadows, 2008, p 98). Conversely, complex systems thinking can be used to integrate the many academic disciplines that study living systems. Because transdisciplinarity requires cross-fertilization, it needs teachers with the previously mentioned systems lens and students who study more than one discipline. Although the intense and early specialization in UK undergraduate degrees stands in the way of such an approach, joint undergraduate degrees or double majors go some way towards cross-training. A student who had just completed a double major in Economics and International Development provided a good example of this in her journey interview when she observed that

'neoclassical economic premises were taught in class as notions that cannot be discussed or put to question, as they are the basis to our economic science, and taught as fixed theories. I started to question these beliefs due to my development modules and the knowledge they imparted. Being able to study the effects of economic policy made me able to question economic policy, and the effects it caused. I realized that the Economics we were being taught was neither real, neither perfect, neither moral.'[14]

Moving beyond double degrees, David Staley has proposed the concept of a Polymath University, where students major in three different disciplines, drawn from the sciences, the arts or humanities and a professional field. Through learning each field's particular ways of thinking, students develop 'cognitive flexibility' to move between them, to integrate multiple perspectives and to negotiate their boundaries as creative spaces (2019, p 190). Rather than clearly delineated blocks of knowledge, academic disciplines become opportunities to explore different ways of thinking:

where transdisciplinary learning is different from traditionally themed or integrated units is that students not only have an opportunity to work in depth, through a range of disciplines, but also recognise, through practice and reflection, the innate value and challenges in applying a range of disciplines to a topic. This quite naturally opens important questions about thinking, and provides a perfect opportunity for students to realise that disciplines are constructed, are continuously changing and can be questioned. (Davies, 2009, p 1)

Integrative learning can also result in what Wals (2010) calls 'gestaltswitching',[15] which involves students moving back and forth across transcultural, trans-spatial, transdiscipline, transtemporal and transhuman mindsets. This is akin to the domain bridging and switching that is an integral part of creativity. Gestaltswitching helps students to cope with the uncertainty that results from the increasing recognition that more knowledge and information lead to more rather than less uncertainty. In general, 'educational spaces should build a culture of learning awash with uncertainty and in which uncertainty provokes transformative yet precautionary commitment rather than paralysis' (Kagwa and Selby, cited in Wals, 2010, p 26). One way to achieve this is to make learning more playful.

Another of Staley's concept universities is the Institute for Advanced Play, which aims to create a space for play in HE, in line with the recognition of serious play and games as learning systems that can help students to practise complex thinking. At the heart of the Institute is asking questions such as 'what if the university were designed to facilitate serious play?' As I have shown in Chapter 3, exploring answers to 'what if' questions involves adopting a beginner's mindset of intellectual curiosity and adventure. Similarly, play involves not being confined to the world as it presents itself, but playing by different rules through appropriating objects and situations in a context different from what they were intended for. Play also entails learning by doing, appropriating and manipulating objects and immersing students in a subjunctive mode. Here, imagining different futures could include designing simulations or virtual worlds inspired by science fiction. Play can be both fun and dangerous, creative and destructive, affirmative and subversive, and it is in this multiplicity that its potential for imagining and creating alternatives lies.

Serious games

In the context of sustain-ability education, systems-games that allow students to 'inhabit the complexities of climate risk' and then explore and test a range of plausible futures are especially effective (De Suarez et al, 2012, p 6). Students can experience various aspects of ecological or climate systems behaviour, playfully understand how these systems function, examine their own assumptions and responses and experiment with rule bending and leverage points. Because games operate in compressed time and therefore allow for the exploration of longer-range futures, they lend themselves to exploring ecological challenges. Their collaborative nature fosters social learning and reinforces the importance of bringing different groups together to effect environmental change (Dieleman and Huisingh, 2006). Games can create positive mental energy that has the potential to counter negative and pessimistic associations of environmental issues and to highlight the innovative aspect of sustain-ability. For games to have these pedagogical effects, they need to be well prepared, executed and evaluated, which includes considerations of group dynamics as well as players' cultural and institutional contexts, clear instructions and an extensive debriefing process during which participants can reflect on their learning. While educators can draw on many resources to find educational games,[16] students designing their own games for others to play goes beyond play to fostering creative learning-by-design, which enables students to assume more ownership of their own and their peers' learning. This is the case for a final-year undergraduate module on Disasters, Environment and Development, taught by my colleague Dom Kniveton, which introduces students to serious games to learn about risk and uncertainty in relation to climate change.

Throughout the term, student groups play and analyse existing games and then design their own game, direct their classmates to play it and evaluate it for assessment.[17] This section is based on my weekly observation of the games seminars in 2017, and subsequent interviews with Kniveton and students. For Kniveton, games allow knowledge to stick better because they facilitate students' own learning in more participatory ways. This includes triple-loop learning, which is an important aspect of complex systems thinking that asks learners to be reflective about the very process of learning. As Kniveton explains to students, single-loop learning means 'are we doing things right?' while double-loop considers 'are we doing the right things?' and triple-loop involves asking 'how do we decide what are the right things?' In other words, the different loops are about following the rules, changing the rules and asking who makes the rules. The latter is a strong leverage point for system change; according to Meadows, 'if you want to understand the deepest malfunctions of systems, pay attention to the rules and who has power over them' (2008, p 158).

Throughout my observations of students designing their games and then playing the final creations, I was struck by how closely this activity linked critical and creative learning. Most groups situated their games in existing countries or frameworks, such as the Sendai game whose description opened this chapter, and conducted in-depth research on local situations that was then translated into playing cards or context sheets. Many of these games' locations came from students' own experiences of natural disasters in their home countries or from having studied abroad. The design of the game materials, which included cards, tokens, boards and other props, and how they were incorporated into overall game structures, showed students' creative abilities to produce something entirely new. When the final games were played by the whole class, I was impressed by their range and diversity.

All games explored the overall themes of uncertainty, risk, vulnerability and resilience and incorporated systems of resource allocation, protection and spending; short- and long-term scenarios; and many different elements of chance such as dice, online randomizers and cards that determined the type and strength of disasters. Some games were modelled after board games and played on giant boards covering the whole room, others incorporated role-playing or physical activities and still others included elements of trade, investments by companies or negotiations for outside aid. Players worked with physical and financial resources differentiated according to particular locations' disaster exposure or level of preparedness and had to make decisions about what crops, programmes or preventative measures to invest in under uncertain and often stressful circumstances. These were viscerally reinforced in the classroom through loud noises, limited time for decision making and restricted movements.

Throughout the game design and playing, I observed a range of emotions and behaviours that showed the affective and experiential learning resulting from this way of teaching. There was initial confusion and overwhelmedness, followed by moving towards tentative making but also paralysis by analysis and eventually reaching creative collaborations among group members. While students still mainly wrote things out, drawing, gathering and making were also part of the design process. This process was not without friction, as students had to navigate a way of working together that was different from researching and putting together academic presentations. The group work was intense and demanding, especially towards the end of term when the games were finalized and trialled; there were stressful moments when groups had got too stuck in the details, when games became overly complicated or when their design ran up against the allotted time of 20 minutes or having to accommodate a certain number of players. There was elation when games were finished and judged to have gone well. Above all, students had fun, albeit more so in the playing than the making.

In the debriefing sessions, which included discussions right after the game and subsequent meetings Kniveton had with each group to determine their marks, he connected the game design back to triple-loop learning by asking students firstly what they had learned in the process of making and playing the game (single loop, factual knowledge), secondly what they would do differently if they had to repeat the process (double loop, think about the design process and outcome itself) and thirdly what surprised them (triple loop, trying to get at the process of learning itself). Some groups had managed to incorporate triple-loop learning as part of the game, by creating opportunities for players to reflect on their choices as they had to explain them to NGO or government representatives. Kniveton also encouraged students to be more confident in drawing out players' own knowledge instead of providing all the answers or solutions, to resist giving too much direction and instead foster open-endedness and flexibility and to be humble in allowing players to question rules and decisions. All of these are elements of complex systems thinking. For Kniveton, because games are themselves complex wholes with many connections and feedback loops, they can convey systems complexity and capture things that are not easily portrayed in more linear educational approaches. Games also create a safe environment in which to experiment, bend or challenge rules, explore different possibilities and fail without consequences. In short, they are vehicles for imagining and trying out alternative futures.

Student comments seconded this. Not surprisingly, almost all students highlighted the creativity of the activity as the thing they enjoyed most about it. One student professed initial scepticism "when hearing that we would be playing games, because I had never thought about games being an educational tool in such a way and it really made me reconsider my idea of learning". In general, the games suited students who said that they learned better through visual, practical and hands-on activities rather than just reading articles. They were seen as a "more accessible" and "more memorable" way of learning that several students described as using a different part of their brains. Students recounted learning lots of factual knowledge about specific places, and some commented that the game had allowed them to bring in skills and knowledges that they had developed outside the university. For one group, having to "reframe the issues and topics in a way that would work as an interactive game" was seen as particularly challenging, as it involved bridging analytical and creative domains of learning. Students also talked about learning a lot from each other, especially as the module brought together international development, human and physical geography students, and being amazed by their team-mates' creativity. One student commented that "you have to learn to be fair and patient with people, but also honest and share tactical criticism when necessary. I found this most challenging but in the end most rewarding."

For another group, "creating the game was the actual game", as they had started off by doing separate research assignments but quickly realized that they had to work together to design their game. Several groups expressed being pleased and surprised at having begun the process with lots of vague ideas and ending up with a game that they liked playing and others enjoyed and became intensely engaged in. In one case, that involved adjusting the playing process when the game was not going as expected and realizing that when they changed certain rules they had to change everything, which showed them the importance of interconnectedness. Another group talked about their delight when the players of their game challenged one of their decisions. For the game designers, this was "a perfect moment of learning" for both groups, as the players had thought of something the designers had not anticipated and the designers were sufficiently confident in their creative abilities to accept the challenge. This was also an example of rules being negotiated and ultimately changed.

One group commented that "it is incredibly hard to make something that is both fun and educational. It was hard to simplify something as complex as disaster risk reduction. Where do you draw the boundary of what to include?" They had come up against the issue of boundaries, which are spaces of potential disruption and creativity. According to Meadows, 'we have to invent boundaries for clarity and sanity; and boundaries can produce problems when we forget that we have artificially created them' (2008, p 97). All students had successfully worked at the boundary between fun and education, while becoming aware that boundaries are not given but produced in the process of knowledge creation. Such insights about interconnectedness, boundary making and simplified models are important elements of complex systems thinking that students learned by designing and playing games.

Students' descriptions of their experiences playing the games, using terms such as immersion, involvement and engagement, reveals whole-person learning. I have already described the multifaceted emotions the games elicited, and many of them also incorporated physical movement that engaged students' bodies. Students characterized their learning as "being confronted with different scenarios" experientially rather than just reading about them, which taught them about themselves, other members of the group and people affected by disasters. While they better understood how they or team members reacted to stressful situations, students also recognized that this could not simply be transferred to people affected by disasters. As one student argued, drawing on his critical knowledge, "games are still a simplification and there needs to be great care in not perpetuating the misrepresentation already faced in the world".

Students were very aware of how far removed their classroom experiences were from real situations of disaster and the people experiencing them, thus realizing the strong limitations of models and the dangers of facile identification I explored in Chapter 3. However, students also said that the game allowed them to "put yourself into the position of people in hazard" and that "immersion increases empathy", as they reflected on what it felt like to be in stressful, time-limited or under-resourced situations when they had to make impulse decisions or felt their instincts kicking in. Experiencing the constraints resulting from operating in situations of uncertainty, from having limited resources or possibilities and from having to work with others were seen as valuable learning moments. These moments also made students understand that in situations of uncertainty, "while the odds are slim it can always be a possibility", as one student put it. This contributed to a sense of hope that was expressed by several students. Serious games therefore exemplify all strands of critical-creative pedagogy: they foster whole-person learning, use creative activities, engage students in praxis and can nurture critical hope. In addition, they foster complex systems thinking and provide a fun and immerse way of learning, in this case about climate change uncertainty. How might such learning be taken outside the classroom?

Mapping campus

The aim of this teaching activity, which was part of my Urban Futures module,[18] was for students to research and map different infrastructures on Sussex campus, to think about how sustain-able they are and propose improvements to senior management. Although the exercise did not explicitly focus on ecological issues, it was a good starting point to explore these. Theoretically, the activity was framed through a seminar discussion of infrastructures as socio-technical systems and how their materiality, (in)visibility and accessibility are shaped by privileges and exclusions. To prepare for the activity, students had picked one of four infrastructures – water, transport, food and energy – the week before and undertaken preliminary research on how these materialized on campus. They had also familiarized themselves with the university's sustainability policy and found out that Sussex is no exception to the many universities that are reframing their teaching, research, campus operations and community engagement around sustainability.

On the day of the workshop, students went in small groups across campus to map their chosen infrastructure. I had introduced them to mapping as a political activity through a video of the MapKibera project, which uses community mapping to make visible the dearth of infrastructures in the informal settlement of Kibera in Nairobi.[19] Building on these theoretical and empirical insights, the aim of the mapping activity was to bring knowledge about infrastructures home to students, all of whom had lived on campus during their first year and in subsequent years were on campus almost daily for classes, in experiential and material ways. To achieve this, clear guidelines were important, especially because the activity included a self-directed, out-of-class element in the form of a walking discussion.

Using copies of campus maps, student groups started by planning their walking route based on the research they had undertaken. During their 30-minute walk they marked sightings of their chosen infrastructures on their maps and also answered questions on a worksheet: In what state are the infrastructures? How are people interacting with them? How sustainable do they seem to you? After writing this chapter, the next time I teach this activity I will also ask how the infrastructures connect with and are embedded in their surrounding natural habitat and what signs of human/environment interaction students can see. Writing things down while walking keeps students focused and provides a record of observations and discussions. Upon returning to the classroom, students used these notes to prepare their presentations. These focused on critical stock-taking and forward-looking sustainability recommendations that the groups presented to fellow students, who role-played a hypothetical senior leadership team.

The transport group had mapped roads, bike lanes, sidewalks, car parks and bike-parking areas, with an emphasis on accessibility, which was generally rated as poor. Suggestions included banning cars from certain parts of campus and instead expanding bike lanes and bike-parking spaces, turning a massive car park into a study area with grass and trees, having buses run on biofuels and supporting the Free Bus petition that one student was already working on. The energy group reported on the general invisibility of energy infrastructures, which allowed them to map only a generator that obstructed a footpath, several substations and a small wind turbine. They could not see the rooftop solar panels they had learned about during prior research, together with the fact that the majority of energy is supplied to campus by French energy giant EDF, which uses nuclear power. Recommendations therefore included finding a more alternative supplier, using more LED bulbs and solar-powered garbage bins and making sure that heating can be turned off by individuals rather than only centrally.

The food group had mapped the many spaces where food can be obtained on campus, noting the good presence of local suppliers. They mentioned various student initiatives such as the campus allotment, the Sussex Food Waste society that had its weekly café that day and the use of food-waste apps in which some campus outlets are participating. Suggestions included communal cooking or cultural food events to use food to bring people together and promote more healthy eating. The most surprising insights came from the water group, which had learned that in older student residences, where most of the students had lived during their first year of study, students shared bathrooms and could shower for only a limited duration, while in newly built halls students paid much higher rents for en-suite bathrooms and unlimited showers. For the students, that was an example of unequal access to infrastructures, in this case based on the ability to pay higher rents. The group had also found dew ponds that some of the students had not noticed before, and had talked to a maintenance person about a water leak between two buildings (Image 5.1). They reported that the on-campus store sells seven different brands of bottled water and recommended restricting this choice and instead installing more water points, as well as setting targets for water reduction in the residences or charging high water users more.

This mapping activity engaged learning in different ways, which one student described as "removing ourselves from the grips of theory". It brought

Image 5.1: Map of water infrastructures on Sussex campus created by students

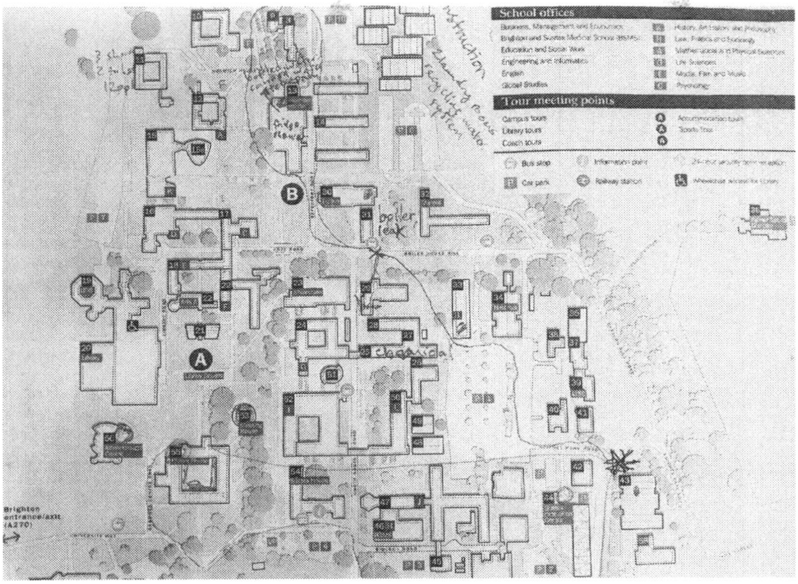

Photo: Author, used with permission.

together a variety of different knowledge sources, such as theoretical articles, policy literatures and the campus environment, and engaged learning through different modalities, including reading, walking and talking, mapping and presenting. Especially, the walking discussions was a new experience for the students, many of whom had never thought before of walking outdoors as a learning opportunity. One student commented that "learning outside the classroom was not something I had done before at university, but it was very welcome and an engaging way to look at everyday sights in a more analytical and systematic way". His quote confirms that outdoor learning can result in new insights, linking with general observations of outdoor education increasing teaching quality and student well-being and physical activity (Bälter et al, 2018). As one student who participated in the journey interviews reflected on a walking seminar she had undertaken for a different class,

'my conceptualisation and experience of nature became even more meaningful and valuable, as a person and a scholar, after being fully immersed in a walking seminar. To be and study outdoors helped immensely with my overall academic performance and well-being. It was through continuous practice, self-discovery and direct engagement with the natural environment when I started noticing real improvements both in my mental and physical health.'

Her comments support research that walking can lead to increased concentration and creativity and encourage discussions by creating more informal environments for students who might not know each other well or might not be comfortable speaking in more formal settings (Bälter et al, 2018).[20]

Walking across campus made students more aware of a place they had been inhabiting for three years but never considered to be part of their actual education. Echoing the last-quoted student's more systematic understanding of campus, another student commented that "I learned a lot about campus, something I thought I knew a lot about already but also about things I had never even thought about before, e.g. who supplies campus with water". In both cases, it was whole-person learning that had facilitated new insights, as students learned about campus experientially by engaging with it in more consciously embodied ways. This also led to an expanded ecological understanding, as shown in one student's comments that she had "a more visceral experience of what it's like to be a student i.e. a human, living in or around campus". She saw her relationship with her place of study in a new light, with the potential for walking with human and non-human others to become a form of convivial sharing, but also as an ethical and political activity (Springgay and Truman, 2017). Students also developed a more conscious connection to infrastructures, commenting on how little they had been aware of their existence; as one student put it "the activity helped me to open my eyes to how much infrastructure we take for granted and realize their enormous complexity". Another student linked this awareness across different scales from campus to cities to the globe, observing that "mapping water resources on campus showed great inequities [between old and new residences]. If these inequalities exist on campus, the difficulty of creating resource equality globally would be a huge urban planning challenge."

In terms of the recommendations students made, many included conventional measures designed to limit consumption or eliminate waste. Students clearly enjoyed this more forward-looking part of the activity, which allowed them to connect their learning to ideas about campus sustainability. For some, this did not go far enough, however. One student suggested to assemble all the infrastructures into a master map and use it to "discuss sustainable interventions that could involve all the infrastructures as a whole, to achieve a holistic point of view, in that way seeing campus functioning as a whole mini society". Here, the student was articulating systems thinking that would integrate the different infrastructures as parts of a whole. How, then, could this activity be expanded to help students imagine more sustain-able, eco-centric alternatives? One possibility would be to give more time and space to the presentation part of the activity; students could have presented their proposals at the first-ever Sussex Sustainability Assembly that took place a few months after this activity. Engaging with senior management, and other campus groups, as knowledge producers and active participants in campus planning would allow students to bridge different domains of learning and engage in praxis. In the next chapter I show how student climate activists did exactly that by using their presentations at the Assembly to advocate for climate justice and a more holistically sustain-able campus.

Another possibility could be to build out the mapping activity itself, for example by asking students to create a final map that would include not only human-made infrastructures but also natural elements. Being located in the South Downs National Park, Sussex campus offers a unique opportunity for students to appreciate its natural beauty and critically study how the park ecosystem has been altered by the presence of the university. Creatively externalizing this learning through working on a 'pluriversal map'[21] could challenge students to think how other-than-human perspectives might be represented, also working with different materials or textures to expand on the two-dimensionality of drawing. Such a map could become a space for students from different disciplines to come together for transdisciplinary discussions, outside learning and collaborative designing, in order to imagine and advocate for sustain-able campus alternatives.

What would such a map look like from an eco-centric perspective that recognizes and represents the intrinsic value of the local ecosystem? How would it manifest the interrelation between Sussex campus and the South Downs? How would it express a definition of sustain-ability not as sustainable development but as 'designing a human community in such a way that its activities do not interfere with nature's inherent ability to sustain life' (Capra, 1996, p 15)? Extending the activity in these ways might also expand hopeful possibilities. As one student wrote in general about the Urban Futures module, of which this activity is a part,

> the module gave me the opportunity to develop new thoughts about how we might live in the future, but personally most important was that it gave me hope I can change something in the world. This I learned by repeatedly applying my knowledge in creative group works. Therefore, the most important thing I learned is that change is possible.

Here, critical hope was fostered through the articulation of critique and creativity.

Conclusion

The student's thoughts resonate with the ongoing debate about whether education and awareness raising about environmental issues actually leads to action, a question I explore in the next chapter. In this chapter, I have focused on critical-creative ways to teach students ecological knowledge that displaces mainstream sustainable development with decolonial and systems-oriented alternatives that argue for recognizing the interconnected and interdependent relationships between humans and the natural world. A discussion of Buen Vivir showed the contested ways in which ideas from the Global South have been inserted into national and global policy discourses and practices, while an introduction to complex systems thinking can help students to better understand the systemic nature of ecological challenges. Especially, the latter can cultivate student orientations towards embracing uncertainty – particularly relevant for the COVID crisis during which this book was written – and transdisciplinary learning. The learning activities of playing and designing serious games and mapping campus infrastructures engaged students with ecological challenges and responses to them through whole-person learning. This can lead to a politics of sustain-ability and eco-centrism that recognizes the intrinsic value of the natural world as well as human responsibility for ecological destruction and its repair.

6

Prefiguring Alternatives

It's a wintry day in February 2020 and I am attending a teach-out on unruly politics organized as part of the ongoing faculty strike at Sussex University. In contrast to the grey weather outside, the atmosphere in the room in the student union building, where about 50 people are sitting in a large circle and chatting, is warm and animated. After a brief introduction of teach-outs as disruptive educational spaces, a colleague from the Institute of Development Studies (IDS)[1] explains that unruly politics are recent forms of direct political engagement that are located outside formal political and institutional structures.[2] They often involve collective prefigurative actions that enact in the here and now changes that people want to make happen. He also talks about the contradictions of research and writing on unruly politics being a site of resistance, one that is located within the academic (and in the case of IDS, development) machinery. This is an ambivalent location with which I can identify. We then turn to our neighbours to discuss our own involvement in collective action, and share these experiences with the larger group, which mainly consists of students. They talk about their participation in movements such as the #Yosoy132 student protests in Mexico against unfair election coverage and for freedom of expression; participation in Occupy and Extinction Rebellion protests; the 2015 referendum in Colombia on the peace agreements; and fighting gentrification in East London. The speakers explain how most of these experiences have made them more committed to the various causes and changed their perceptions of authority.

This leads into a more tricky and contentious discussion of the current strike, which begins with staff members again explaining the reasons for the strike, but also what their experiences of standing on the picket lines have been.[3] Some students describe the strike as "a political re-education", while others discuss the question of students' multiple and sometimes contradictory identities as citizens and consumers. Can they both ask for refunds and support striking staff? How effective is it to be striking again when the first two strikes have not been successful? Could the union do more to acknowledge students' missed learning and to bring them along in building solidarity? Even though some of these questions remain unanswered, the teach-out models an alternative educational space where more horizontal relations between teachers and students lead to collective knowledge production. As one student comments afterwards, "teach-outs are an incredibly collaborative experience of political learning and one of my favourite times to be at the university. They are an alternative space of what the university could be outside of rigid assessment structures." Similarly, another student reflects that during teach-outs "people realize how teaching could be different, how it should be different to how it is now, where the teacher is in front of the class quickly delivering the content they have prepared and then rushing off to the next class."

The teach-out, and the strikes for better pensions, pay and working conditions during which it took place, are a good starting point for this chapter, in which I shift my attention to how students apply their learning inside and beyond the university to enact change. Faculty strikes are a potent opportunity for both students and staff to express their opposition to the neoliberal university and for students to show their solidarity with staff. While they can include intense conviviality on the picket line, strikes are also times when emotions run high, tempers flare and individuals are forced to assess their political positions. All of this is relevant for a critical-creative pedagogy. As one of its aims is to enable students to work towards alternative futures, the question of what, if anything, students do with the knowledge they are gaining at university is an important one. In exploring possible answers, this chapter shows how students are introduced to new concepts such as prefiguration, which refers to 'the creation of alternatives in the here and now [that] enacts an interplay between theory and practice' (Maeckelbergh, 2011, p 3). Rather than bringing about change through analysis, planning and predetermination, or through demanding future reforms from the state, for prefigurative practitioners 'the struggle and the goal, the real and the ideal, become one in the present' (p 4). Prefiguration can lead to student orientations of being hopeful and transgressive and to a politics of possibilities.

I begin the chapter by decentring employability approaches that aim to prepare students for post-university work and ask how skills and work experience programmes can be taught in critical-creative ways that challenge employability's market-focused agenda. I then investigate decolonial teaching and related student action to show not only how teaching shapes students but also how students are changing what and how they are being taught. Drawing on my own experiences of teaching a postgraduate module on activism, I go on to explore the possibilities of combining theory and practice to craft a critical-creative activist pedagogy. Finally, a description of climate change activism among Sussex students shows how they take their learning outside the classroom to demand and prefigure alternative futures.

Decentring employability

One of the most prominent aspects of the corporatization of universities described in Chapter 1 is the growth of the employability agenda, which focuses on students' workforce readiness and success. Indeed, in the UK employability has become a new HE buzzword (Arora, 2015), operating similarly to buzzwords in other domains that 'gain their purchase and power through their vague and euphemistic qualities, their capacity to embrace a multitude of possible meanings, and their normative resonance' (Cornwall, 2007, p 472). A report published by Universities UK and the Confederation of British Industries defines employability as 'a set of achievements, skills, understandings and personal attributes that make individuals more likely to gain employment and be successful in their chosen occupation ... Employability is a curriculum issue and the acquisition of subject specific knowledge and employability skills are complementary and not oppositional' (cited in Arora, 2015, p 637).

This quote shows that employability is seen by UK government and industry to cut across the entire curriculum and to complement rather than take away from academic learning. Both actors explain the need for employability with the failure of universities to produce graduates with the right skills. This is echoed in the media, where headlines such as 'Businesses Warn that Graduates Lack Skills' reinforce public perceptions about the inadequacies and irrelevance of universities (cited in Arora, 2015, p 643). All of this results in increasing pressure on universities to expand their employability work and to institutionalize dedicated staff and careers services, the teaching of practical skills, placements and other work experience programmes, and alumni mentoring networks. Advertising their employability programmes is becoming an integral part of universities' recruitment drives, reinforced through the use of indicators that track leaver destinations and feed into league tables (Chadha and Toner, 2017). There are two aspects of the employability agenda that are of particular relevance to challenge-focused social sciences: the acquisition of employability skills and work experience programmes.

There is no doubt that fostering students' capabilities and orientations that help to prepare them for life after university is an important part of university education. To deny this would be dishonest towards students' aspirations and ignorant of their needs, especially in light of the high debt burden faced by many graduating students and their families that makes earning money after, and increasingly during, university studies crucial.[4] And it would overlook that some elements of a critical-creative pedagogy, especially the project-based, applied and practical learning that is part of the praxis strand, are a mainstay of employability programmes. There is a significant difference, however, because praxis, as practice informed by theory, combines such teaching with developing students' critical thinking abilities. By contrast, a look at the employability skills outlined in the aforementioned report shows a glaring absence of such abilities. Skills such as 'self-management, positive attitude, enterprise and entrepreneurship, team-working, business and customer awareness and numeracy' are a far cry from the analytical questioning, critical self-reflection and social engagement that are the goals of university education according to critical educators (cited in Arora, 2015, p 637). These goals are being discredited and displaced as the employability agenda becomes ever more central for university managers. A focus on employability is also increasingly shaping what students want to learn and how they are expecting this knowledge to be delivered and assessed, resulting in a Freirean banking-style education. Finally, a dominant focus on employability, situated within broader value-for-money discourses, contributes to students' perceptions of themselves as customers and of staff as service providers. This in turn reinforces transactional employability-focused programmes, to the detriment of transformational and emancipatory teaching.

In the challenge-focused social sciences, and in global development in particular, employability takes on particular contours. As I have shown previously, many students enter their studies with plans to work for mainstream development organizations after graduating. When critical teaching makes students aware of these institutions' shortcomings, they begin to question their former aspirations. As one student explained, "you learn where not to engage, where to draw the line, such as working for the UN". Becoming disillusioned with the development industry often goes along with becoming more interested in smaller, local organizations or grassroots initiatives, although some students cannot help but question every action they learn about. One student observed that "I don't want to be very cynical but every time you hear about somebody who wants to do something good, start an NGO, you ask 'are you part of the problem?'" Like many others, this student came to 're-envision development practice beyond the interventionist approach to helping ... [and] to focus on approaches based on solidarity and justice' (Cameron et al, 2013, p 356). Here, practice itself becomes interrogated, alongside its relationship to theory.

Given the problem-focused nature of global development, this relationship is more dynamic and entangled in this field than in other social sciences. It therefore shows more clearly the challenges posed by collaborations among critical scholars, policy makers and practitioners, with their different goals, organizational and methodological modes of operation and philosophical and ontological orientations. This also opens up the question of what is considered valid knowledge, where academic knowledge can be perceived as impractical, irrelevant and slow, while academics regard practitioners as uncritical, instrumental and donor driven. Further complexities arise from North–South dynamics that still structure global development and heightening power, knowledge and resource access differentials. Within this complex ensemble, there is scope for the critical teaching of skills that prompts students to question the development tools and methods they are learning about and experimenting with in university classrooms.

At Sussex, this happens in a popular third-year undergraduate module called Development Tools and Skills, taught by my colleague Lyndsay Mclean, who is also a consultant working on gender and inclusion, gender-based violence and children and youth. The module is built around students learning different tools, approaches and skills that are used in the development and related sectors to identify, design and evaluate programmes, including theories of change, stakeholder analysis, log frames and risk assessments. McLean's teaching style aims to approximate a professional work environment through an intense hands-on and group-work approach and assignments that mirror professional activities. However, even in such practice-based classes it is important that 'the managerial procedures of the mainstream development industry are [not] offered up as constitutive of what it means to practice development' (Cameron et al, 2013, p 356). In this regard, the Tools and Skills module handbook explains that

> many of the methods and approaches we will address in this course are Euro-centric and intellectually problematic. But the objective of this module is to make sure that you understand how these methods are used in the development world, that you are able to use them and to recognise their strengths and weaknesses. This will provide a foundation for the second objective of the module which is to start to unpack the epistemological and ontological problems that these approaches entail, critique their relationship to a particular view of what 'development' is and consider alternative approaches which de-centre and challenge these Northern, positivist approaches.

Such alternative approaches can range from human-centred design and social network analysis to participatory approaches and outcome mapping. The module therefore joins critical analysis and learning-by-doing, whereby students come to interrogate development tools through applying them to an example development scenario. At the start of term, students are allocated into groups and given a project that is often informed by McLean's own work. Through ongoing group work, students deepen their knowledge of that scenario and apply the different tools and approaches. They thus learn about the benefits and challenges of tools and methods through their use, rather than just thinking about them in the abstract or reading about their shortcomings. Each week, as well as in their two assessments, students have to critique the tools they have used, both by engaging critical readings and by reflecting on their own practice. While this does not escape the rendering technical that comes with development interventions (Li, 2007), it subjects this rendering to critical analysis.

The module was frequently mentioned by students in their journey interviews as not only simulating the high-pressure, deadline-driven and team-focused work of social change organizations but, more importantly, giving students an understanding of the language and tools of the development industry that they need in order to be able to challenge things. One student said that "without this module we would not understand what needs to change", while another liked that the module asked them to also think about alternative approaches: "if this tool is not effective, what do you propose, including looking at tools from other countries". For a third student, it was important that they could explore different methods and their limitations in a safe and supportive classroom space, "otherwise it could be soul-crushing in the workplace if we were not prepared for [these challenges]". She liked that these explorations were guided by a convenor who is a practising consultant and "real and honest about [her] struggles of working with DfID [Department for International Development]" and other mainstream organizations. These comments show that students appreciate McLean's critical-creative teaching that combines practical learning with critical reflection on this learning. Such teaching can have a significant impact on the second component of the employability agenda, which are work experience programmes.

Work experiences

By work experiences, I refer to a plethora of activities offered to students as part of their university education, including internships, work placements, service learning and volunteering (abroad) opportunities. Calling them work experiences acknowledges students' multifaceted labour during these programmes, whose physically and emotionally immersive environments connect students directly to the phenomena being studied rather than merely thinking about them. Over the years, four broad approaches to such experiential learning have emerged (Weil and McGill, 1989). The first focuses on its connection to employment, the second examines how it can shape education programmes, the third sees it as a way towards emancipatory social and community change and the final approach emphasizes learners' personal growth. While many programmes might start with more alternative orientations, increasingly it is the first and last approaches that are dominating university thinking within the hegemonic employability context (Langdon and Agyeyomah, 2014). This shift marks a crucial difference between work experiences and those aspects of critical-creative pedagogy, particularly its whole-person learning strand, that regard students' past and present experiences as an important part of students' own knowledge creation. Because whole-person learning focuses on students exploring alternatives to mainstream interventions, work experiences with organizations that question and destabilize the status quo are best placed to stimulate such explorations. By contrast, employability-focused work experiences that often take place in mainstream organizations can reinforce hegemonic relationships between students and host groups.

These problematic relations are particularly salient when Northern students travel to faraway places 'to help', which legitimizes unskilled young people from the Global North providing services and solutions to the Global South (Simpson, 2004). This not only undermines local efforts and may impact on livelihoods, but often can reinforce Northerners' feelings of importance and superiority, and more generally replicates hierarchical international development relations. The short-term nature of many international work placements means that meaningful relationships that could lead to deeper learning cannot be established. This can also lead to further marginalization, when local immersion, however superficial, becomes a source of authority for students who feel that they have been there and can now speak for locals, who are silenced in the process (Pedwell, 2012). The results are inappropriate 'quick moves that students (and teachers) will often make from observation to narratives that claim knowledge or expertise', and from there to action (MacDonald, 2014, p 218).

Because work experiences are located within the institutional constraints of universities, the good intentions of educators who design them are often subsumed by bureaucratic calculations (Cameron et al, 2018). Where legal, liability and risk considerations of university administrators dominate, they undermine the pedagogical and decolonial efforts of educators, which can erode trust and thwart the potential for mutual collaboration with host organizations. The danger is that 'international experiential learning programs, without employing critical self-reflexivity or confronting dominant ideologies, are inherently colonial with their impetus to know and encounter difference and to experience the other' (p 10). In international encounters, students must therefore go beyond analysing their own positionalities and privileges to also look at historical complicities and legacies that might connect their home and host countries (MacDonald, 2014). As programmes are usually set up to benefit students first and foremost, they can place extra burdens on host communities and organizations. Even when placements take place closer to home, the exploitative potential of using marginalized communities as resources to teach affluent students does not disappear (Huish, 2015).

Students' own accounts add nuance to these critiques and emphasize the two-way relationship between classroom learning and work experiences. On the one hand, especially international volunteering can galvanize young people to learn more; there was more than one student who told me that they had come to study at Sussex after their own volunteering stints, usually during a gap year, left them with misgivings and questions that then motivated their studies and gave them personal relevance. One student was particularly articulate about her doubts when she realized that orphanage or school walls were being painted six times a year by young Westerners who had raised tens of thousands of pounds to travel abroad, money which could have been better spent on local initiatives. Admittedly, many of these trips are organized by commercial companies not interested in their customers' learning or meaningful engagement, but these volunteering experiences nevertheless shape young people's perceptions of the Global South. It takes careful consideration and ethical commitment to ensure that university field experience programmes do not become development tourism by another name.

On the other hand, having *in situ* experiences can remind students of why they decided to study in the first place and rekindle their passions for change work. One student told me that after studying for several years she had come to feel detached and demotivated from what had brought her initially to global development, which had been working with a local NGO in Nicaragua. Building on the work she was doing with a Brighton refugee organization and a campus refugee advocacy group, she decided after much soul searching to volunteer in a refugee camp on a Greek island, although this went against her beliefs that she should work for refugee rights in the UK and support initiatives abroad from afar. However, when the opportunity arose to work with a small, local organization, she went to see the conditions of refugees in Greece. She reflected that "going to Greece pushed me back into wanting to be as active as I can be"; it also reanimated her work with refugees' mental health back in the UK and gave her a better understanding of the situations people have to face during their hazardous journeys to the UK. Upon graduating from a development-focused MA, she set up an organization connecting asylum seekers with volunteers for English classes and in the process changing the conversation about refugees.

Another student observed that she was more critical of her work placement in a UK-based gender consultancy organization because of her studies, being able to identify a lack of intersectionality in its practices and reports. Thus, critical thinking in the classroom can sharpen and enhance students' learning during their work experiences. Last but not least, these experiences can also help students to become more certain of what they want to do after graduation. In this regard, a student who spent eight months on a self-organized internship with a research organization in South-East Asia reflected that

> 'it was integral to me really figuring out what I want to do after my degree. Learning how politically and financially influenced research can be, I began to ask myself what role donor organizations, funders and host organizations played in influencing research and its outcomes. I think gaining experience in the field is so important in order to contextualize learnings from the course. I think gaining that perspective has allowed me to think more critically and with more conviction than just by studying.'

Her work experience led the student to co-found a student mental health organization, but also to undertake a graduate programme with a major auditing company. She told me that "I am still very, very apprehensive about the graduate programme I'll be taking on. I think I have realized though that for me it will be the best way to ever have a chance of making change in the corporate sphere, in terms of big business' role in development." For her, it was working in the belly of the beast where she hoped to make a difference, while also realizing that there was no guarantee of changing things (cf Kapoor, 2004). These varying accounts show that work experiences and the whole-person and praxis-focused learning they facilitate, if buttressed by critical reflection, can allow students to apply, question and enrich their classroom education in a two-way relationship between both. For this to happen to the fullest degree possible, it is important to consider where work experiences take place and how students learn from them.

As argued earlier, placement locations matter geographically, with, especially, overseas experiences potentially replicating hierarchical development binaries. It also matters institutionally, with university administrators preferring large, established organizations that are easier to verify for insurance and risk-reduction purposes. These also often maintain the status quo, while smaller, local organizations and social movements can be better for students to experience, and to support where appropriate, local struggles for social transformations. Another option would be for students to remain in their classrooms and aim for a 'stationary global connectivity' (Huish, 2015, p 2). Huish describes an undergraduate class where Canadian students supported the struggles of North Korean refugees and learned through fundraising, organizing and coordinating events rather than travelling and volunteering. Students 'approached the topic through a path of curiosity and humility as non-experts ... positioned as allies to those in need rather than as experts on the issue' (p 7). This was partly by pedagogical design but also resulted from the scarcity of information and scholarly research about North Korea, which meant that students had to rely on activist organizations to learn about the situation there. The module also had creative elements in that students crafted speeches, music, photos and a social media campaign to inform others about their work.

This raises the question of what role technology can play in potentially establishing global classrooms, a possibility made more urgent by the COVID-19 pandemic.[5] However, just having a technological infrastructure in place does not guarantee learning; instead it is important to ask how learning spaces can be opened up in meaningful ways. This necessitates the intentional design, integration and facilitation of technologies to support learning aims, which can encompass communication among students for information exchange or, more ambitiously, enable student collaboration and co-creation of knowledge (Lock, 2015). Students who are 'committed to learning something together and cooperating in the achievement of a goal that they cannot achieve individually' can make use of collaborative online tools, which have the potential to 'create an awareness of "us" and generate a climate of belonging' (Manso and Garzon, 2011, p 33). To foster such a sense of togetherness, students' virtual engagements need to be sustained over a period of time and based on an understanding of the affordances of different technologies, which many educators have been developing in the COVID teaching context. Besides more technical questions of availability, access and skills, other capabilities such as cross-cultural communication, an openness to diverse viewpoints and a willingness to learn from others might be even more important in global classrooms, which can generate insights that go beyond interacting with in-class peers.

Support for student work experiences is most often provided through a before and after approach, where preparatory teaching should include students developing a strong grounding in ethics, and post-experience work usually focuses on written assessments (Merlino and Steward, 2015). In this approach, student engagement with teachers during a placement is more perfunctory, ensuring that students are safe and indeed participating in the specified activities. By contrast, critical-creative teaching calls for an ongoing reflective learning cycle that does not treat the work experience itself as a decontextualized time apart. Instead, such a cycle asks students for continuous analysis of their experiences and, especially, of the 'disorienting dilemmas' that are bound to occur as students apply their learning outside the classroom (Langdon and Agyeyomah, 2014, p 56). It is not the work experience itself that does the teaching, but its embeddedness in a continuous process of reflection–action–reflection, coupled with hyper-self-reflexivity (Kapoor, 2004). The latter is important because self-reflexivity alone can produce merely descriptive accounts of work done, lead to superficial recounting of personal experiences or 'dead-end in the simplified narrative of becoming a better person/citizen' (Langdon and Agyeyomah, 2014, p 52). Instead, Freirean praxis and critical consciousness lead students to reflect on their positionalities and privileges, to interrogate and unsettle power relations that flow from these and to destabilize how they might see themselves as helpers or, indeed, saviours.

There are, then, many pitfalls to work experiences, especially when they are enacted within employability agendas that mainly focus on developing students' work-ready skills. However, when harnessing values and practices of justice and solidarity and practices of hyper-self-reflexivity, work experiences can become modes of learning 'that engage students with the complexity of the contemporary world and with challenges of contemporary problems … [Students] are confronted with a world that will bear the consequences of their actions and with which they need to negotiate and collaborate to create ethical futures' (Facer, 2018a, p 15). The whole-person learning and praxis strands of critical-creative pedagogy can provide valuable ideas and tools to work towards fulfilling this potential. Moving beyond work experiences, there are other, more disruptive ways in which students have been extending their learning beyond university classrooms.

Decolonial movements

bell hooks has described teaching as a form of political activism that 'enables transgressions – a movement against and beyond boundaries' (1994, p 12). Teaching students to transgress, to go beyond the limits of what is normative and acceptable, implies questioning disciplinary, institutional and social boundaries as a central strategy of critical-creative pedagogy. The aim is to encourage students to trespass into imagined alternatives that destabilize personal certainties, question academic orthodoxies and challenge the social status quo. One area where this has happened most visibly is the movement to decolonize universities and their curricula. In Chapter 2 I described a first-year core module for all development-related students in the school of Global Studies called Colonialism and After, which many students find both eye opening and unsettling. A complement to this is a third-year specialist option called Decolonial Movements, which introduces students to social and political movements that try to de-link from the legacies of coloniality, understood as the persisting impacts of colonialism.

Taught by my colleague Anna Laing, who herself is engaged in research and activist work with indigenous peoples in Bolivia, the module combines critical analysis of key theoretical perspectives, such as decoloniality, intersectionality and subalternity, with examining diverse ways of decolonizing knowledge. Students also learn about emancipatory struggles for alternative futures, including Latin American indigenous autonomy movements, Black Lives Matter and feminist struggles. Drawing on formats like films, indigenous poetry and activist blogs and declarations that are marginalized within Eurocentric knowledge frames, the module not only introduces students to activist voices but also decentres written texts as the sole source of authoritative knowledge. By making such marginalized perspectives and decolonial movements the central focus of her module, Laing moves beyond the 'just add and stir approach' that is still common to many decolonizing curricula efforts but insufficient to dispel Eurocentrism (Langdon and Agyeyomah, 2014). Still, Laing acknowledges her discomfort at the potential danger that her own White British 'authority and legitimacy shape and redefine what is meant by the decolonial project in the classroom ... [and] could actually work to re-embed the hegemonic geo-politics of knowledge production' (2020, p 3). However, indigenous scholars such as Cree/Salteaux/Dakota Shauneen Pete argue that decolonizing work in the academy 'is not my work alone; the longer I do this work the more I am convinced that this is white work' (2018, p 187). Decoloniality cannot only come from subaltern positions, while, conversely, non-Western and Global South perspectives are not necessarily decolonial or emancipatory.

Laing argues that decolonizing includes substantial reflection on what is being taught and how it is taught. As part of her module, she conducted a mind-mapping exercise with students to decolonize teaching in the School of Global Studies, in order 'to challenge the institutional authority that academic faculty hold over students by recognizing the value of student standpoints, particularly on issues where they may have more experiential understanding of how colonial structures of power, control and hegemony work to disenfranchise certain [students] over others' (2020, p 3). Students proposed ideas such as normalizing diverse teaching staff, using decolonial pedagogies in the classroom and ensuring that students draw on decolonial scholars in their essays. Suggestions to introduce more creative and innovative teaching tools and to encourage forms of praxis are especially relevant for critical-creative pedagogy. For example, during a week studying the history of decolonial solidarity movements from Bandung[6] and the non-aligned movement to pan-Africanism and the World Social Forum, students could themselves start to engage in acts of solidarity with decolonial campaigns. As one student remarked, "it's not enough to just speak from an ivory tower ... you have to actually engage in making a change" (cited in Laing, 2020, p 12).

The module was frequently mentioned as transformational during my journey interviews. One student described how it completely changed his thinking towards "less linear and conventional ideas of development ... Having had to unlearn in third year was truly beneficial but I wish I had known sooner." Several students agreed that the decolonial approach of the module resulted in them questioning some of their critical ideas about development, as they were introduced to alternative approaches emerging from marginalized struggles. They explained that the teaching about (post-)colonialism they had received prior to this module had not sufficiently shown them the persistent effects of colonialism, and especially that there are movements actively working to undo colonial legacies. This was not only the case for White students.

One student from the Global South recounted that "the module assured me that it was possible to follow a path which uses creative pedagogic approaches to work towards positive change, outside a more Westernized approach to education". Another student told me how the module "challenged me as a person as I looked at my own learning experience as a black student studying international development. I realized that I am part of the colonial system and that blew my mind. I have the same knowledge and value set as everyone else because I have been part of the system for 18 years." She had originally intended to go to her family's African home country after graduation "to help", but decided to further her studies in the UK to better understand the implications of her saviourism. Decolonial teaching can therefore contribute to students 'attain[ing] an awareness that implicates their own values, biases, senses of entitlement, and previous training and upbringing in the entire educational process itself' (Cameron et al, 2018, p 3). But students also felt challenged to ask 'what can you do about the situation?' and described the module as a more hopeful and positive end to their studies.

Decolonizing the curriculum is of course one area where students have actively protested and campaigned for change. Most prominently, the Rhodes Must Fall movement that started in 2015 in South Africa received widespread attention and was taken up by students around the world.[7] At Oxford University, students demanded the removal of a Rhodes statue from Oriel College, which was resisted for some time in part due to pressure from alumni donors (Srinivasan, 2016), but was finally voted for by university governors a result of the Black Lives Matter protests in 2020.[8] These campus movements 'have challenged HE institutions for disproportionally representing White, male Western voices and consequently marginalizing other voices and forms of knowledge, as well as for re-embedding structural inequalities that create barriers for some students and faculty to get an equitable institutional experience' (Laing, 2020, p 4). At Sussex there have been several student- and faculty-led initiatives to decolonize curricula, including working groups and a three-day workshop in collaboration with School of Oriental and African Studies, London on Decolonial Transformations: Imagining, Practising, Collaborating, where the body-mapping workshop that opened Chapter 2 took place. Student action has been central in these initiatives, with the student society Decolonise Sussex being a key actor, organizing student–staff fora as well as privilege and creative arts workshops.

One of these initiatives was the Co-producing Sussex Curriculum project, which, in its own words, was 'created to be disruptive, through experimental intervention into our pedagogical practices' that aimed to engage students as active agents in their own learning.[9] The project brought together a small number of staff and student volunteers for informal interactions that forged closer links between them. As a prefigurative practice, whereby workshop participants enacted the non-hierarchical relations they wanted to see in the classroom, projects like this can give students a sense of hope and agency (Ojala, 2017). One participating student described how she and two fellow students proposed a comprehensive alternative reading list, comprised mainly of academics in the Global South. While the student clearly saw value in being able to offer input in this way and in connecting with staff members more directly, one staff participant was concerned that the project 'exploits [students'] knowledge and time with no financial remuneration or reward, re-embedding the power inequalities between student and educator that it seeks to challenge' (quoted in Laing, 2020, p 11). Another wondered whether the project promised things that could not be delivered in the face of logistical constraints such as difficult access to non-English texts, lack of funds for translation and time pressures on teaching staff. If alternative visions could not be realized, would students feel let down and faculty become disillusioned? In addition, because meaningful decolonization asks educators to unlearn their own academic training and remake their pedagogical practice, it 'is unlikely to be popular at a time when lecturing staff are increasingly overworked' (p 11).

Such campaigns can also be co-opted by university administrators, who see them conveniently feeding into top-down managerial inclusiveness, multicultural or internationalization agendas, with de-radicalizing effects. While these dangers are ever present, a generative theory shows that they do not condemn such initiatives from the outset. Potential appropriation demands vigilance and self-awareness but is not a necessary effect of decolonial work. Rather, because that work is linked to an interrogation of power relations, it frequently involves contestations of and opposition to bureaucratic agendas and systems. It also involves praxis. According to Bolivian subaltern theorist and activist Silvia Rivera Cusicanqui, 'there can be no discourse of decolonization, no theory of decolonization, without a decolonizing practice' (2012, p 100). Practice is frequently brought into university classrooms through case studies or guest speakers, both of which remain at a theoretical level. A more involved way is the teaching of activism itself, which I have done since 2014.

Teaching activism?

I was assigned the MA-level Activism for Social Change and Development module when I first joined Sussex in 2014, with the freedom to completely redesign it. I used this opportunity to realize a long-held vision for a module where theory and practice would complement each other. While the first half of the module introduces students to concepts and case studies of activism, including the already-mentioned unruly politics, in the second half they undertake group work to design an activist campaign and produce a report for assessment. In designing the module, I was aware that teaching activism can be regarded as too radical by university administrators, colleagues or the public, or as too conformist by practising activists who see it as an elitist exercise that diverts energies from real action (Hodkinson, 2009). Both positions are based on a misrecognition of what activist pedagogies are trying to do, which is to give students concepts, tools and critical hope by showing them what has been done and what can be done. In such modules, students learn about activist work 'as a process of challenges and moral dilemmas more than as an experience that brings clear answers and solutions to social problems' (Huish, 2015, p 10). Students also recognize the various forms of agency they themselves have to engage with structures of power, and can experiment with how they might enact this agency. Having taught this class for several years now, in this section I draw on close to 40 campaign reports, as well as students' personal reflections on the pedagogical, methodological and interpersonal aspects of the campaign design activity, to reflect on the potentials and pitfalls of a critical-creative activist pedagogy.

The premise of the module is that activism, broadly defined as active work by individuals and collectives for emancipatory and transformative change,[10] can take many forms, from day-to-day encounters such as being handed a leaflet downtown, to receiving online campaign information or calls to e-mail one's MP via social-networking platforms, to becoming actively involved in a campaign. Such actions can be planned and organized or random and eclectic, and students may ignore them or can be moved by them emotionally and physically. Throughout the class, students consider such different approaches and responses, often drawing on their own experiences. Class discussions often focus on who an activist is, especially in the context of the academy, and what that means for educator and student subjectivities. While each year some students are completely new to activism, others identify as allies, individuals who use their own power and privilege 'to advocate for anti-oppressive and anti-racist social justice project' (Thomas and Chandrasakera, 2014, p 103). Students further develop their understandings through studying historical and contemporary experiments in which activists fight for and implement alternative models to tackle inequalities and achieve social and economic justice. The theoretical part of the module ends with a class on alternative worlds that introduces students to the work of Gibson-Graham and pluriversal and prefigurative politics, and invites them to consider their roles in imagining and building alternative futures.

This leads directly into the second half of the term, during which students apply their theoretical knowledge to the development of their own activist campaign, which students often describe as 'bringing the course to life'. Campaign work begins with a design workshop during which student groups iterate ideas for the target of their campaigns, using techniques such as brainstorming, random association, collective idea generation[11] and mind mapping. Like the design workshops described at the end of Chapter 3, this introductory workshop is supported by thinking and making materials and encourages students to draw, map and visualize. Once groups have chosen their topics, they develop their campaigns through a series of hands-on workshops that introduce various campaign tools, from problem-tree and stakeholder analysis, SMART goals and budgeting to monitoring/evaluation frameworks. Like McLean in the Tools and Skills module described earlier, I explain to students that these are mainstream tools and that, after experimenting with them in the full awareness of their origins and limitations, they can decide how useful they are, or not.

In the personal reflections students write as part of the assessment, they must critically evaluate the tools, and while some find their institutional origins too problematic, others write that they have been helpful to move their campaigns from vague ideas to finished plans, to organize thoughts and actions and to frame decision making. Especially, the problem tree, an image of which must be included in the final report, is a helpful visual device that allows students to unpack the roots, causes and effects of the issues they are targeting, which are often broad and undefined at the outset of the campaign. This can become the basis for a solutions tree (Image 6.1). Applying these tools, groups refine and focus their ideas, understanding of the issues and best approaches to addressing them. This is not a purely hypothetical exercise, as groups have to research their topic extensively, identify existing possible collaborators and funding sources and draw up realistic budgets and timelines. That they do not go on to approach organizations, apply for funding or implement their campaigns does not diminish the work,[12] and the extent to which campaigns are properly contextualized and grounded is one of the assessment criteria.

The module involves intense group work over several hours each week. I ask students to write down their personal and professional backgrounds, skills, experiences and interest and on the basis of this information pre-select the groups to ensure experiential diversity and evenly distribute expertise. Because it is offered to MA-level students across a range of programmes, from anthropology to global development to gender, human rights, environmental policy and media practice, the module brings together students with various academic and professional backgrounds. In addition, MA programmes at Sussex have a high number of international students, many coming from

Image 6.1: Solutions tree designed by students for the Teach British Colonialism campaign

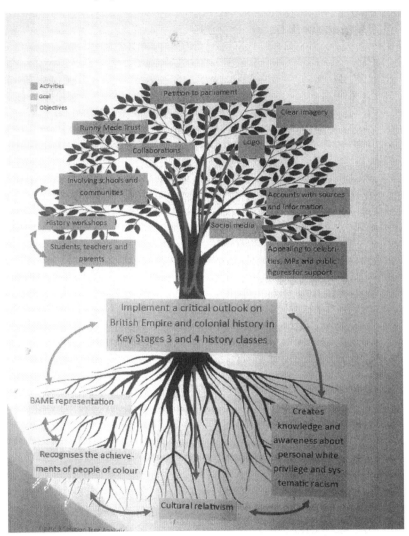

Photo credit: Author, used with permission.

the Global South supported by scholarships, and the groups therefore have to negotiate different learning and working styles as well as diverse understandings of concepts such as decolonization or political work. In their personal reflections, students often write that as a result they learn how to be more open to others' ideas, achieve compromises and agreements, overcome frustrations and resolve conflicts; patience is a word frequently used as an orientation students cultivate with each other. Group work is seen by many as an opportunity for personal growth, based on students unlearning some of their established ways and reorienting themselves towards the future.[13]

Students' campaign work is assessed in the form of a written campaign report produced by each group and an individual reflective account. This is a crucial component of the module's critical-creative activist pedagogy, as teaching that combines theory and practice cannot (only) be assessed by conventional essays.[14] Developing the activist campaign is when most of the experiential and praxis learning takes place, which needs to be reflected both in the form of the assessment and in the grade given for the report, which is shared by all members of the group to reflect collective efforts and responsibility. In addition, the personal reflections of each student on the pedagogical, methodological and interpersonal aspects of the campaign work enable peer assessment, whereby each group member evaluates their own and other group members' work.[15]

Students become collective producers of knowledge and its practical application, as evidenced by the high quality of the reports that show students' substantial engagement with their campaign topics. A quantitative analysis of the 39 campaign reports designed to date reveals a commonality of themes reflecting students' interests and passions. Nine projects addressed issues relevant to Sussex University, including housing, sexism on campus, the commodification of education and campus spaces, digital inequality and dependency and the use of slave labour. Seven projects advocated for changes in how the British public, and especially Brighton residents, learn about and interact with refugees and migrants, ranging from setting up a community cooking club, children's play classes and awareness-raising events. Six projects targeted homelessness in Brighton, through providing better services, advocating for the council to fulfil its legal commitments and educating people about the complexities of homelessness.

These projects also show the intense localization of the campaigns that resonates with previous observations of students wanting to 'dig where they stand' (Gebrial, 2018, p 34). Seventy per cent of the projects were based either on Sussex campus or in Brighton, with the remainder being UK based and only three international campaigns. This is especially remarkable because in many campaign groups at least half of the members were non-UK students, and addressing local issues came from their own experiences of living in Brighton. For example, international students from the Global South would frequently express their shock at the sight of rough sleepers, which does not correspond to the image of the UK they previously held. Similarly, the presence of refugees and immigrants in Brighton, as a City of Sanctuary with whom Sussex as a University of Sanctuary has close connections, is something students are aware off. There are also a number of student societies that work with local homeless and refugee support organizations. Not surprisingly, in 2021 several campaigns addressed COVID-related issues, such as digital exclusions experienced by some students and the gendered unequal care work exposed and exacerbated by the pandemic. Other campaign targets were workplace-related discrimination, such as mental health stigmatization and the gender wage gap, and reflected the participation of a significant number of students with professional backgrounds in the module. There were also four campaigns related to environmental sustainability, especially around food production, consumption and waste, and four campaigns focused on changing education. The latter are of particular interest to a critical-creative pedagogy, together with campaigns that made use of artistic methods.

Several projects directly engaged creative and artistic expressions. One group proposed to organize workshops during which Brighton artists would guide homeless people in creating their own artworks, as a way of expressing their experiences, stories and hopes. The art would be sold during a day-long festival. The aim of the (In)visible Artists campaign was to use the arts to bring homeless and housed people together, encourage conversations, increase understanding and combat stigma and social isolation. The campaign also involved public performances, where on the day of the festival volunteers would lie down on sidewalks wrapped in black bin bags, to show the negative connotations of homelessness in unsettling ways. The performers would invite residents to the festival, where they could meet homeless people as artists. The juxtaposition between social outcasts and artistic creators could encourage residents to query their own attitudes towards homeless people and thereby engage in 'ontological reframing to produce the ground of possibility' on which action can take place (Gibson-Graham, 2008, p 620).

Educating people around homelessness was also the aim of Homefull campaign. Because a member of the group had designed a serious game as part of his final-year undergraduate studies the previous year,[16] the group decided to organize participatory workshops during which former and current homeless people, organizations working with them and Brighton residents would design a board game as a creative, non-linear way to make people aware of the complexities of homelessness and to envision responses to it. The aim was to position all participants as both holders and receivers of knowledge, while also acknowledging existing ignorance about homelessness. The workshops would produce a number of theme-based game cards that would represent the personal experiences of participants, as well as structural, social and governance aspects of homelessness. The game would be launched to the Brighton public on World Homelessness Day, and the students also planned to make it available on the internet. Both campaigns show students' creativity in bringing together insights from different domains, generating new ideas and applying them to areas where they could be useful. For Gibson-Graham (2008), this is a technique of doing thinking that can be used to cultivate oneself as an ethical subject of new possibilities.

Artistic creation was central to a student group that constituted itself as the Active Empathy Collective and proposed a campaign called Yarl's Wood Speaks. In response to a hunger strike of women detainees at the Yarl's Wood immigration removal centre who were protesting against inhumane conditions,[17] the campaign aimed to raise public awareness of the UK immigration system through an interactive art exhibition on the theme of home, belonging and freedom. Its central focus was the use of testimony by former detainees, participants in a detainee visitor programme and visitors of the exhibit. Using a feminist approach, the campaign conceived of testimony as an active process of meaning-making, a personal and political platform for enacting change and a catalyst for generating self-reflection, empathy and a critical collective consciousness towards immigration injustices. The campaign's objective was to make these experiences actionable by connecting people to relevant advocacy organizations and urging them to contact their MPs to pressure Parliament to extend legal protections for refugees and terminate indefinite detentions. The campaign report included a mock-up of the gallery space, throughout which exhibition items had been thoughtfully placed to enhance visceral audience engagement and participation.

There were also a number of campaigns that targeted various aspects of education from a decolonial perspective. The campaign Teach British Colonialism advocated to change the current 'white-washing' in the UK's secondary school history curriculum, which makes minimal reference to slavery, colonialism and empire. Proposing a pilot project with two Brighton secondary schools, the campaign aimed to combat institutional racism and privileged ignorance and bring about structural change through a petition to Parliament to review the national history curriculum. The group also planned a social media outreach campaign, and its final report included sample social media posts, showing non-White activists and historical figures, such as Olaudah Equiano, whose autobiography I mentioned in Chapter 4. A group that included a Mexican student campaigned to decolonize STEM education at schools in Chiapas. The aim was to recognize and incorporate the scientific knowledge and achievements of indigenous communities and to allow Chiapas youth to learn about STEM subjects without compromising their cultural heritage.

A third campaign, called Newversity, drew on weak theorizing and prefiguration to redefine the role of universities in UK society. Departing from a critique of the neoliberal university model, the campaign proposed to bring academics, students, local communities and policy makers together in horizontal and open-ended workshops in five locations across the UK to co-write a collective manifesto laying out alternative ways of teaching and researching. Similar to the Co-constructing the Curriculum project and the teach-out described earlier, the students imagined the workshops to prefigure alternative pedagogies, which included unlearning existing teaching strategies and operating without guarantees and predetermined goals. The students thereby directly applied theoretical knowledge and conceptual learning to the practical design of their campaign, resulting in praxis-focused learning.

In their personal reflections, students frequently described their learning journey from initial reluctance and anxiety about the module's campaign design component, which is a completely new activity for many of them, to seeing that it is possible, to eventually realizing the work. Some of them articulated how the activity allowed them to reflect on what activism is and what it can achieve, as well as on their personal roles, "not by reading about it" but by aiming to practise it. Those students who think about engaging with activism outside university because they "have had a simulated experience guided by a teacher" realized that "being an activist can only happen through action". Others felt that they had gained valuable confidence and skills for their life journeys, including future work. Even though enhancing employability is not one of the module's aims, undertaking praxis work endows students with capabilities and orientations that many see as useful for future endeavours. This shows that critical–creative pedagogy contributes to preparing students for life after university, without subscribing to neoliberal agendas. On the contrary, teaching (about) activism can impart knowledge that challenges the current HE regime and its conformist campus culture (Huish, 2013). This becomes especially clear when talking to students who do engage in activism outside the classroom.

Student activists

I came across many examples of student activism in my research, where in their journey interviews students commented on their involvement in campaigns ranging from supporting refugee students to campaigning against sweatshop labour or for better student housing, often through student societies that connected them to like-minded individuals. Sometimes identification with activism happened through the articulation of learning and practice, as in the case of a student who came to recognize her work lobbying Sussex University leadership to become an affiliate of Electronics Watch, a technology industry monitoring organization, as activism after writing an essay on the topic and subsequent conversations with the lecturer.[18] Other struggles have included students occupying buildings to protest the privatization of campus services or the deportation of a fellow student, demanding that the university divest from unethical financial instruments or fossil fuel use, supporting staff during pension and pay strikes and organizing a rent strike during the COVID-19 pandemic. This has often been in direct opposition to senior management and outside the purview of a student union that at times has been seen as too conformist.

However, there is one issue in particular that has galvanized young people's activism in recent years in powerful and visible ways. Climate change activism brings together many of the themes articulated in previous chapters. It is *the* contemporary challenge, *the* defining condition of our age, caused by anthropogenic design. Addressing it calls for pluriversal and complex systems thinking, including fundamental changes to current economic systems. It is inherently future oriented by actively demanding alternative ways of knowing, being and doing – of running the economy, governing the planet, living everyday lives and engaging with others. Describing climate change activism through the lens of participating Sussex students is therefore a fitting final activity to reflect on how critical-creative pedagogy can enable students not only to better understand global challenges but also to imagine and start enacting alternative responses to them.

The importance of educating young people about climate change is undeniable, while a lack of environmental education has been identified as a predictor for climate change scepticism among young adults (Ojala, 2015). This education can take various forms. When I asked Sussex students about the influence their university studies had on their climate activism, it was general contextual and critical knowledge rather than specific information about climate change that had shaped their engagements. This was most prominently expressed in the concept of climate justice through which all students framed their activism, and which is informed by the eco-pedagogies described in the previous chapter.[19] One student explained that learning about issues such as identity, gender, class and race had given her and fellow activists a language of inclusiveness and intersectionality that informed the way they wanted to organize themselves and others. Learning about geographical scales, political economy and debt relations also offered important conceptual scaffoldings. Another student told me how learning about environmental justice, and its connections to colonialism and capitalism, helped her to clarify what principles and values were important to her. Being at university also instilled confidence and provided access to resources, through student societies and personal student loans, which were seen as essential for successful organizing. As one student explained, "university is the perfect space to disrupt and partake in activism. It allows you to be radical." Another argued that "I've been able to do this activist work so relentlessly because I'm a student. The academia is enough to make me angry, and my spare time is enough to make me active."[20]

The School of Global Studies, where all the students I interviewed have been studying, was described by students as being particularly sociable, including having access to a physical space where students would bump into each other, study together and have discussions.[21] University life was therefore recognized as an opportunity that afforded and provoked activist involvement, at the same time as students were frustrated and disillusioned by the university's leadership. They saw campus as a space where advocacy and activism could be experimented with and where theories could be imbued with life and emotional and embodied salience. Students sometimes found surprising institutional collaborators, such as the university procurement team, which strongly supported the aforementioned Electronics Watch association.

In regard to environmental teaching per se, several students had taken a module on Environmental Perspectives on Development, which provided them with important historical contexts such as the colonial foundations of conservation work and national parks. As one student explained, "understanding the convoluted and painful history of environmentalism, something I had never before considered, opened my eyes to the idea that concepts many of us consider to be an all-round good, such as saving the planet, are fraught with moral relativism, spiritual clashes, agendas and bureaucratic nonsense". Another student, while also appreciating this critical historical perspective, felt that the module's language of sustainability was becoming outdated and that alternative perspectives that better spoke to the immanent threats of climate emergencies were necessary. I have introduced some of these perspectives, such as eco-centrism and sustain-ability, in the previous chapter.

Because of the absence of teaching focused specifically on climate change, especially in 2016/17 when many of the students I interviewed had first joined the university, a small group of them established a student society as a place for discussion and debate. According to one of the co-founders, the society is "a place for youth-based climate action practically and theoretically. We don't just do things, we provide a space for students to present ideas and think critically about environmental discourses and identify their limitations in order to overcome them." During the weekly meetings, students present topics of interest to them, often drawing on research they are undertaking for their essays. They thus establish a two-way relationship between formal and student-run learning spaces, showing students as active generators of knowledge that feeds back into classrooms. They also make use of that knowledge, as another aim of the society is to empower students to undertake activism through teaching campaigning skills and co-organizing workshops. Such student action has been taking different forms.

Two students set up the Youth Strike 4 Climate in Brighton, putting climate justice at the heart of the strikes. Without much experience in organizing or being fully aware of the work they were taking on, but also the effects they were to have, the students and a small group of co-organizers coordinated monthly strikes that at their height in September 2019 brought together 10,000 school strikers (Image 6.2). For the organizers, the strikes showed the importance of mass mobilizations for expressing discontent and anger, but also hope, and the student frequently commented on the

Image 6.2: Youth Strike 4 Climate in Brighton, September 2019

Photo: Sussex University climate campaign, used with permission.

incredible energy of the marches. Their descriptions resonate closely with elements of whole-person learning, from the felt sensations of positive and negative emotions to the embodied conviviality experienced during protests or direct action that cannot be replicated in the classroom.[22] Several students contrasted the strikes' collective positive energy with the negative and individualizing messaging of Extinction Rebellion, a group all students had engaged with either practically or conceptually. As one student explained, "activism should incite joy and hope. It should not motivate people by fear, doom and gloom". Joining activist groups or collective action can also counter feelings of powerlessness, which relates directly to the importance of critical hope as one of the strands of critical-creative pedagogy. In this case, it is a hope informed by the awareness of colonialism and capitalism's impacts on environmental degradation and the importance of highlighting and supporting struggles by groups, especially in the Global South, who are acutely affected by climate change.

The students subsequently travelled to Brussels to meet with Members of the European Parliament and fellow climate change activists. While they welcomed the opportunity to discuss climate change with politicians, they felt that some of their engagements in Brussels were "too tokenistic. If politicians were already doing enough, we would not need to be here." To get this message, which echoes the words of Greta Thunberg who started the school climate strikes in 2018, across more forcefully, the students loudly voiced their demand for climate justice in the plenary hall, "an action that turned a lot of heads but was quite necessary". Tokenism was a word often used to describe the superficial performance of transformative work, against which students reacted with anger, disobedience and unruliness. Instead they argued for the need to creatively communicate the urgency of climate change action to reach diverse audiences; one student described it as "finding new ways to make a point and being heard by the right people, to make them realize that there is a problem". For her, this connected to breaking down the boundaries of the academy and validating other knowledges. Similarly, another student talked about the work with a local gallery organizing various climate change-related exhibits and workshops, which for her created moving and sociable ways to communicate both environmental destruction and action to counter it. This gallery, which plays an important role in the Brighton activist movement, is another example of the importance of physical spaces to bring people together and support their work. In addition to the strikes, students also engaged more formal structures in their fight for climate justice.

Through the already-mentioned student society, two students joined a legal challenge against the UK government. As one of them explained, "obviously it's good if you lead your life with a low carbon footprint. But I would rather green the political sphere. Turning off lights is fine, but climate change requires dramatic political action." Based on their belief in the importance of holding governments to account and partly inspired by Brighton's Green Party MP, Caroline Lucas,[23] the students partnered with a charity that successfully took the government to court over the expansion of Heathrow Airport. They argued that ministers had not adequately taken into account the government's legal commitments to tackle climate change, and particularly its goal for net zero emissions by 2050. The ruling in their favour, which effectively stopped planning for a third runway, was the first major ruling in the world to be based on the Paris Climate Agreement and could be used to stop other high-carbon projects.[24] The two students were among 12 claimants named in the lawsuit; in his witness statement one student made a connection between his previous humanitarian work, which had shown him extreme human suffering, and the research and learning about climate change through his studies. The students also explained that, in spite of the legal success, "we're not going to solve climate change in a courtroom. It's going to be this much wider societal process of changing the opinions and culture until the politics doesn't fit the culture any more, and then the politics will change."

Universities are undeniably part of this broader transformation, and students also pursued change on campus. One group conducted a campaign for Ecosia, a social enterprise planting trees for internet searches, to become the default search engine on campus computers. After their success at Sussex, the students have been offering advice and support to students at other universities. Other students engaged with formal structures set up by the university leadership, albeit in ambivalent ways. Several students spoke at the first Sussex Sustainability Assembly, co-organized by the Student Union to discuss how the university should respond to the climate emergency declared by the vice-chancellor partly in response to student mobilizations.[25] In his presentation, one student showed a slide of a new campus expansion project that involved cutting down mature trees; he characterized the university's planting of new trees as tokenism and instead suggested responses that included cooperation with international movements fighting for climate justice and a campus ban on companies that are investing in fossil fuels. In addition, a new green deal for the university should include shifting investment from building new, expensive student residences into sustainable living-wage jobs, renewable energy and working with ethical suppliers.[26] He also asked those present "to value the skills of Sussex students".

Another student speaker connected climate change and mental health, based on research she was undertaking for her undergraduate thesis (Vaičiulionytė, 2020). Throughout her presentation she was highly critical of the university's 'greenwashing' marketing measures and quick-fix solutions and advocated for more holistic understandings of both issues and for building support communities among students, with staff and with nature. Bridging different domains, she argued that "I know you might not associate [anxiety over] getting a seat in the library with climate anxiety but this university cut down a forest to build accommodations for hundreds of new students, disregarding the fact that students already studying here desperately need more space, attention and care." Another point of critique was that the interdisciplinary education necessary to understand climate change is taking place only in student-created spaces such as the aforementioned student society, while the separation of the social and natural sciences into different schools stands in the way of this integration in formal instruction. The student finished her presentation with calling on those present to support the staff strikes which started the next day, because "overworked and underpaid staff" were not able to provide the support students needed. Little wonder that students in the audience clapped while senior managers looked much less pleased.

These actions show that students see the importance of participating in formal structures, including the university sustainability committee set up as a result of the assembly. On the one hand, they regard such participation as opportunities to hold management to account, while remaining suspicious of the effectiveness of top-down initiatives and sceptical of getting things done through bureaucratic channels. On the other hand, students are effectively using these channels to disrupt management-speak, call out leadership hypocrisy and propose more radical solutions. As one of them explained, radical activism at Sussex is, and has always been, enacted by students, often in opposition to or defiance of management. For her, the current university leadership trying to take credit for it is similar to Earth Day, which began as university teach-outs modelled on anti-Vietnam War protests, being commodified by companies to sell green products.[27]

Both forms of appropriation need to be resisted, and students educated through critical-creative pedagogy are in a good position to do this. One student spoke for everybody I interviewed when she wondered, "how can you learn about injustices and inequalities and not want to do anything about it?" I am aware that I spoke to only a small number of mostly self-selected students and that my sample is in no way representative of the entire student body, where apathy, indifference or passivity might be more common. Critical-creative teaching on its own is therefore not sufficient to bring about, nor will it automatically lead to, student action, but I believe that it lays important ground work by teaching new heterodox knowledge, nurturing transgressive orientations and advocating prefigurative politics. It creates a hopeful environment in which students can better understand current challenges, imagine alternative responses to them and engage in bringing about these changes.

Students often focus their activism on areas that are of particular importance to them, from decolonizing what they are learning and how they are learning it, to climate change that is affecting their futures in direct and urgent ways. Looking at the experiences of Sussex students in these areas, it becomes clear that formal instruction, while important, is only one avenue through which students learn. Just as important are student-led and student-centred spaces that show students as active knowledge producers and sharers. There is much we can learn from these spaces to enrich our own pedagogical practice. Students use this learning to create alternative futures, often in prefigurative ways that enact in the here and now the changes they want to bring about. To do so they strategically use the opportunities provided by universities, from student societies to financial and logistical resources to formal spaces in which they can hold senior managers accountable and counter bureaucratic limitations with radical alternatives. While not all students I interviewed are leaving the university as activists, those who do are showing the potential of critical-creative pedagogy in inspiring and powerful ways.

Conclusion

In this chapter I have shown how students are using the knowledge they gain through their studies and through their own learning spaces to imagine and work towards alternative futures. This is necessarily praxis work, which takes learning outside university classrooms while remaining anchored in critical-creative teaching that combines theory and practice within them.

I began by arguing that, in contrast to the market-driven employability agenda that focuses on students' work skills, incorporating practical, applied and problem-focused learning that has critical thinking as a central element results in praxis as the articulation of theory, reflection, dialogue and action. Similarly, while the many initiatives that go under the name of work experience can easily reinforce the status quo and students' stereotypes and normative assumption about who enacts change and at whom it is directed, these experiences can also become sources of experiential learning about social struggles that stand in a mutually enriching relationship with classroom learning, making the latter real while providing critical reflection on the former. I then turned my attention to activism as an important expression of students' engagement with the world. While it is possible to teach activism in ways that show students the challenges and potentials of activist work, especially if such teaching combines theory and practice, it is students' own activist work that best reveals how they are imagining and working towards alternative responses to global challenges.

7

Capstones

Capstones are prominent bricks laid on top of built structures or the outside walls of buildings for everyone to see. They are manifestations of completed work that showcase to the world the culmination of a project. Over the last decade, the term has been adopted for educational use; capstone projects are final projects undertaken by more and more university students in their last year of study.[1] Drawing together many different elements of learning, they are the crowning accomplishments of students' learning journeys. They are also catalysts that launch students into their lives after university and therefore often linked to the employability agenda I critiqued in the previous chapter. However, from a generative theory perspective, capstones can open up spaces for students to imagine and work towards radical alternatives to current challenges.

I therefore see capstones as a fitting end to my book on critical-creative pedagogy, especially as their spelling encapsulates the main elements of this pedagogy – creative, analytical, practical – CAPstones.[2] By presenting the conclusion to *Creative Universities* as a series of experimental capstone projects, as prototypes of potential future uses of critical-creative pedagogy, I also shift from imagining in steps to dreaming in leaps. I move from the small-scale, careful, classroom-focused approach of the preceding chapters to imagining larger utopian initiatives that bring together students from different disciplines, schools or faculties across universities to work on ambitious capstone projects. In formulating these projects, I draw on arguments and activities from previous chapters as well as the literature cited throughout the book and articulate these insights into thought-experiments that enact generative theorizing of new possibilities within expansive and participatory universities. I do so in a critically-hopeful way, inspired by Freire's observation that 'my hope is necessary but it is not enough. Alone, it does not win. But without it, my struggle will be weak and wobbly. We need critical hope the way a fish needs unpolluted water' (1994, p 2).

After a brief introduction, I present several examples of possible projects and initial ideas for how they could be undertaken. My hope is that readers will follow my final imaginative leap and consider possible capstone projects at their own institutions. The projects are conceived as open-ended action research, carried out within universities that become experimental spaces supported by adequate resources. This includes not only making available the spaces and materials I have shown to be crucial to critical-creative pedagogy in Chapter 3, but also funding to bring scholars, practitioners and activists to campus for longer stays that allow for in-depth engagement with students, including teaching, workshops and mentoring. Funding is also available for student grants to carry out project ideas. These are realized by groups that encompass student members from as many different disciplinary backgrounds as possible and are supported by staff and PhD researchers from at least three faculties. They guide students in identifying, researching and addressing challenges that affect universities – effectively asking students to dig where they stand – but have further-reaching impacts.

Project work begins with collectively formulating a challenge, researching it from a decolonial perspective, iteratively designing possible responses to the challenge and then implementing one of them. During this process, students work with research groups and student societies on campus, as well as with community organizations, activist collectives or other institutions that advocate for alternative futures. These diverse groups become active collaborators rather than just placeholders for internships; they engage with students in collective labour from projects' inception to their implementation. The following examples of possible projects are grouped into three broad themes of opening up learning, sustain-able campuses and reimagining universities. These are by no means exhaustive but, rather, meant to serve as jumping-off points for readers to imagine projects that are relevant for their own contexts and situations.

Opening up learning

The emphasis of the first theme is on connecting universities, and learning within them, to both their immediate surroundings and wider worlds. In Chapters 2 and 6 I have unpacked the dynamics of students engaging beyond the university, and the project proposals presented here consider how these engagements can be extended. For the first project, students would design and undertake a *decolonized field module*. They begin by thinking about the pedagogical foundations of a fieldtrip that would not replicate development tourism or nature edu-tainment but enable collective learning about social, ecological and other transformations with partner organizations. This includes experimenting with different forms of collaborations, for example with international universities, research groups or social movements. Students would start by asking what is to be learned, where, by whom, in what ways and toward what ends? If students decide on international locations, considerations include how such a module is made accessible to students who cannot afford to pay for international travel, for example through cross-subsidization or crowdfunding. Students must also consider how two-way travel can bring international partners to their home universities. In addition, preparatory work engages with historical relationships between institutions and countries and students' own entanglements within those. Other questions include how field engagements can be opened up to epistemic diversity and enact whole-person learning. How do students position themselves as learners rather than helpers, decentre themselves, unlearn their certainties and become open to being challenged? How can they ask questions and listen deeply before suggesting actions, if any? How can meaningful learning and cooperation take place among both students and host organizations? How, in other words, can decolonial field engagements be imagined, created and enacted in theory and practice, in praxis?

A second, related project would focus on designing a global classroom around a current challenge. In Chapter 6 I have explore how students can engage in stationary connectivity, and in this project they experiment with technological possibilities to bring them together with students and educators around the world. During the COVID-19 pandemic many students were learning from their home locations, but global classrooms go far beyond remote access to classroom instructions. After agreeing on a challenge with their international co-learners, students research how it has been addressed in their own locations and then explore to what extent local responses could be transplanted, or alternatively how global initiatives might be incorporated into local responses. What is the potential to connect and amplify local responses through pluriversal modes of engagement that work with multiple ways of being, learning and making in diverse worlds? How can these different modes be maintained rather than flattened or homogenized? How can epistemic diversity be ensured in global classrooms? Particular attention is paid to how all students, with diverse abilities and modes of engagement, can participate. That might include decentring writing and encouraging other forms of knowledge production and communication. It also raises the question of how collaborative learning platforms and spaces are governed, besides more mundane challenges such as time zone and linguistic differences. Students could work with international student societies on their home campuses and could combine individual, pen-pal type connections and collective working groups. In the process, they learn that working with the most appropriate technologies is important, but only the starting point for ensuring meaningful and mutually enriching collaborative learning in the service of addressing global challenges.

Sustain-able campuses

This second theme takes its inspiration from the ecological learning introduced in Chapter 5. The emphasis here is on students developing deep ecology, sustain-ability and systems approaches to university campuses and their surroundings, and the multiple and diverse labours and lives that take place on them. Two possible project areas are mobilities and food. For the first, students could prototype an integrated mobility plan, starting for example with the campus transport mapping exercise described in Chapter 5. Mobility is seen as a transdisciplinary issue with far-reaching effects that impact on human and non-human campus inhabitants in interconnected ways. Students begin by thinking about different means of transportation and their effects on the natural and human environments of campuses and their environs, and then extend these to design in elements of accessibility and safety, physical and mental health, creative and community aspects. This process can be guided by design questions: What if commuting to university could itself become a learning experience? What if mobility was not merely an instrumental necessity but became an enriching, convivial experience? What if diverse means of mobility were generous, not only not polluting the environment but instead releasing clean air or water into it? Answering these questions can help student groups to reconceptualize mobility as a sustain-able complex system that can contribute to ecological well-being for all inhabitants of university campuses and beyond.

A second possible project is inspired by the future food exercise described in Chapter 3, and extends it to university campuses. This can begin with the redesign of campuses around allotments as central spaces of whole-person learning and well-being (Image 7.1 of Sussex campus allotments, closed during the pandemic). Rather than being tucked away and precariously dispensable, allotments can become meeting and working places, research facilities and jumping-off points for nutritional and biological experiments, projects on mental and physical health, deeper understandings of ecological and environmental issues and collective labour.

Student groups also work to imagine future food scenarios for universities that involve locally grown food, local suppliers, cooperative food outlets and on-campus waste recycling and composting facilities. Students research the various aspects of campus food systems, get involved in planning, building and growing, connect with existing initiatives such as zero-waste cafés or food distribution apps. In the process, they explore how food can be reconceptualized as a holistic means for economic, ecological and social sustain-ability. How can food bring students and staff together? How can growing and distributing food enable economic alternatives? How can cooking and eating generate conviviality on campuses? Because of its location at the nexus of personal and political practices, food has the unique potential

Image 7.1: What if allotments became central to university campuses rather than being seen as expendable?

Photo: Author.

to nurture bodies, intellects and souls and to foster critical hope through individual actions amplified into systemic change.

Reimagining universities

In the third theme, student groups would experiment with radically rethinking universities through the lens of economic and social justice. They draw on insights especially from Chapters 2 and 4 and on ideas of ecological universities 'that take seriously both the world's interconnectedness and the university's interconnectedness with the world' through civic engagement (Barnett, 2011, p 451, Wright, 2017). The projects in this theme challenge students to reflect on their personal and institutional identities and locations, and to imagine different ways of being students and engaging with universities. For the first project student groups generate a comprehensive history of the present of their university and its connections to the world. In the case of Sussex, for example, research would go beyond its radical past that is a frequent reference point, and include the university's impact on its immediate surroundings, given that it was built in the vicinity of a small village and in the middle of the South Downs National Park. How have this building activity and the resulting mini-city of several thousand residents altered the landscape, ecological systems and human–non-human relations?

How has the continuous growth of universities impacted on neighbouring towns and affected urban dynamics, house prices and gentrification? How have universities helped to shape creative environments, through collaborations with other local universities or international networks? How have universities engaged with community groups and local governments and to what purposes and effects? To answer these questions, student groups conduct primary and secondary research, and then creatively present their universities as long-standing neighbours, good or bad, to many different communities, human and non-human. From such a historically grounded perspective, students then develop future scenarios that might not involve the usual growth ambitions but, rather, focus on the quality of relationships and the meaningful contributions universities can make, while also being honest about their detrimental effects. Ultimately, this project challenges students to interrogate what it means to be a university student in multiple, often ambiguous, ways.

Last but not least, another project could explore what radically inclusive universities would look like. Starting with the question of what does that mean and what does it take to make them so, students consider a wide variety of intersecting elements. What if university education were to become free again? How would it be funded? What alternative governance modes would that enable? This includes research focusing on how universities used to be publicly funded in the UK and on funding models in other countries, and helping students to develop an understanding of how government policies are made and interlink with broader regimes such as neoliberalism. Students can also investigate existing experiments such as popular universities around the world, cooperative universities like the Mondragon University and the Free Universities that have been established in cities such as Brighton. What would the effects of non-commodified HE be? What are its potentials to address and abolish structural hierarchies and exclusions, based on race, gender, class, abilities? What else needs to happen to make universities radically inclusive? One possibility could be for groups to experiment with campus-wide basic income schemes that ensure all students and staff the financial means to cover their basic needs. Such schemes could work with alternative campus currencies, taking their inspiration from the local currency schemes that are in existence in many towns. Through such multifaceted questions, student groups address pragmatic, political and philosophical questions of responsibility, equality and justice.

These six potential capstone projects are but an indication of what is possible when staff and students work together in the spirit of critical-creative pedagogy. I conclude by considering some initial ideas of how these projects can realize the four strands of this pedagogy: whole-person learning, design and arts methods, praxis and critical hope. When first coming together in their groups, students could introduce themselves to each other using a creative artefact, similar to the artefacts students produced about their lives in Brighton described in Chapter 2. That would set the tone of what's to come, showing students that being creative will be an important aspect of their work. In formulating their project challenges, groups need to find ways in which their diverse interests, backgrounds, abilities and experiences can inform mutual choices; design exercises described throughout this book can help to ensure that all group members participate in this process.

Making projects decolonial, in the many ways laid out in the preceding chapters, includes students reflecting on their positionalities, privileges and power and ensuring that potential inequalities and hierarchies in their groups are addressed and overcome through collective work. Decolonial work also entails attention to epistemic diversity, for example in the research that groups undertake to learn more about their challenges. Investigating how and by whom challenges have been formulated and measured, what questions have been asked and assumptions made about them, as well as previous responses and future solutions, gives students an in-depth understanding that contextualizes and frames their projects. Alongside academic literature from the Global North and South, marginalized perspectives and non-academic knowledges also provide material for interrogating key concepts, sources and authors. In addition, students draw on their personal experiences of the challenges to include experiential learning; keeping a learning diary throughout the project to engage in the reflection–action–reflection cycle and critical self-reflexivity described in Chapters 2 and 6 enriches that learning.

Projects also entail a praxis component for which students work with diverse collaborators; as I argued earlier, these are an integral part of the work from the outset. In these collaborations, reciprocity and continuous engagement in the spirit of mutuality and equality are key elements, including both student presence at the organizations and the latter's engagement on campus. Praxis leads to learning-by-doing, informed by theoretical analysis and whole-person learning. Last but not least, the projects are future oriented and focused on exploring alternative responses to challenges that unsettle and change rather than replicate the status quo. Students can engage in personal or collective experiments, scenario building or design activities, in the process reflecting on multiple possible futures and on decisions about which ones are desirable for whom. Students also participate in working towards materializing their responses by redirecting their own ways of knowing, being and making in the world.

Given the substantial amount of work entailed, assessment is another factor to consider, which could be allocated on a pass/fail basis. If marks are given, students can be invited to formulate and apply assessment criteria, similar to the serious games activity in Chapter 5, to give them ownership in the process. Final outcomes are opportunities to highlight the creative aspects of the groups' work, by challenging students to go beyond written reports or standard presentations to produce multimedia, artistic and experimental creations. These are presented during a final, public forum to which all staff and students, collaborators as well as universities' neighbours are invited. The event becomes a manifestation of critical–creative learning and a showcase for the heterodox possibilities and pluriversal alternatives that can be created within mainstream institutions and, above all, serve as a celebration of critical hope.

Notes

Chapter 1

1. Microfinance makes small loans to mainly low-income women to help them start or grow businesses. There is a large debate around the effectiveness of microfinance, which I have summarized in Schwittay (2011). Criticism of microfinance ranges from its potential to further indebt poor people to its questionable impact for women recipients and its links to market-driven development agendas.
2. All quotes are from interviews conducted with students at Sussex for this research.
3. Many other disciplines outside the social sciences are also addressing global challenges, but lie outside my expertise.
4. As I show throughout this book, there have been important and sustained critiques of international development, for example by postdevelopment scholars who have argued that it is a top-down technocratic imposition of Western discourses and practices on the Global South (Escobar, 1995). It has failed to improve living conditions for the majority of aid recipients and instead reproduced and deepened political imbalances and economic inequalities.
5. Following UK terminology, I use the term modules to refer to individual units that make up a degree course, in effect referring to what in many other countries are called courses.
6. My own research on Information and Communication Technologies for Development (ICTD) and crowd-sourcing platforms has made me aware of technological possibilities and limitations in a more general sense.
7. I am adopting Gibson-Graham's ethical stance, which they developed in the context of their diverse economies programme, for the project of teaching.
8. Here I draw only on Anglo-American writings, which neglects cultural and other factors.
9. More attention to outcomes is necessary if creative practice is part of course assessments, which is a difficult and much-discussed issue in the literature. The activities I am describing here have, with two exceptions, been non-assessed to allow students to experiment without worrying about grades.
10. Mātauranga Māori refers to Māori knowledge, culture and philosophy, for more information see https://kep.org.nz/assets/resources/site/Voices7–16.Matauranga-Maori.pdf.
11. The university's Sackler Centre for Consciousness Science is funded by the Sackler family, who are in the opioid business.
12. Available at https://www.sussex.ac.uk/webteam/gateway/file.php?name=chucl-report-4-july-2018.pdf&site=291.
13. For more information, see https://activelearningnetwork.com/.
14. With the advice of Harvard economist Jeffrey Sachs, in 1985 Bolivia underwent dramatic economic changes to control hyperinflation. The results included an end to government subsidies, mass unemployment and a steep rise in poverty.

[15] Workshop of Andean Oral History, for a good summary of its work in English see Stephenson, 2002.

[16] As I explain in Chapter 5, I take the notion of sustain-ability from Tony Fry (2018).

Chapter 2

[1] In spring 2021, Education secretary Gavin Williamson suggested that funding for arts, design and media courses be cut by up to 50 per cent, labelling them 'dead-end university courses that leave students with nothing but debt.' The money would be redirected to 'high-value STEM subjects' among others (https://www.theguardian.com/education/2021/may/06/plans-for-50-funding-cut-to-arts-subjects-at-universities-catastrophic).

[2] Critical pedagogy is a large, established field of educational scholarship; rather than providing an exhaustive overview here I highlight those aspects that are of particular relevance to my critical-creative pedagogy.

[3] Important feminist, decolonial and ecological critiques of critical pedagogy have been made over the years (Darder et al, 2009).

[4] The development of a critical consciousness was originally developed in the work of anti-colonial writer and revolutionary Frantz Fanon.

[5] Freire's thinking was shaped by his own experiences of hunger and deprivation as a child in Brazil, when his family suffered from the ravages of the Great Depression.

[6] Postdevelopment is a school of thought within development studies and anthropology emerging in the 1980s, which completely rejects mainstream development as a Western project (Ferguson, 1990, Escobar, 1995).

[7] Voluntourism refers to young people from the Global North going to countries in the Global South to volunteer, often for short periods of time. In the UK, this often happens during a gap year before the start of university.

[8] Gardener's multiple intelligences include verbal-linguistic, logical-mathematical, visual-spatial, musical, bodily-kinaesthetic, personal and naturalistic intelligences.

[9] The padlet can be accessed at https://creativeuniversities.com/2021/02/13/teaching-urban-futures-again/.

[10] This could also be combined with body mapping for a more embodied perspective following Sweet and Ortiz Escalante (2015).

Chapter 3

[1] In October 2020, EU President Ursula von der Leyen launched a new European Bauhaus movement to realize a European Green Deal, showing the enduring force of the Bauhaus ideals (https://ec.europa.eu/commission/presscorner/detail/en/AC_20_1916).

[2] All student quotes are from Friedewald, 2009, p 18. Other references consulted for this section include Droste, 1971 and Forgács, 1991.

[3] Design anthropology, with its systematic interest in history and context, critical use of theory and attention to the perspectives of, especially, marginalized people affected by design projects, is one field that can provide important correctives to mainstream design's defuturing tendencies focused on the ever-new and modernists' visions of progress and innovation that accompany it (Gunn et al, 2013).

[4] These scenarios range from Conventional Worlds, in which companies or governments continue the status quo, to Barbarization, marked by breakdown or retreat, to Great Transitions that present visionary alternatives focused on natural preservation, material sufficiency and social justice.

[5] The donor is German businessman Hasso Plattner, co-founder of the software company SAP. In addition to the Stanford d.school he also established the Hasso Plattner Institute

at the Universität Potsdam on the outskirts of Berlin, which is applying design thinking to software solutions to social issues. I was due to visit there in March 2020 but could not because of COVID-19.

6 This InQbate Learning Space, together with two others at the University of Brighton, was funded by a Centre for Excellence in Teaching and Learning in Creativity grant from the Higher Education Founding Council for England in 2005.

7 I distinguish between a studio and a workshop, with the latter being a place of practice filled with specialist machinery to work on particular materials. It was the Bauhaus that made workshops central to design education.

8 The quotes are from the notes I took while attending the conference panel as an audience member.

9 The growing maker movement shows a shift from do-it-yourself to do-it-together approaches. Such forms of communality also connect to practices focusing on material sustainability such as repairing and recycling (Gauntlett, 2013).

10 I am aware that extra-curricular activities like the design workshops entail extra faculty labour and time, which is another manifestation of resource politics. I had organized them because of my own interest in the role of design in global development and creative teaching.

11 These visuals were inspired by my visit to the Stanford d.school.

12 LEGO Serious Play®, a method developed by the LEGO® company, is often used to introduce serious play into university classrooms (Nerantzi and James, 2019).

13 https://www.ed.ac.uk/studying/postgraduate/degrees/index.php?r=site/view&id=951, accessed 1 April 2020.

14 Victor Papanek's book *Design for the Real World: Human Ecology and Social Change* (1971) was one of the first books calling for a socially responsible design.

15 Cradle-to-cradle design mimics natural processes of reusing all products rather than creating waste (McDonough and Braungart, 2002).

Chapter 4

1 https://web.archive.org/web/20130102063356/http://hpronline.org/harvard/an-open-letter-to-greg-mankiw/, accessed 20 May 2020.

2 There are historical parallels when 'the twinned crisis of the Great Depression and the second world war set the stage for the modern welfare state' (Baker, 2020).

3 The 1918 Spanish flu epidemic helped to create national health services in many European countries (Baker, 2020).

4 This has been the case in Germany, for example (Alves and Kangraven, 2020).

5 I thank my colleague Demet Dinler for drawing my attention to Gudeman's work.

6 The Universidad de la Tierra (University of the Earth, also called Unitierras) was first set up in Oaxaca in 1999 by Gustavo Esteva, to assert distinctive indigenous values and identities apart from government and market rule. The Chiapas Unitierras is called Centro Indígena de Capacitación Integral.

7 This activity is engaging ideas presented in *Take Back the Economy* (Gibson-Graham et al, 2013).

8 The idea of the inventory is adapted from Gibson-Graham (2006).

9 While the activity could also be located in a Global North country, waste-collection services in many of these are formalized and leave no roles for the informal waste pickers this exercise focuses on.

Chapter 5

[1] For more information about the Sendai Framework, see https://www.undrr.org/publication/sendai-framework-disaster-risk-reduction-2015-2030.

[2] Throughout the chapter, I use sustain-ability and sustain-able to refer to ideas and approaches that propose decolonial, relational and eco-centric alternatives to mainstream environmental interventions, and sustain-ability education to signal the environmental dimension of critical-creative pedagogy.

[3] At the time of its publication, the *Limits to Growth* report was met with some criticism, including from the University of Sussex Science Policy Research Unit (SPRU). SPRU researchers argued that the report's key assumptions had been overly pessimistic and that its methodology, data and projections were faulty and did not accurately reflect reality (Cole et al, 1973).

[4] ESD has given rise to its own large academic research field, exploring issues such as definitions and boundaries of the environment and the place of humans within it, the roles of science, technology, culture and values and the overall goals of ESD and how best to assess them.

[5] In 2018, the *Times Higher Education* introduced a global impact ranking of universities' performance linked to the SDGs; the University of Auckland, where I taught for five years, has occupied the top spot in the last two years. https://www.timeshighereducation.com/rankings/impact/2020/overall#!/page/0/length/25/sort_by/rank/sort_order/asc/cols/undefined, accessed 6 July 2020.

[6] Competencies are not unique to ESD, but more generally an important focus of the Bologna Process for European universities (Lozano et al, 2012).

[7] While the more common term in Bolivia is Vivir Bien, I will use Buen Vivir, as it is more internationally recognized. The concept's indigenous origins encompass the Andean Aymara notion of *suma qamaña* (good living) and Quechua *sumac kawsay* (living well) as well as the Amazonian Guaraní *ñandereko* (harmonious living) and Kichwa *alli kawsay* (good living).

[8] This process of de-radicalization is not unique to Buen Vivir but happens to many terms that become development buzzwords and fuzzwords (Cornwall, 2007).

[9] Interdependence refers to the relationships between elements of a system, where complex systems depend on other systems to operate.

[10] Self-organization is a process of interactions between parts of a system, giving rise to an overall order without the control of an external agent. Flocks of birds are a good example.

[11] Emergence refers to an entity having properties that its parts do not have on their own. Rather, these properties emerge only when the parts interact in a wider whole.

[12] A non-linear relationship between elements of a system produces a non-proportional effect, in contrast to the straight line of a linear relationship (Meadows, 2008).

[13] Meadows (2008) and Capra (1996) – both of these could be good primers for students.

[14] The student also wrote a blog post on the topic, which can be found at https://creativeuniversities.com/2020/07/23/double-trouble-in-a-good-way/.

[15] Gestalt is the German word for organic form.

[16] Resources include the *Systems Thinking Playbook* (Sweeney and Meadows, 1995), the Red Cross Red Crescent Climate Centre and the Pardee Centre for the Study of the Longer-range Future.

[17] This is one of two learning activities in the book that was assessed. Kniveton developed the assessment criteria, which included interesting game setting, clear learning outcomes, game facilitation and engagement and originality, together with the students. Students were also involved in discussing their marks. Both of these steps were important to reassure

students, as the game was a completely new form of assessment for them and co-designing the assessment criteria gave them a sense of control and took away some of the anxiety.

18 Other activities from this module are the urban manifesto (Chapter 2), the big build (Chapter 3) and the co-op design (Chapter 4).

19 https://mapkibera.org/, accessed 7 July 2020.

20 A variation of this are twalks, as walking seminars that use Twitter for students to capture their discussions (Middleton and Spiers, 2019).

21 I borrow this idea of a pluriversal map from Garduño Jiménez (2019a).

Chapter 6

1 IDS is an international development think-tank co-located on Sussex campus. There are many research and teaching collaborations between the two institutions.

2 For unruly politics, see Khanna (2012).

3 The 2019/20 strikes focused on four demands: the sustainability of the pension scheme and improvements on pay, equality, casualization and workloads (https://www.ucu.org.uk/article/10621/UCU-announces-14-strike-days-at-74-UK-universities-in-February-and-March).

4 A survey conducted among students in Global Studies in 2019 showed that more than 40% of students work 11–20 hours per week, and 18% work more than 21 hours per week alongside their full-time studies (https://blogs.sussex.ac.uk/global/2018/11/19/how-does-the-necessity-of-paid-work-impact-our-students-learning-from-the-global-studies-student-employment-survey/).

5 Global connections are tied up with larger debates around global citizenship education and universities' internationalization agendas that, while important, are beyond the scope of this chapter.

6 The Bandung conference was the first large-scale meeting of leaders of newly independent Asian and African countries. It took place in 1955 in Bandung, Indonesia, focused on Afro-Asian cooperation and resistance to colonialism and led to the eventual creation of the non-aligned movement.

7 Rhodes Must Fall started when South African student Chumani Maxwele threw human excrement at a statue of Cecil Rhodes at the University of Cape Town (UCT) to condemn his racism and role in the construction of apartheid and to protest against ongoing institutionalized racist and colonial attitudes at UCT.

8 https://www.bbc.co.uk/news/education-53082545.

9 https://coproducing.wixsite.com/thecurriculumproject/about.

10 I am aware that there are conservative groups that consider themselves activist, too.

11 For this, each student writes their idea for the campaign on the top of the sheet of paper and then passes it to their neighbour, who must add onto the idea in constructive ways and then pass on the sheet. At the end of the exercise, each group member has had their idea considered and expanded by all other members, meaning that quieter students who might not speak up during group discussions also had the opportunity to provide input. All initial ideas will have been equally considered and have thus fed into the collective decision process. This activity is also useful as an icebreaker for students who do not know each other very well.

12 The campaigns cannot be implemented because immediately after the module ends students begin intensive summer dissertation work. Upon finishing, many return to their home countries and start to work.

13 In the spring of 2020 and 2021, campaign work was carried out online via Zoom break-out rooms, jam boards and Google Docs. This did not stand in the way of all groups producing high-quality campaign reports. As one student reflected, "completing this

project within the midst of a pandemic has reinforced to me that positive change can be achieved with collaborative work and collective action, even in challenging times".

14 Because, due to university regulations, a large percentage of the grade has to be individually based, students submit a short essay at the end of the module's theory part, analysing a campaign of their choice through applying one of the conceptual frameworks discussed in class.

15 Ten per cent of the personal reflection mark depend on peer evaluation, with the possibility of students loosing marks if they were consistently scored low by their group members. This allows for an element of fairness, as I can take into account when group members do not participate in the campaign work in equal measure, which happens very rarely.

16 I describe these serious games in Chapter 5.

17 Yarl's Wood is a detention centre near Gatwick airport, where mainly female detainees awaiting decisions on their asylum applications, often for long periods of time, have been protesting against inhumane conditions for several years.

18 https://creativeuniversities.com/2020/07/15/academia-and-activism-a-students-story/.

19 Climate justice argues that climate change disproportionately affects people in the Global South but is caused by policies of Northern governments and exacerbated by the ongoing effects of colonial and other exploitative relations.

20 While this section mainly draws on interviews with students, I have also included information from newspaper articles. To protect anonymity I am not citing the latter.

21 This is also the space where I ran my design workshops. It remains to be seen what impact the lack of student socializing due to COVID-19 will have on activism and other student activities.

22 In her work, Maria Ojala shows that emotions can be a motivating force for pro-environmental action, but only when students' emotions are taken seriously and actively engaged by their teachers, including facing rather than ignoring or downplaying negative emotions.

23 Brighton, where most students live, has the UK's only Green Member of Parliament, a significant source of pride for many residents.

24 https://amp.theguardian.com/environment/2020/feb/27/heathrow-third-runway-ruled-illegal-over-climate-change?fbclid=IwAR1cCYUlpsQvwx4EYJzQmvAmn_8mJSN_-isKEsJBP-H30IyfNrlunvYSQq0. In December 2020, the UK Supreme Court overturned this ruling, on the grounds that taking the UK climate commitments into account was not necessary (https://www.theguardian.com/environment/2020/dec/16/top-uk-court-overturns-block-on-heathrows-third-runway).

25 https://universitybusiness.co.uk/news/sussex-university-declares-climate-emergency/.

26 Many of the student's observations resonate with the low scorecard Sussex University received for its environmental sustainability work from the student-run People and Planet website (https://peopleandplanet.org/university/129410/ul19).

27 The Sussex 2025 Strategic Framework, developed by the current vice-chancellor, is full of references to the university's 'pioneering spirit', 'distinguished tradition of disruptive and experimental interventions' that 'has challenged convention since 1961' and 'dares to be different' (https://www.sussex.ac.uk/strategy/).

Chapter 7

1 Capstone projects originated in the US but have now become widespread in other countries, including the UK.

2 I thank Paul Braund for spotting this correspondence.

References

AAA. 2018. Lab/field/studio/archive: Speculative designs for a lateral anthropology. (Conference panel) https://www.eventscribe.com/2018/AAA-Annual/agenda.asp?day=11/16/2018&theday=Friday&h=Friday%20%20November%2016&BCFO=P%7CG

Achtenberg, E. 2017. Contested development: The geopolitics of Bolivia's TIPNIS conflict. NACLA Reporting on the Americas Since 1967.

Altmann, P. 2019. The commons as colonisation: The well-intentioned appropriation of Buen Vivir. *Bulletin of Latin American Research*, *39*(1), pp 83–97.

Alves, C. and Kvangraven, I.H. 2020. Changing the narrative: Economics after Covid-19. *Review of Agrarian Studies*, *10*(1), pp 147–163.

Amsler, S. 2009. Embracing the politics of ambiguity: Towards a normative theory of 'sustainability'. *Capitalism Nature Socialism*, *20*(2), pp 111–125.

Amsler, S. 2011. Beyond all reason: Spaces of hope in the struggle for England's universities. *Representations*, *116*(1), pp 62–87.

Amsler, S. 2014. 'By ones and twos and tens': Pedagogies of possibility for democratising higher education. *Pedagogy, Culture & Society*, *22*(2), pp 275–294.

Amsler, S. 2015. *The Education of Radical Democracy*. Routledge.

Amsler, S. and Facer, K. 2017. Contesting anticipatory regimes in education: Exploring alternative educational orientations to the future. *Futures*, *94*, pp 6–14.

Andreotti, V.d.O., Stein, S., Ahenakew, C. and Hunt, D. 2015. Mapping interpretations of decolonization in the context of higher education. *Decolonization: Indigeneity, Education & Society*, *4*(1), pp 21–40.

Arora, B. 2015. A Gramscian analysis of the employability agenda. *British Journal of Sociology of Education*, *36*(4), pp 635–648.

Baker, P. 2020. 'We can't go back to normal': How will the coronavirus change the world? https://www.theguardian.com/world/2020/mar/31/how-will-the-world-emerge-from-the-coronavirus-crisis, accessed 13 May 2020.

Bälter, O., Hedin, B., Tobiasson, H. and Toivanen, S. 2018. Walking outdoors during seminars improved perceived seminar quality and sense of well-being among participants. *International Journal of Environmental Research and Public Health*, *15*(2), pp 303–314.

Barcan, R. 2016. *Academic Life and Labour in the New University: Hope and Other Choices*. Routledge.

Barnett, R. 2011. The coming of the ecological university. *Oxford Review of Education*, *37*(4), pp 439–455.

Beichner, R.J. 2014. History and evolution of active learning spaces. *New Directions for Teaching and Learning*, *2014*(137), pp 9–16.

Beling, A.E., Cubillo-Guevara, A.P., Vanhulst, J. and Hidalgo-Capitán, A.L. 2018. Buen vivir (good living): Glocal genealogy of a Latin-American utopia for the World. *Latin American Perspectives*, *48*(3), pp 17–34.

Beloff, M. 1970. *The Plateglass Universities*. Fairleigh Dickinson University Press.

Berglund, E. 2015. Time for design anthropology: Reflections from the point of view of environmental change. *Suomen Antropologi: Journal of the Finnish Anthropological Society*, *40*(4), pp 29–36.

Bessant, S.E., Robinson, Z.P. and Ormerod, R.M. 2015. Neoliberalism, new public management and the sustainable development agenda of higher education: History, contradictions and synergies. *Environmental Education Research*, *21*(3), pp 417–432.

Bhambra, G.K. 2016. Whither Europe? Postcolonial versus neocolonial cosmopolitanism. *Interventions*, *18*(2), pp 187–202.

Blakey, S. and McFadyen, J. 2015. Curiosity over conformity: The Maker's Palette – a case for hands-on learning. *Art, Design & Communication in Higher Education*, *14*(2), pp 131–143.

Bloom, P. 2017. *Against Empathy: The Case for Rational Compassion*. Random House.

Boys, J. 2010. *Towards Creative Learning Spaces: Re-thinking the Architecture of Post-compulsory Education*. Routledge.

Bresler, L. (ed) 2013. *Knowing Bodies, Moving Minds: Towards Embodied Teaching and Learning* (Vol 3). Springer Science & Business Media.

Buchanan, R. 1992. Wicked problems in design thinking. *Design Issues*, *8*(2), pp 5–21.

Burman, A. 2012. Places to think with, books to think about. *Human Architecture: Journal of the Sociology of Self-knowledge*, *10*(1), pp 101–120.

Burman, A. 2016. Notes on the coloniality of reality in higher education in the Bolivian Andes and beyond. In *Decolonizing the Westernized University: Interventions in Philosophy of Education from Within and Without*. Lexington Books, pp 71–94.

Cadena, M.D.L. 2012. Indigenous cosmopolitics: Dialogues about the reconstitution of worlds. In *Seminar Abstract*. John E. Sawyer Seminar on the Comparative Study of Cultures. University of California, Davis.

Callahan, M. 2020. (Insubordinate) conviviality of the COVID-19 conjuncture. Blogpost on https://www.convivialthinking.org/index.php/2020/04/24/insubordinateconviviality/, accessed 27 April 2020.

Cameron, J., Quadir, F. and Tiessen, R. 2013. A changing landscape for teaching and learning in international development studies: An introduction to the special issue. *Canadian Journal of Development Studies/Revue canadienne d'études du développement*, *34*(3), pp 349–363.

Cameron, S., Langdon, J. and Agyeyomah, C. 2018. Service learning and solidarity: Politics, possibilities and challenges of experiential learning. *Journal of Global Citizenship & Equity Education*, 6(1), 1–23.

Capra, F. 1996. *The Web of Life: A New Synthesis of Mind and Matter*. Flamingo.

Capra, F. 2005. Speaking nature's language: Principles for sustainability. In *Ecological Literacy: Educating Our Children for a Sustainable World*. Sierra Club Books, pp 18–29.

Chadha, D. and Toner, J. 2017. Focusing in on employability: Using content analysis to explore the employability discourse in UK and USA universities. *International Journal of Educational Technology in Higher Education*, *14*(1), p 33–57.

Chikarmane, P. and Narayan, L. 2005. *Organising the Unorganised: A Case Study of the Kagad Kach Patra Kashtakari Panchayat (Trade Union of Wastepickers)*. KKPKP.

Cole, H.S.D., Freeman, C., Jahoda, M. and Pavitt, K.L.R. (eds) 1973. *Models of Doom: A Critique of the Limits to Growth*. Universe Publishing.

Cornwall, A. 2007. Buzzwords and fuzzwords: Deconstructing development discourse. *Development in Practice*, *17*(4–5), pp 471–484.

Cornwall, A. 2020. Decolonizing development studies: Pedagogic reflections. *Radical Teacher*, *116*, pp 37–46.

Corsín Jiménez, A. 2014. Introduction: The prototype: More than many and less than one. *Journal of Cultural Economy*, 7(4), pp 381–398.

Cowden, S. and Singh, G. 2013. *Acts of Knowing: Critical Pedagogy In, Against and Beyond the University*. Bloomsbury Publishing USA.

Cusicanqui, S.R. 1986. Taller de historia oral andina: proyecto de investigación sobre el espacio ideológico de las rebeliones andinas a través de la historia oral (1900–1950). In *Estados y naciones en los andes: hacia una historia comparativa Bolivia-Colombia-Ecuador-Perú*. Instituto de Estudios Peruanos, pp 83–99.

Cusicanqui, S.R. 2012. Ch'ixinakax utxiwa: A reflection on the practices and discourses of decolonization. *South Atlantic Quarterly*, *111*(1), pp 95–109.

Darder, A. 2009. Teaching as an act of love: Reflections on Paolo Freire and his contributions to our lives and our work. In *The Critical Pedagogy Reader*. Routledge, pp 567–578.

Darder, A., Baltodano, M. and Torres, R.D. (eds). 2009. *The Critical Pedagogy Reader*. 2nd edn. Routledge.

Davies, D. 2009. Currillum is a constrict. www.inclueded.net/writing/curriculum.html

Demaria, F., Schneider, F., Sekulova, F. and Martinez-Alier, J. 2013. What is degrowth? From an activist slogan to a social movement. *Environmental Values*, *22*(2), pp 191–215.

de Sousa Santos, B. 2016. Epistemologies of the South and the future. *From the European South: A Transdisciplinary Journal of Postcolonial Humanities*, 1, pp 17–29.

de Sousa Santos, B. 2017. *Decolonising the University: The Challenge of Deep Cognitive Justice*. Cambridge Scholars Publishing.

De Suarez, J., Suarez, P., Bachofen, C., Fortugno, N., Goentzel, J., Gonçalves, P., Grist, N., Macklin, C., Pfeifer, K., Schweizer, S. and Van Aalst, M. 2012. Games for a new climate: Experiencing the complexity of future risks. *Pardee Center Task Force Report*, pp 9–67.

Dewey, J. 1938. *Experience and Education*. Touchstone.

Dewey, J. 2005. *Art as Experience*. Pedigree Books.

Dieleman, H. and Huisingh, D. 2006. Games by which to learn and teach about sustainable development: Exploring the relevance of games and experiential learning for sustainability. *Journal of Cleaner Production*, *14*(9–11), pp 837–847.

Dinerstein, A. 2017. Co-construction or prefiguration? Rethinking the 'translation' of SSE practices into policy. In *Towards Just and Sustainable Economies: The Social and Solidarity Economy North and South*. Policy Press, pp 57–71.

Dinerstein, C. and Deneulin, S. 2012. Hope movements: Naming mobilization in a post-development world. *Development and Change*, *43*(2), pp 585–602.

Dinler, D. n.d. *Utopia and Development*. Unpublished course handbook.

Dinler, D.Ş. 2016. New forms of wage labour and struggle in the informal sector: The case of waste pickers in Turkey. *Third World Quarterly*, *37*(10), pp 1834–1854.

DiSalvo, B., Yip, J., Bonsignore, E. and Carl, D. 2017. *Participatory Design for Learning*. Routledge.

Droste, M. 1971. *Bauhaus, 1919–1933*. Taschen.

Du Pisani, J.A. 2006. Sustainable development – historical roots of the concept. *Environmental Sciences*, *3*(2), pp 83–96.

Ehn, P. 1993. Scandinavian design: On participation and skill. *Participatory Design: Principles and Practices*, *41*, p 77.

Ehn, P., Nilsson, E.M. and Topgaard, R. 2014. *Making Futures: Marginal Notes on Innovation, Design, and Democracy*. The MIT Press.

Eisenmenger, N., Pichler, M., Krenmayr, N., Noll, D., Plank, B., Schalmann, E., Wandl, M.T. and Gingrich, S. 2020. The Sustainable Development Goals prioritize economic growth over sustainable resource use: A critical reflection on the SDGs from a socio-ecological perspective. *Sustainability Science*, *15*, pp 1101–1110.

Elgin, D. 1991. Creating a sustainable future. *Revision*, *14*(2), pp 77–79.

Escobar, A. 1995. *Encountering Development: The Making and Unmaking of the Third World*. Princeton University Press.

Escobar, A. 2007. Worlds and knowledges otherwise: The Latin American modernity/coloniality research program. *Cultural Studies*, *21*(2–3), pp 179–210.

Escobar, A. 2015. Transiciones: A space for research and design for transitions to the pluriverse. *Design Philosophy Papers*, *13*(1), pp 13–23.

Escobar, A. 2017. *Designs for the Pluriverse: Radical Interdependence, Autonomy, and the Making of Worlds*. Duke University Press.

Escobar, A. 2018. Autonomous design and the emergent transnational critical design studies field. *Strategic Design Research Journal*, *11*(2), pp 139–146.

Escobar, A. 2020. *Pluriversal Politics: The Real and the Possible*. Duke University Press.

Facer, Keri. 2018a. The university as engine for anticipation: Stewardship, modelling, experimentation, and critique in public. In *Handbook of Anticipation: Theoretical and Applied Aspects of the Use of Future in Decision Making*. Springer, pp 1–20.

Facer, K. 2018b. Governing education through the future. In I. Grosvenor and L.R. Rasmussen (eds) *Making Education: Material School Design and Educational Governance*. Springer International Publishing, pp 197–210.

Ferguson, J. 1990. *The Anti-Politics Machine: 'Development', Depoliticization and Bureaucratic Power in Lesotho*. CUP Archive.

Fischer, L., Hasell, J., Proctor, J.C., Uwakwe, D., Perkins, Z.W. and Watson, C. (eds) 2017. *Rethinking Economics: An Introduction to Pluralist Economics*. Routledge.

Forgács, É. 1991. *The Bauhaus Idea and Bauhaus Politics*. Central European University Press.

Freire, P. 1993. *Pedagogy of the City*, trans D. Macedo. Continuum.

Freire, P. 1994. *Pedagogy of Hope*, trans Robert R. Barr. Continuum.

Freire, P. 2000. Pedagogy of the Heart, trans. D. Macedo and A. Oliveira. Continuum.

Friedewald, B. 2009. *Bauhaus*. Prestel.

Fry, T. 2018 [2009]. *Design Futuring: Sustainability, Ethics and New Practices*. Bloomsbury.

Gardener, H. 2006. *Multiple Intelligences: New Horizons in Theory and Practice.* Basic Books.

Gardiner, S. and Rieckmann, M. 2015. Pedagogies of preparedness: Use of reflective journals in the operationalisation and development of anticipatory competence. *Sustainability*, 7(8), pp 10554–10575.

Garduño Jiménez, D. 2019a. Design for technical change: Component One storyboard. Project submitted to the MA in Design for Change at the University of Edinburgh.

Garduño Jiménez, D. 2019b. Design for technical change: Component Two scenario. Project submitted to the MA in Design for Change at the University of Edinburgh.

Gauntlett, D. 2013. *Making Is Connecting.* John Wiley & Sons.

Gebrial, D. 2018. Rhodes must fall. In *Decolonising the University*. Pluto Press, pp 19–36.

Gibson-Graham, J. K. 2006. *A Postcapitalist Politics.* University of Minnesota Press.

Gibson-Graham, J.K. 2008. Diverse economies: Performative practices for other worlds. *Progress in Human Geography*, 32(5), pp 613–632.

Gibson-Graham, J.K. and Dombroski, K. (eds) 2020. *The Handbook of Diverse Economies.* Edward Elgar.

Gibson-Graham, J.K. and Roelvink, G. 2010. An economic ethics for the Anthropocene. *Antipode, 41*, pp 320–346.

Gibson-Graham, J.K., Cameron, J. and Healy, S. 2013. *Take Back the Economy: An Ethical Guide for Transforming Our Communities.* University of Minnesota Press.

Gilbert, P.R. 2018. Sovereignty and tragedy in contemporary critiques of investor state dispute settlement. *London Review of International Law, 6*(2), pp 211–231.

Gilman, N. 2003. *Mandarins of the Future: Modernization Theory in Cold War America.* Johns Hopkins University Press.

Giroux, H.A. 2014. *Neoliberalism's War on Higher Education.* Haymarket Books.

González-Gaudiano, E.J. 2016. ESD: Power, politics, and policy: 'Tragic optimism' from Latin America. *The Journal of Environmental Education, 47*(2), pp 118–127.

Greene, M. 1995. *Releasing the Imagination: Essays on Education, the Arts, and Social Change.* Jossey-Bass.

Greene, M. 1997. Teaching as possibility: A light in dark times. *Journal of Pedagogy, Pluralism and Practice, 1*(1), pp 14–24.

Greene, M. 2009. Teaching as possibility: A light in dark times. In *Critical Pedagogy in Uncertain Times*. Palgrave Macmillan, pp 137–149.

Grosfoguel, R. 2012. The dilemmas of ethnic studies in the United States: Between liberal multiculturalism, identity politics, disciplinary colonization, and decolonial epistemologies. *Human Architecture: Journal of the Sociology of Self-Knowledge, 10*(1), pp 81–89.

Gudynas, E. 2009. Diez tesis urgentes sobre el nuevo extractivismo: contextos y demandas bajo el progresismo sudamericano actual. In F.R. Dávila (ed) *Extractivismo, política y sociedad.* CAAP/CLAES, pp 187–225.

Gudynas, E. 2011. Buen Vivir: Today's tomorrow. *Development, 54*(4), pp 441–447.

Gudeman, S.F. 1986. *Economics as Culture: Models and Metaphors of Livelihood.* Routledge.

Gunn, W., Otto, T. and Smith, R.C. 2013. *Design Anthropology: Theory and Practice.* Bloomsbury Academic.

Halse, J. 2013. Ethnographies of the possible. In W. Gunn, T. Otto and R.C. Smith (eds) *Design Anthropology: Theory and Practice.* Bloomsbury, pp 180–198.

Hammond, C.A. 2017. *Hope, Utopia and Creativity in Higher Education: Pedagogical Tactics for Alternative Futures.* Bloomsbury Publishing.

Harcourt, W. 2017. The making and unmaking of development: Using post-development as a tool in teaching development studies. *Third World Quarterly, 38*(12), pp 2703–2718.

Harcourt, W. 2018. 'People and personal projects': A rejoinder on the challenge of teaching development studies. *Third World Quarterly, 39*(11), pp 2203–2205.

Harding, J. and Hale, L. 2007. Anti-creativity, ambiguity and the imposition of order. Conference paper presented at Building Cultures of Creativity in Higher Education Conference, University of Wales Cardiff, January 2007.

Heron, B. 2005. Self-reflection in critical social work practice: Subjectivity and the possibilities of resistance. *Reflective Practice, 6*(3), pp 341–351.

Hidalgo-Capitán, A.L. and Cubillo-Guevara, A.P. 2017. Deconstrucción y genealogía del 'buen vivir' latinoamericano. El (trino) 'buen vivir' y sus diversos manantiales intelectuales. *International Development Policy/Revue internationale de politique de développement, 9*(9), https://journals.openedition.org/poldev/2517

Hillenkamp, I. 2014. *La economía solidaria en Bolivia: entre marcado y democracia.* CIDES-UMSA.

Hodkinson, S. 2009. Teaching what we (preach and) practice: The MA in activism and social change. *ACME: An International Journal for Critical Geographies, 8*(3), pp 462–473.

hooks, b. 1994. *Teaching to Transgress.* Routledge.

Huish, R. 2013. Dissent 101: Teaching the 'dangerous knowledge' of practices of activism. *Canadian Journal of Development Studies/Revue canadienne d'études du développement, 34*(3), pp 364–383.

Huish, R. 2015. Going where nobody should go: Experiential learning without making the world your classroom. *Journal of Global Citizenship & Equity Education*, *6*(1), pp 1–20.

Ijeh, I. 2015. University of Sussex: The second act. https://www.building.co.uk/buildings/university-of-sussex-the-second-act/5078742.article, accessed 26 August 2020.

Ingold, T. 2000. *The Perception of the Environment: Essays on Livelihood, Dwelling and Skill*. Psychology Press.

Ingold, T. 2013. *Making: Anthropology, Archaeology, Art and Architecture*. Routledge.

Jackson, N. and Shaw, M. 2006. Developing subject perspectives on creativity in higher education. In *Developing Creativity in Higher Education: An Imaginative Curriculum*. Routledge, pp 89–108.

James, A. and Brookfield, S.D. 2014. *Engaging Imagination: Helping Students Become Creative and Reflective Thinkers*. John Wiley & Sons.

Judson, G. 2015. Re-imagining sustainability education: Emotional and imaginative engagement in learning. In D. Selby and F. Kagawa (eds) *Sustainability Frontiers: Critical and Transformative Voices from the Borderlands of Sustainability Education*. Barbara Budrich Publishers, pp 205–220.

Kahn, R. 2009. Towards ecopedagogy: Weaving a broad-based pedagogy of liberation for animals, nature, and the oppressed people of the earth. In *The Critical Pedagogy Reader*. Routledge, pp 522–540.

Kapoor, I. 2004. Hyper-self-reflexive development? Spivak on representing the Third World 'Other'. *Third World Quarterly*, *25*(4), pp 627–647.

Khanna, A. 2012. Seeing citizen action through an 'unruly' lens. *Development*, *55*(2), pp 162–172.

Killick, E. 2020. Extractive relations: Natural resource use, indigenous peoples and environmental protection in Peru. *Bulletin of Latin American Research*, *39*(3), pp 290–304.

Kopnina, H. 2012. Education for sustainable development (ESD): The turn away from 'environment' in environmental education?. *Environmental Education Research*, *18*(5), pp 699–717.

Kopnina, H. and Gjerris, M. 2015. Are some animals more equal than others? Animal rights and deep ecology in environmental education. *Canadian Journal of Environmental Education*, *20*, pp 108–122.

Kothari, A., Demaria, F. and Acosta, A. 2014. Buen Vivir, degrowth and ecological Swaraj: Alternatives to sustainable development and the green economy. *Development*, *57*(3–4), pp 362–375.

Laing, A.F. 2020. Decolonising pedagogies in undergraduate geography: Student perspectives on a Decolonial Movements module. *Journal of Geography in Higher Education*, pp 1–19.

Lake, R. and Kress, T. 2017. Mamma don't put that blue guitar in a museum: Greene and Freire's duet of radical hope in hopeless times. *Review of Education, Pedagogy, and Cultural Studies*, *39*(1), pp 60–75.

Langdon, J. 2013. Decolonising development studies: Reflections on critical pedagogies in action. *Canadian Journal of Development Studies/Revue canadienne d'études du développement*, *34*(3), pp 384–399.

Langdon, J. and Agyeyomah, C. 2014. Critical hyper-reflexivity and challenging power: Pushing past the dichotomy of employability and good global citizenship in development studies experiential learning contexts. In *Globetrotting or Global Citizenship: Perils and Potential of International Experiential Learning*. University of Toronto Press, pp 43–70.

Latour, B. 2008. A cautious Prometheus? A few steps toward a philosophy of design (with special attention to Peter Sloterdijk). In *Proceedings of the 2008 Annual International Conference of the Design History Society*, pp 2–10.

Lave, J. and Wenger, E. 1991. *Situated Learning: Legitimate Peripheral Participation*. Cambridge University Press.

Li, T.M. 2007. *The Will to Improve: Governmentality, Development, and the Practice of Politics*. Duke University Press.

Light, A. 2018. Ideas of autonomía: Buzzwords, borderlands and research through design. *Strategic Design Research Journal*, *11*(2), pp 147–153.

Lock, J.V. 2015. Designing learning to engage students in the global classroom. *Technology, Pedagogy and Education*, *24*(2), pp 137–153.

Lopes-Cardozo, M.T. 2012. Decolonising Bolivian education: Ideology versus reality. In *Logics of Socialist Education*. Springer, pp 21–35.

Lotz-Sisitka, H. 2017. Decolonisation as future frame for environmental and sustainability education: Embracing the commons with absence and emergence. In *Envisioning Futures for Environmental and Sustainability Education*. Wageningen Academic Publishers, pp 46–62.

Lozano, J.F., Boni, A., Peris, J. and Hueso, A. 2012. Competencies in higher education: A critical analysis from the capabilities approach. *Journal of Philosophy of Education*, *46*(1), pp 132–147.

Lugones, M. 2010. Toward a decolonial feminism. *Hypatia*, *25*(4), pp 742–759.

Lyon, P. 2011. *Design Education: Learning, Teaching and Researching through Design*. Gower Publishing.

MacDonald, K. 2014. (De) colonizing pedagogies: An exploration of learning with students volunteering abroad. In *Globetrotting or Global Citizenship?: Perils and Potential of International Experiential Learning*. University of Toronto Press, pp 209–229.

Macedo, D. 1997. An anti-methods pedagogy: A Freirian perspective. *Counterpoints*, *60*, pp 1–9.

MacGregor, H. and Mills, E. 2011. Framing rights and responsibilities: Accounts of women with a history of AIDS activism. *BMC International Health and Human Rights*, *11*(3), pp 1–11.

Maeckelbergh, M. 2011. Doing is believing: Prefiguration as strategic practice in the alterglobalization movement. *Social Movement Studies*, *10*(1), pp 1–20.

Mäkelä, M. and Löytönen, T. 2017. Rethinking materialities in higher education. *Art, Design & Communication in Higher Education*, *16*(2), pp 241–258.

Maldonado-Torres, N. 2007. On the coloniality of being: Contributions to the development of a concept. *Cultural Studies*, *21*(2–3), pp 240–270.

Mansell, J.L. 2013. Naming the world: Situating Freirean pedagogics in the philosophical problematic of Nuestra América. In *Education and Social Change in Latin America*. Palgrave Macmillan, pp 17–33.

Manso, M. and Garzón, M. 2011. Multidisciplinary-designing effective global collaborative projects. *Learning and Leading with Technology*, *39*(3), pp 32–35.

Manzini, E. 2015. *Design, When Everybody Designs: An Introduction to Design for Social Innovation*. MIT Press.

McDonough, M. and Braungart, W. 2002. *Cradle to Cradle: Remaking the Way We Make Things*. North Point Press.

McGregor, S.L.T. 2015. Transdisciplinary consumer pedagogy: Insights from a panoply of pioneering, sustainability-related pedagogies. In *Sustainability Frontiers: Critical and Transformative Voices from the Borderlands of Sustainability Education*. Barbara Budrich Publishers, pp 79–102.

Meadows, D.H. 2008. *Thinking in Systems: A Primer*. Chelsea Green Publishing.

Meadows, D.H., Meadows, D.L., Randers, J. and Behrens, W.W. 1972. *The Limits to Growth*. Club of Rome.

Meijers, F. and Kopnina, H.N. 2014. Education for sustainable development (ESD): Exploring theoretical and practical challenges. *International Journal of Sustainability in Higher Education*, *15*(2), pp 188–207.

Melhuish, C. 2010. Ethnographic case study: Perceptions of three new learning spaces and their impact on the learning and teaching process at the Universities of Sussex and Brighton. Unpublished report, CETLD/InQbate.

Merlino, D. and Stewart, S. 2015. Creating the global network: Developing social and community practice in higher education. In *The Everyday Practice of Public Art*. Routledge, pp 101–118.

Middleton, A. and Spiers, A. 2019. Learning to twalk: An analysis of a new learning environment. In C. Rowell (ed) *Social Media in Higher Education: Case Studies, Reflections and Analysis*. Open Book Publishers, pp 223–236.

Molina-Motos, D. 2019. Ecophilosophical principles for an ecocentric environmental education. *Education Sciences*, *9*(1), pp 37–52.

Murphy, K. and Marcus, G. 2013. Epilogue: Ethnography and design, ethnography in design . . . ethnography by design. In W. Gunn, T. Otto and R.C. Smith (eds) *Design Anthropology: Theory and Practice*. Bloomsbury, pp 251–268.

Naess, A. 1973. The shallow and the deep, long-range ecology movement: A summary. *Inquiry*, *16*(1–4), pp 95–100.

Nerantzi, C. and James, A. 2019. *LEGO® for University Learning: Inspiring Academic Practice in Higher Education*. https://doi.org/10.5281/zenodo.2813448

New, S. and Kimbell, L. 2013. Chimps, designers, consultants and empathy: A 'theory of mind' for service design. In *2nd Cambridge Academic Design Management Conference*. Cambridge University Press, pp 4–5.

Nieusma, D. 2004. Alternative design scholarship: Working toward appropriate design. *Design Issues*, *20*(3), pp 13–24.

North, P. and Scott Cato, M. (eds) 2017. *Towards Just and Sustainable Economies: The Social and Solidarity Economy North and South*. Policy Press.

Ojala, M. 2015. Hope in the face of climate change: Associations with environmental engagement and student perceptions of teachers' emotion communication style and future orientation. *The Journal of Environmental Education*, 46(3), pp 133–148.

Ojala, M. 2017. Hope and anticipation in education for a sustainable future. *Futures*, *94*, pp 76–84.

Papanek, V. 1971. *Design for the Real World: Human Ecology and Social Change*. Thames and Hudson.

Pedwell, C. 2012. Affective (self-) transformations: Empathy, neoliberalism and international development. *Feminist Theory*, *13*(2), pp 163–179.

Pete, S. 2018. Meschachakanis, a Coyote narrative: Decolonising higher education. In G.K. Bhambra, D. Gebrial and K. Nişancioğlu (eds) *Decolonising the University*. Pluto Press, pp 173–189.

Polanyi, K. 1944. *The Great Transformation*. Farrar and Reinhardt.

Pope, R. 2005. *Creativity: Theory, History, Practice*. Routledge.

Postero, N. 2013. Protecting Mother Earth in Bolivia: Discourse and deeds in the Morales administration. In *Amazonia: Environment and the Law in Amazonia: A Plurilateral Encounter*. Sussex Academic Press, pp 78–93.

Pupavac, V. 2010. From materialism to non-materialism in international development: Revisiting Rostow's stages of growth and Schumacher's small is beautiful. In *Challenging the Aid Paradigm*. Palgrave Macmillan, pp 47–77.

Raworth, K. 2017. *Doughnut Economics: Seven Ways to Think Like a 21st-Century Economist*. Chelsea Green Publishing.

Reinaga, F. 1970. *La revolución india*. Ediciones Fundacion Amautica.

Revollo, P.R. 2018. El vivir bien como alternativa al desarrollo y no como modelo de desarrollo alternativo. In P.R. Gerritsen, S. Rist, J.M. Hernández and N.T. Ponce (eds) *Multifuncionalidad, sustentabilidad y buen vivir. Miradas desde Bolivia y México*. Departamento de Ecología y Recursos Naturales –IMECBIO, Centro Universitario de la Costa Sur, Universidad de Guadalajara, pp 67–74.

Richards, R. 2007. Everyday creativity and the arts. *World Futures, 63*(7), pp 500–525.

Roberts, J. 2008. From experience to neo-experiential education: Variations on a theme. *Journal of Experiential Education, 31*(1), pp 19–35.

Robinson, K. 2001. *Out of Our Minds*. Tantor Media, Incorporated.

Sandri, O.J. 2013. Exploring the role and value of creativity in education for sustainability. *Environmental Education Research, 19*(6), pp 765–778.

Schwittay, A.F. 2003. From peasant favors to indigenous rights: The articulation of an indigenous identity and land struggle in northwestern Argentina. *Journal of Latin American Anthropology, 8*(3), pp 127–154.

Schwittay, A. 2014. Designing development: Humanitarian design in the financial inclusion assemblage. *PoLAR: Political and Legal Anthropology Review, 37*(1), pp 29–47.

Schwittay, A. 2015. *New Media and International Development: Representation and Affect in Microfinance*. Routledge.

Schwittay, A. and Boocock, K. 2015. Experiential and empathetic engagements with global poverty: 'Live below the line so that others can rise above it'. *Third World Quarterly, 36*(2), pp 291–305.

Sen, A. 1999. *Development as Freedom*. Anchor Books.

Shreeve, A. and Austerlitz, N. 2008. Editorial for ADCHE special issue. *Art, Design & Communication in Higher Education, 6*(3), pp 139–144.

Simpson, K. 2004. 'Doing development': The gap year, volunteer-tourists and a popular practice of development. *Journal of International Development: The Journal of the Development Studies Association, 16*(5), pp 681–692.

Solomon, J. 2002. *'Living with X': A Body Mapping Journey in Time of HIV and AIDS. Facilitator's Guide*. Psychosocial Wellbeing Series.

Spannring, R. 2019. Ecological citizenship education and the consumption of animal subjectivity. *Education Sciences, 9*(1), p 41.

Springgay, S. and Truman, S.E. 2017. *Walking METHODOLOGIES in a More-than-Human World: WalkingLab*. Routledge.

Srinivasan, A. 2016. Under Rhodes. *London Review of Books, 38*(7).

Staley, D.J. 2019. *Alternative Universities: Speculative Design for Innovation in Higher Education*. Johns Hopkins University Press.

Steele, C.S. 2016. Education in the age of complexity: Building systems literacy. PhD thesis at the university of Vermont. https://scholarworks. uvm.edu/cgi/viewcontent.cgi?referer=https://scholar.google.com/ scholar?hl=en&as_sdt=0%2C5&q=steele+caitlin+Education+in+the+a ge&btnG=&httpsredir=1&article=1587&context=graddis

Stein, S. and Andreotti, V.D.O. 2016. Decolonization and higher education. In *Encyclopedia of Educational Philosophy and Theory*. Springer Science+ Business Media, pp 978–981.

Stephenson, M. 2002. Forging an indigenous counterpublic sphere: The Taller de Historia Oral Andina in Bolivia. *Latin American Research Review*, pp 99–118.

Stilwell, F. 2006. Four reasons for pluralism in the teaching of economics. *Australasian Journal of Economics Education*, *3*(1), pp 42–55.

St Martin, K., Roelvink, G., Gibson, K. and Graham, J. 2015. Introduction: An economic politics for our times. In *Making Other Worlds Possible: Performing Diverse Economies*. University of Minnesota Press, pp 1–25.

Straubhaar, R. 2015. The stark reality of the 'White Saviour' complex and the need for critical consciousness: A document analysis of the early journals of a Freirean educator. *Compare: A Journal of Comparative and International Education*, *45*(3), pp 381–400.

Suchman, L. 2011. Anthropological relocations and the limits of design. *Annual Review of Anthropology*, *40*, pp 1–18.

Svampa, Maristella. 2013. Resource extractivism and alternatives: Latin American perspectives on development. In M. Lang and D. Mokrani (eds) *Beyond Development: Alternative Visions from Latin America*. Transnational Institute, pp 117–143.

Sweeney, L.B. and Meadows, D. 2010. *The Systems Thinking Playbook: Exercises to Stretch and Build Learning and Systems Thinking Capabilities*. Chelsea Green Publishing.

Sweet, E.L. and Ortiz Escalante, S. 2015. Bringing bodies into planning: Visceral methods, fear and gender violence. *Urban Studies*, *52*(10), pp 1826–1845.

Tassi, N. and Canedo, M.E. 2019. *Una pata en la chacra y una en el mercado*. CIDES-UMSA.

Thomas, L. and Chandrasekera, U. 2014. Uncovering what lies beneath: An examination of power, privilege, and racialization in international social work. In *Globetrotting or Global Citizenship: Perils and Potential of International Experiential Learning*. University of Toronto Press, pp 90–111.

Tignor, R.L. 2006. *W. Arthur Lewis and the Birth of Development Economics*. Princeton University Press.

Tuck, E., McKenzie, M. and McCoy, K. 2014. Land education: Indigenous, post-colonial, and decolonizing perspectives on place and environmental education research. *Environmental Education Research*, 20(1), pp 1–23.

Tuhiwai-Smith, L. 2013. *Decolonizing Methodologies: Research and Indigenous Peoples.* Zed Books Ltd.

Tunstall, D. 2013. Decolonizing design innovation: Design anthropology, critical anthropology and indigenous knowledge. In W. Gunn, T. Otto and R.C. Smith (eds) *Design Anthropology: Theory and Practice.* Bloomsbury, pp 232–250.

UNESCO. 2002. Education for Sustainable Development Information Brief. United Nations Educational, Scientific and Cultural Organisation. Available at http://www.unesco.org/education/tlsf/extras/img/DESDbriefWhatisESD.pdf

Vaičiulionytė, K. 2020. Balancing hope and despair: The transformative role of emotions in climate change action. Unpublished thesis, University of Sussex.

Wals, A.E. 2010. Mirroring, Gestaltswitching and transformative social learning: Stepping stones for developing sustainability competence. *International Journal of Sustainability in Higher Education, 11*(4), pp 380–390.

Walsh, C. 2007. Shifting the geopolitics of critical knowledge: Decolonial thought and cultural studies 'others' in the Andes. *Cultural Studies, 21*(2–3), pp 224–239.

Wanderley, F. 2019. Bolivian cooperative and community enterprises. In L.I. Gaiger, M. Nyssens and F. Wanderley (eds) *Social Enterprise in Latin America: Theory, Models and Practice.* Routledge, pp 58–86.

Wanderley, F., Sostres, F. and Farah, I. 2015. *La Economia solidaria an le economia plural: discursos, practicas y resultados en Bolivia.* HEGOA-CIDES.

Webb, D. 2007. Modes of hoping. *History of the Human Sciences, 20*(3), pp 65–83.

Weil, S.W. and McGill, I. 1989. A framework for making sense of experiential learning. In *Making Sense of Experiential Learning: Diversity in Theory and Practice.* Open University Press, pp 3–24.

White, P. 1996. *Civic Virtues and Public Schooling: Educating Citizens for a Democratic Society.* Teachers College Press.

Whitehead, A. 1929. *The Aims of Education and Other Essays.* The Macmillan Company.

Willis, A.M. 2014. Designing back from the future. *Design Philosophy Papers, 12*(2), pp 151–160.

World Commission on Environment and Development. 1987. *Our Common Future.*

Wright, S. 2017. Can the university be a liveable institution in the Anthropocene? In *The University as a Critical Institution?* Brill Sense, pp 15–37.

Yelavich, S. and Adams, B. (eds) 2014. *Design as Future-making.* Bloomsbury Publishing.

Index